Christ the Key

Through the intensely intimate relationship that arises between God and humans in the incarnation of the Word in Christ, God gives us the gift of God's own life. This simple claim provides the basis for Kathryn Tanner's powerful study of the centrality of Jesus Christ for all Christian thought and life: if the divine and the human are united in Christ, then Jesus can be seen as key to the pattern that organizes the whole, even while God's ways remain beyond our grasp.

Drawing on the history of Christian thought to develop an innovative Christ-centered theology, this book sheds fresh light on major theological issues such as the *imago dei*, the relationship between nature and grace, the trinity's implications for human community, and the Spirit's manner of working in human lives. Originally delivered as the Warfield lectures at Princeton Theological Seminary, it offers a creative and compelling contribution to contemporary theology.

KATHRYN TANNER is Dorothy Grant Maclear Professor of Theology at the University of Chicago Divinity School. She is the author of *Economy of Grace* (2005) and *Jesus, Humanity and the Trinity: A Brief Systematic Theology* (2001).

CURRENT ISSUES IN THEOLOGY

General Editor:

Iain Torrance
Professor in Patristics and Christian Ethics, Master of Christ's College, and Dean of the Faculty of Arts & Divinity, University of Aberdeen

Editorial Advisory Board:

David Ford   *University of Cambridge*
Bryan Spinks   *Yale University*
Kathryn Tanner   *University of Chicago*
John Webster   *University of Aberdeen*

There is a need among upper-undergraduate and graduate students of theology, as well as among Christian teachers and church professionals, for a series of short, focussed studies of particular key topics in theology written by prominent theologians. *Current Issues in Theology* meets this need.

The books in the series are designed to provide a "state-of-the-art" statement on the topic in question, engaging with contemporary thinking as well as providing original insights. The aim is to publish books that stand between the static monograph genre and the more immediate statement of a journal article, by authors who are questioning existing paradigms or rethinking perspectives.

Other titles in the series:

Christ and Horrors   Marilyn McCord Adams
Divinity and Humanity   Oliver D. Crisp
The Eucharist and Ecumenism   George Hunsinger

KATHRYN TANNER

Christ the Key

CAMBRIDGE
UNIVERSITY PRESS

CAMBRIDGE
UNIVERSITY PRESS

University Printing House, Cambridge CB2 8BS, United Kingdom

Cambridge University Press is part of the University of Cambridge.

It furthers the University's mission by disseminating knowledge in the pursuit of education, learning and research at the highest international levels of excellence.

www.cambridge.org
Information on this title: www.cambridge.org/9780521732772

First published 2010
4th printing 2013

A catalogue record for this publication is available from the British Library

ISBN 978-0-521-51324-1 Hardback
ISBN 978-0-521-73277-2 Paperback

Cambridge University Press has no responsibility for the persistence or accuracy of URLs for external or third-party internet websites referred to in this publication, and does not guarantee that any content on such websites is, or will remain, accurate or appropriate.

Contents

Preface

This book is the promised sequel to my brief systematic theology, *Jesus, Humanity, and the Trinity.*[1] The central theological vision of both books is the same: God wants to give us the fullness of God's own life through the closest possible relationship with us as that comes to completion in Christ. In the incarnation one finds the immediate convergence of the most disparate things – God and humanity suffering under the weight of sin and death – as the means by which the goods of God's own life are to be conveyed to us in fulfillment of God's original intentions for us.

The first book developed the basic import of this Christ-centered theological vision by showing how it could be productively used to talk about almost anything of Christian interest in an integrated way. By carrying it through a number of different topics and thereby interconnecting them, my intent was to give readers a general sense of this overall vision and sufficient confidence about its fruitfulness to employ it themselves, if they so chose, on topics the book either did not raise or fully explore. The present book takes the heart of that theological vision – Christ – and shows in less systematic fashion how this understanding of Christ throws fresh light on otherwise tired theological topics and opens up new avenues for approaching them by breaking through current impasses in the theological literature. This understanding of Christ illuminates and unlocks discussion of these topics, and in that sense provides a key to them.

---

[1] Kathryn Tanner, *Jesus, Humanity and the Trinity* (Minneapolis, Minnesota: Fortress, 2001).

It does so by making evident what might not otherwise be clear: that, in order to give us the entire fullness of what God enjoys, God must give us God's very own life and not simply some created version of it. God cannot give us everything that God has to give by merely transforming human life itself into some created approximation of divinity. God must attach us, in all our frailty and finitude, to God.

As the culmination and completion of what is true generally of God's interactions with us, Christ is the key, this book suggests, to what God is doing everywhere. Christ clarifies and specifies the nature, aim, and trustworthiness of all God's dealings with us because Christ is where those dealings with us come to ultimate fruition. For example, as I have argued elsewhere, from the supreme fashion in which God achieves intimacy with us in Christ we gain a new confidence about, and have a more definite sense of the point and manner in which, God has always been present with the world as its creator and providential guide. If God saves by taking the radical step of uniting the whole of human nature to itself, we can be sure that God is responsible for the created goodness of our world through quite direct involvement with every aspect of it.[2]

Christ epitomizes in supreme form God's overall intent with respect to us; and thereby gives that intent a concrete shape we can follow. The whole of who God is for us as creator and redeemer, which in its varied complexity might simply overwhelm and mystify us, is found in concentrated compass in Christ. Christ in this way provides, we shall see, a clue to the pattern or structure that organizes the whole even while God's ways remain ultimately beyond our grasp.[3]

Like its predecessor, this book is highly eclectic in its use of the history of Christian thought (although because of its focus on

[2] For Christ as key in this way to God's creation and providential guidance of the world, see Kathryn Tanner, "Is God in Charge?" in William C. Placher (ed.), *Essentials of Christian Theology* (Louisville, Kentucky: Westminster John Knox, 2003), pp. 119, 121–2, 128, 130.

[3] See Thomas F. Torrance, *Theology in Reconciliation* (London: Geoffrey Chapman, 1975), pp. 258–60; and his *Divine Meaning: Studies in Patristic Hermeneutics* (Edinburgh: T & T Clark, 1995), pp. 121–3.

attachment to God in Christ it trades more heavily than the first book on specifically Neo-Platonic strands of early Christian theology). In this respect it imitates much of the earlier Christian thought it employs. Rather than find me an "eclectic compiler" because of it, and the book "a syncretistic concoction of pre-existing givens," the reader, I hope, will extend to me the courtesy now afforded someone like Gregory of Nyssa, in which "looking backward towards the sources and the basic elements" does not "replace a looking forward that endeavors to grasp the synthesis that has been effected, the irreducible novelty that has been attained." "The fruit of these labors, even though ... contained in the roots," is, I hope to convince the reader, "something new and unexpected."[4]

While I do not believe I have distorted any of the material I directly or indirectly quote, my thinking often pushes that material in directions beyond its own explicit statement, without any great defense of the uses to which it is thereby put.[5] While I welcome specialist interest in the question of my faithfulness to sources, my main intent is simply to show the fruitfulness of a kind of internalizing of the history of Christ thought for its creative redeployment. In much the same way scripture (particularly the Psalms) was internalized (through repeated direct reading, liturgical recitation, and theological commentary) and redeployed in earlier Christian thought – for example, in Anselm's poetry and prose meditations, which for all their prayerfulness took a quite analytical and rigorous form not unlike this book.[6]

[4] Hans Urs von Balthasar, *Presence and Thought: An Essay on the Religious Philosophy of Gregory of Nyssa*, trans. Mark Sebanc (San Francisco: Ignatius, 1995), pp. 16–17, 79. He is defending the eclecticism of Gregory of Nyssa's thought, which he thinks unfairly led to its dismissal.
[5] Note that I have routinely altered archaisms of capitalization and grammar in nineteenth-century translations of early Christian sources in order to ease comprehension by the contemporary reader.
[6] See Benedicta Ward, "Introduction," in *The Prayers and Meditations of St. Anselm with the Proslogion*, trans. Benedicta Ward (London: Penguin, 1973), pp. 28–9, 43, 46.

In large part because of the particular sources utilized most often, the book is also full of references to pre-critical scriptural interpretation. While I know of current efforts to resuscitate forms of biblical interpretation common in the early church, I do not intend my own work here (with the exception of Chapter 4's highly qualified remarks) to be a contribution to such efforts.[7] There is much more to be said on this score of course. But suffice it to say now that I am principally interested in the theological claims that result from such interpretation, and believe the theological merits of those claims to be separable from biblical commentary that at least in its particulars is often dubious from a modern historical-critical perspective.

The chapters of this book came together as the Warfield lectures at Princeton Theological Seminary in 2007. I am deeply grateful to Iain Torrance, the President of Princeton Theological Seminary, and to my faculty host, Daniel Migliore, for the invitation to deliver them. Several chapters are revisions of papers written prior to that occasion and in earlier forms have been previously, or are now in process of being, published. Chapter 1 is a substantially revised version of a paper written for a conference organized under the auspices of Catherine Keller at Drew University in 2006 and presented again in 2007 both at the University of Otago, New Zealand, for a conference on "Christian Salvation," and at a conference on "The Self" at the University of Chicago organized by Jean-Luc Marion. Different

In his *Confessions*, of course, Augustine also develops Neo-Platonic themes in language that is a "pastiche of the Psalter," as Henry Chadwick puts it. See his "Introduction" in Augustine, *Confessions*, trans. Henry Chadwick (Oxford University Press, 1992), p. xxii.

[7] See, for example, some of the contributions in Ellen F. Davis and Richard B. Hays (eds.) *The Art of Reading Scripture* (Grand Rapids, Michigan: Eerdmans, 2003), especially the first of the Nine Theses of the combined contributors, p. 1, and the essay by Robert Jenson, "Scripture's Authority in the Church," pp. 28–9, 33–6. See also Lewis Ayres, "Patristic and Medieval Theologies of Scripture: An Introduction," in Justin S. Holcomb (ed.), *Christian Theologies of Scripture* (New York University Press, 2006), pp. 11–12.

versions are published under the titles, "In the Image of the Invisible," in Christopher Boesel and Catherine Keller (eds.), *Apophatic Bodies* (New York: Fordham University Press, 2009), and "Creation and Salvation in the Image of an Incomprehensible God," in Ivor Davidson and Murray Rae (eds.), *God of Salvation: Essays in Systematic Theology* (Aldershot, England: Ashgate, forthcoming). A much compressed treatment of material from Chapters 1 and 3 is published as "Grace without Nature," in David Albertson and Cabell King (eds.), *Without Nature? A New Condition for Theology* (New York: Fordham University Press, 2009) and was delivered as a lecture in that combined form at a conference organized by them on this theme at the University of Chicago in 2007. A much different version of Chapter 5 appeared as "The Trinity," in William Cavanaugh and Peter Scott (eds.), *Blackwell Companion to Political Theology* (Oxford: Blackwell, 2003). A shortened version of Chapter 5 was published under the title "Kingdom Come: The Trinity and Politics," *Princeton Seminary Bulletin* 27/2 (2007), pp. 129–45; this same version was revised for a conference on "Christology and Ethics," organized by Brent Waters and L. LeRon Shults at Garrett Evangelical Theological Seminary in 2008, and is to be published under the title "Trinity, Christology, and Community" in a book edited by them on that theme (Eerdmans, forthcoming). Chapter 6 was originally presented at a meeting of the Society for the Study of Theology in Newcastle, England, in 2003, delivered in 2004 at Yale University as the Pitt Lecture and at Kampen Theological University, Netherlands, and published under the title "Incarnation, Cross, and Sacrifice: A Feminist-Inspired Reappraisal," *Anglican Theological Review* 86/1 (2004), pp. 35–56. A version of Chapter 7 appeared as "Workings of the Spirit: Simplicity or Complexity?" in Michael Welker (ed.), *The Work of the Spirit* (Grand Rapids, Michigan: Eerdmans, 2006). I would like to thank everyone who attended these lectures and asked questions, and the editors of these volumes for suggested revisions. I am especially grateful for the extended responses to the written manuscript that I received from Paul DeHart, Kevin Hector, Catherine Keller, Ian McFarland, Joy McDougall, David Newheiser, Jean Porter, John Thiel, and the Yale–Princeton Theology Group. This book and the lectures upon which it is based could not have been written without the unwavering support of my family; my greatest debt of gratitude is to them.

[Handwritten notes at top:]

- Defining what "image" of God means, we are portraying in what we are not, t/f cannot be a perfect image as the Son is of the Father; we more strongly image God when we are conformed to God
- The HS molds us to be able to better image God
- Characteristics of human nature that make us open to Christ's transformation

1 | Human nature   work (37-39)

- How we are open to transformation (39 -

What light might be thrown on the well-worn idea that humans are created in the image of God, if Christ were the key to understanding it? Theological treatments of the topic often concentrate on human nature in and of itself, in the effort to specify some set of well defined and neatly bounded characteristics that both make humans like God and clearly distinguish them from other creatures. Humans are created in the image of God, as the Genesis verses say, because unlike other creatures they have reason, free will, or the ability to rule over others as God does. In contrast to these theological tendencies, I show that a Christ-centered treatment of our creation in the image of God turns attention initially away from the human altogether; and when attention returns to the human what is of theological interest about it is its lack of given definition, malleability through outside influences, unbounded character, and general openness to radical transformation. A whole Christ-centered account of humanity, from creation to salvation, we shall see, might be fruitfully developed on this basis.

[Handwritten margin note:] method

What humans are thought to image – God, the trinity, or the Word – determines in great part whether theologians focus primarily on human nature in and of itself as the image of God. When human beings are thought to image God generally, without, that is, the need for any further trinitarian specification of who or what God is, general human characteristics tend to be identified with the image of God. Humans are higher on the ontological scale of created beings by possessing certain faculties such as intelligence and will; their rationality, freedom from necessity, and capacity for self-determination make them like God.

1

This need not mean God is at the top of a single ontological scale that includes creatures: the most immaterial and intelligent being among others, for example. The difference between God and creatures is usually not understood to be a mere difference in kind of the sort that holds within the created order. These theologians are merely saying that when the absolute fullness, beyond kinds, of God's own perfection is communicated to creatures it takes the form of a ranked order of different created perfections. Humans are more like God than other creatures, then, simply by being among the more perfect of them.

Given the same general identification of God with what humans image, theologians can buck this focus on human nature in and of itself by considering "image" a mere designation of relationship.[1] When the Genesis verses (1:27 and 5:1) say that human beings are created in the image of God that means, not that human beings have something in them that images God, but simply that they were made for a relationship with God, one perfected in Christ. Emphasis can be placed on God's decision to have a special relationship with humans rather than on the character of human nature that warrants it. It is simply the special relationship that God chooses to have with them that singles them out from other creatures. Moreover, since the whole human being is made for such a relationship, little interest need be expressed in particular characteristics or dimensions of their nature that distinguish humans from other creatures.

Nonetheless, relationality is often isolated as the human characteristic that forms the presupposition for fellowship with God.[2] Human beings are made for fellowship with God by being made

[1] See, for example, Jürgen Moltmann, *God in Creation: A New Theology of Creation and the Spirit of God*, trans. Margaret Kohl (Harper San Francisco, 1991), pp. 216–25; and Karl Barth, *Church Dogmatics 3/1*, ed. G. W. Bromiley and T. F. Torrance (Edinburgh: T & T Clark, 1958), pp. 183–7, 191–200, 289–95; and *Church Dogmatics 3/2*, ed. G. W. Bromiley and T. F. Torrance (Edinburgh: T & T Clark, 1960), pp. 323–4.
[2] See Moltmann, *God in Creation*, pp. 222–3; Barth, *Church Dogmatics 3/1*, pp. 185–7, 194–6, 289–90; and *Church Dogmatics 3/2*, p. 324.

for fellowship with one another. This essential sociability makes them the image of God in the usual way. The reference to male and female in Genesis 1:27, considered alongside the Adam and Eve story, suggests that human beings are the image of God by being social beings, through their need for human companionship, by their not being made to be alone. The trinity enters the picture rather late at this point to show, once again, that something about human nature considered in itself images God. The essentially social character of human persons is an analogue for the essentially relational character of persons within the trinity.

The simple identification of what humans image with the trinity need not, then, fundamentally interrupt isolated theological attention to humans in and of themselves, attention that seeks to locate the image of God *in* them, in the form of some set of peculiarly human properties and capacities. What Augustine attempts in Books 8–11 of *De trinitate* would be a prime case in point – at least if one considers the influence those particular books have had on thinking about the image of God in the West.[3]

Augustine tries to support the intelligibility of rules for trinitarian speech – for example, the rule that persons of the trinity are really distinct in virtue of their relations with one another but one and equal in their divinity – by finding analogues for those rules in the more familiar character and dynamics of the human mind and heart. The effect of this in these books is often to make human nature seem a self-contained image of God in and of itself. Human consciousness, it appears, can be an image of God in isolation from anything else, apart from relations with anything not itself, whether above the human (God) or below it (sense objects). Only the internal dynamics of human consciousness – the self's relations with itself – can mimic, for example, the perfect equality and union of distinct things which

---

[3] "On the Trinity," trans. Arthur West Haddan and William Shedd, in Philip Shaff (ed.), *Nicene and Post-Nicene Fathers*, vol. III (Grand Rapids, Michigan: Eerdmans, 1956), Books 8–11, pp. 115–55.

is the rule for the trinity; in relations with anything else there is, if not distance or disunity, then at the very least a marked lack of equivalence among the things related. For these reasons, Augustine goes so far as to suggest that the mind is a *better* image of God when knowing itself rather than God.[4] The strong impression from such discussion is that human consciousness is the image of God all by itself, in an ideally self-enclosed self-sufficiency – for example, when knowing, loving, or remembering only its own pure productions.

In subsequent books of *De trinitate* Augustine dispels this impression by affirming that the soul's relations to itself become the image of God in the strongest sense only when informed by an actual relationship with God: "The true honor of man is the image and likeness of God, which is not preserved except in relation to him by whom it is impressed."[5] Humans are the image of God, properly speaking, only when actually contemplating God face to face in heaven. "The likeness of God will then be perfect in this image, when the sight of God shall be perfected."[6] Considered apart from such a relationship, humans would image God in only a secondary, less proper way in virtue of the characteristics that are the prerequisite for such relationship (for example, in virtue of the cognitive capacities that God's grace might expand to enable contemplation of God). Thus, "it is made after the image of God in respect to this, that it is able to use reason and intellect in order to understand and behold God."[7]

Another sort of trinitarian reading of the Genesis verses, the dominant one I believe in the early church, produces, however, a much more radical deflection from preoccupation with human nature itself. Whatever its merits as biblical exegesis, its theological import holds great promise. On this way of reading those verses, the second person of the trinity is what human beings are created to

[4] "On the Trinity," Book 9, chapter 11, section 16, p. 132.
[5] *Ibid.*, Book 12, chapter 11, section 16, p. 161.
[6] *Ibid.*, Book 14, chapter 17, section 23, p. 196. [7] *Ibid.*, chapter 5, section 6, p. 186.

4

image. Indeed, that divine person, rather than human nature, is the very image the Genesis verses are discussing. Humans are not simply said to be the image in Genesis 1:27 but to be made "in" or "after" or "according to" it, because the image primarily being referred to here is a divine one and not a human one at all. The kind of relationship that human beings have to that divine image is not specified by the passages; at best it would seem to involve being a secondary image of this other image.

For theological reasons, Augustine in *De trinitate* rejects this way of understanding the verses.[8] The plural terms in "let *us* make man in *our* image" refer to all three persons of the trinity taken as a whole. Since the second person of the trinity images the first person and not the whole of the trinity, these verses must mean man, and not the second person of the trinity, when they talk about the image of that whole.

Augustine seems to fear that if humans are in the image of only the second person of the trinity and not of all the others as well, the second person of the trinity will appear to be something less than the others.[9] But the premise of such a worry is strongly disputed by most theologians who identify the image with the Word: it is by being in the image of the second person of the trinity that we come to be in the image of the trinity as a whole. A relationship with the second person brings with it relationships with the others, since, as Augustine himself maintains in earlier books, the persons of the trinity are never without one another.

Unlike Augustine, these early church theologians read the Genesis passages through New Testament ones, in which Christ is talked about in frequently cosmic terms as the image of God.[10] The image of

---

[8] *Ibid.*, Book 7, chapter 6, section 12, pp. 113–14; and Book 12, chapter 6, sections 6–8, pp. 157–8; and Book 14, chapter 19, section 25, p. 197. See also his "The Literal Meaning of Genesis," trans. Edmund Hill, in John E. Rotelle (ed.), *On Genesis, The Works of Saint Augustine*, Part I, vol. XIII (Hyde Park, New York: New City Press, 2002), Book Three, section 29, p. 234.

[9] "On the Trinity," Book 12, chapter 6, section 7, p. 157.

[10] See, for example, Rom 8:29; 2 Cor 4:4; and Col 1:15. Most are from the Pauline epistles.

God consequently takes on for them a primarily intra-trinitarian sense. Christ is said to be the image of God in these New Testament passages, because, it is thought, the divinity with which he is identified – the second person of the trinity – is itself the image of the first person of the trinity. The image most properly speaking – the express or perfect image of God (Heb 1:3) – just is the second person of the trinity, the perfect manifestation of all that the first person is. When the Genesis verses talk about the image of God they are not, then, referring in the first place to human beings but to an imaging relationship that occurs within the trinity itself.

Because these theologians worry that Christ will be confused with a creature by Arians, they stress that the second person of the trinity, incarnate in Christ, images God in a way human beings themselves cannot match. A perfect image of God can be only a divine image. To be perfect, that image must be the equal of its archetype, reproducing it from top to bottom, in every dimension inclusive of its very nature. Such an image must, in other words, share or participate wholly in what its archetype is – not in part.[11] For this reason perfect imaging requires a community of nature.[12] Creatures by definition do not share the divine nature; and consequently human beings simply cannot be images of God in this way.

In virtue of having a shared nature, the second person of the trinity, one could say, is a natural image of the first in the way a natural son is the spitting image of his father, or the way the radiance surrounding a source of light manifests the light-filled nature of its source. The second person is therefore nothing like an image

---

[11] Athanasius, "Four Discourses against the Arians," trans. John Henry Newman and Archibald Robertson, in Philip Schaff and Henry Wace (eds.), *Nicene and Post-Nicene Fathers*, vol. IV, Second Series (Grand Rapids, Michigan: Eerdmans, 1957), Discourse 1, chapter 5, section 16, pp. 315–16.

[12] Gregory of Nyssa, "Against Eunomius," trans. H. C. Ogle, William Moore, and Henry Austin Wilson, in Philip Schaff and Henry Wace (eds.), *Nicene and Post-Nicene Fathers*, vol. V, Second Series (Peabody, Massachusetts: Hendrickson, 1994), Book 2, section 12, p. 123.

produced in a foreign medium – for example, nothing like the portrait of a flesh and blood person painted on a canvas.[13] But that is all that human beings who are not divine can be – images of God produced in a medium of a radically different, indeed inferior, sort.

Because the divine image is all that its archetype is, it is not an image by participation at all, if participation means sharing in something that one is not.[14] Rather than being something other than what it images, the second person of the trinity simply is it. Its imaging of another does not therefore involve its being a composite of what it properly is by nature and something extra, foreign and external to it, received from without in order to make it an image. Being the image of the first person of the trinity is not an accidental acquired quality, added to the second person; the simplicity of the divine nature rules that out. Unlike other images, the second person of the trinity does not acquire the capacity to image something by, say, being impressed by it; nor, as a merely acquired property, can that image be lost.

The second person of the trinity does not in any sense borrow from the first what it does not have of itself. One cannot say that the second person of the trinity "is made illustrious by the mere addition to himself of features that were not originally his own, so that he shines as it were by reflected light from glories bestowed upon him, and not by his own natural luster."[15] Instead, whatever the second person gets from the first is properly its own by nature. The second person of the trinity is divine in and of itself and not simply in virtue of being the image of the first person. As Cyril of Alexandria points out: what is "the very image and likeness and effulgence" of the

---

[13] *Ibid.*; and Cyril of Alexandria, *Commentary on the Gospel according to John*, trans. P. E. Pusey (Oxford: James Parker, 1874), Book 2, chapter 8, pp. 265–6 (John 5:23); and Book 3, chapter 5, pp. 348–50 (John 6:27).

[14] See Athanasius, "Against the Heathen," trans. Archibald Robertson, in Philip Schaff and Henry Wace (eds.), *Nicene and Post-Nicene Fathers*, vol. IV, Second Series (Grand Rapids, Michigan: Eerdmans, 1957), p. 29. See also his "Four Discourses," Discourse 3, chapter 23, section 1, p. 394; section 6, p. 396; and chapter 25, section 15, p. 402.

[15] Cyril of Alexandria, *Commentary on John*, Book 9, chapter 14, p. 255 (John 14:9).

Father must be "bearing innate within himself the proper characteristics of his Father's essence, and possessing in all their beauty the attributes that are naturally the Father's."[16]

Contrary to what has just been said about the second person of the trinity, human beings image God only by participating in what they are not – God. Because they are not God, they come to image God only by receiving what is not their own. In virtue of being received in something not itself divine, what humans have from God does not exist in them in the way it does in God, in perfect or divine fashion – fully, unchangeably, and without susceptibility of loss.

This idea that humans image God through participation can mean, however, two very different things. In a first quite weak sense, participating in God means nothing more than being a creature of God. Not just human beings, but everything in the world gets all that it is – inclusive of its existence, good qualities and capacities, and well-performed acts, over the whole of its existence – from what it is not – God. This is simply what it means to be a creature. Creatures participate in God by leading a derived life in that sense, a life derived from a God who does not derive from another as they do. What creatures are and have for their own they neither are nor have of themselves but through another who, unlike themselves, is and has all that it is through itself. God is, for example, life itself in virtue of having life through itself, while everything else receives its life from God, without simply being it in and of itself. Any creature therefore has life in some degree or fashion and can lose it.

Expressing much the same thing in explicitly Thomistic fashion, one can say God does not participate in being but *is* it: to be *God* just is to *be*. In God there is no distinction between what God is – God's essence – and God's existence. To participate in being is, by definition, not to be it, if participation means participating in what one is

---

[16] *Ibid.*, Book 2, chapter 6, p. 246–7 (John 5:19), where Cyril is discussing Christ, but the point remains the same.

not; and therefore with participation arises a distinction between essence and existence, the very composite character that constitutes created things.[17]

What creatures get from God pre-exists in God in exemplary, perfect fashion, and therefore when they participate in God in virtue of their creation creatures also image God. This is a Christian version of a basically Platonic understanding of participation: all that derives from a perfect exemplar for that reason approximates it. On a Platonic understanding of participation, imperfectly round things within the world, for example, would owe what they are to that paradigm of the absolutely round they all strive to approach in being themselves.[18] According to the Christian version, God in creating things other than God is trying to give them the good of God's own life, and therefore God contains in perfect fashion all that creatures become. Creatures form created approximations of God's own goodness, following (for example) the principle that a cause contains its effects in a superior fashion. Creatures image God in that God as their cause contains in a super-eminent divine fashion what they are.[19]

This imaging of God in virtue of creation involves an imaging of the second person of the trinity in particular. The paradigms for created things exist in the second person, God's own Word or Wisdom. That Word or Wisdom holds the idea or plan for all that God creates. In that Word or Wisdom God knows, one might say, all the different ways that God's own goodness can be imitated by what is not divine, and chooses, out of love for what is not God, to bring those things into existence. God therefore creates in and through this Word or Wisdom of God, which establishes the pattern for the

---

[17] See Cornelio Fabro, *Participation et causalité selon S. Thomas d'Aquin* (Paris: Beatrice-Nauwelaerts, 1961), pp. 468, 610.

[18] See R. G. Collingwood, *The Idea of Nature* (Oxford University Press, 1960), pp. 68, 71–2.

[19] See Fran O'Rourke, *Pseudo-Dionysius and the Metaphysics of Aquinas* (University of Notre Dame Press, 2005), chapters 7 and 9.

world.[20] The whole of creation becomes an image of the second person of the trinity in this way: "That what came into being might not only be, but be good, it pleased God that his own Wisdom should condescend to the creatures, so as to introduce an impress and semblance of its image on all in common and on each, that what was made might be manifestly wise works and worthy of God."[21]

Creatures themselves – their own existence, characteristics and capacities – become the focus here; what they are in themselves forms an image of the second person of the trinity. But equally focal is the fact that they are not such independently of God. This, indeed, is just the point of saying creatures image God through participation. This imaging is not an accidental mirroring of God, by chance or happenstance in virtue of what a creature has become independently of God, on its own steam apart from any relation to God, the way a pumpkin might by chance or happenstance have grown of itself into the image of a human face. Something images God because it comes from God. Indeed, it images God only by participating in God, that is, by continuing to receive what it has from God. To be a creature just means to lead an insufficient life of oneself, to lead a continually borrowed life.

Different creatures can be more or less the image of God in virtue of their particular created characteristics. Human beings in virtue of their rationality, for example, might naturally be better images of God's own Word and Wisdom than creatures without intelligence. Not only can they reflect the divine idea of themselves in the Word or Mind of God in virtue of what they are; they also have the capacity, at least in principle, of knowing what that idea for themselves and everything else is. "For as the Son of God, considered as the Word, our word is an image, so of the same Son considered as

[20] Thomas Aquinas, *Summa Theologica [Theologiae]*, trans. Fathers of the English Dominican Province, 5 vols. (Westminster, Maryland: Christian Classics, 1948), vol. I, Q44 a2, p. 230; see also Q34 a3, pp. 180–1.
[21] Athanasius, "Four Discourses," Discourse 2, chapter 22, section 78, p. 390. See also sections 79–82, pp. 391–3.

Wisdom is the wisdom which is implanted in us an image; in which wisdom, we having the power of knowledge and thought, become recipients of the all-framing Wisdom; and through it we are able to know its Father."[22]

But this is still a general form of imaging shared with everything that exists and as such imaging at the lowest possible level. What is in creatures, the image of God that their own capacities and acts constitute, is a mere "copy" and "shadow" of the image of God that is God's own Wisdom.[23] God contains the good that God wishes to communicate to creatures in a supreme fashion that finite creatures can resemble only remotely. Thus, God contains all the good found in the created world but with an intensive fullness and simplicity beyond any distinctions of this or that to be found there. The goodness of God cannot be contained in any genus; it is beyond all distinctions in kind. And this is just what cannot be communicated to finite creatures. Even in our world, what causes communicate of themselves to others may not exist in their effects in anything like the way it exists in the cause. Cause and effect may be of the same species, as when a human being produces another human being. But other causes that communicate themselves do not reproduce themselves. The sun, for example, communicates its own light and heat to others without producing another sun; and therefore in this case cause and effect share only a generic resemblance. If there is a cause that is not contained in any genus – God – its effects – creatures – will that much more distantly reflect their cause, lacking not just a specific but even a generic resemblance.[24]

This weakness of resemblance between creatures and God results not from the weak power of the communicating cause – God – but from the necessarily inferior quality of the medium when God is

---

[22] *Ibid.*, p. 390.

[23] *Ibid.*, p. 392. Once again Athanasius' downplaying of the character of the world's imaging is an attempt to distinguish clearly the Word itself as the image of the Father from the world as the image of the Word.

[24] Aquinas, *Summa Theologica*, vol. I, Q4, pp. 20–3.

communicating the goodness of God to what is not God. In short, the difference between God and creatures requires this first sort of imaging through participation to be quite weak. The difference in underlying media, so to speak, between the human image and its divine archetype makes too big a difference here; the divine simply cannot be imitated very well in what is not divine. There is nothing in between God and creatures, no ontological continuum spanning the difference between them, despite what the idea of one creature better imitating God than another might suggest; and therefore there can be no real approximation to the divine on any creature's part.

God finds a way, however, to communicate the goodness of God's own life to creatures without abolishing or mitigating the difference between them and God. In a second, much stronger way of being an image through participation in what one is not, creatures would receive the divine image itself for their own, and end the futile struggle, so to speak, to approximate God in and through what they are simply in themselves. Creatures would receive from God what is beyond themselves – the divine image itself – and be considered the image of God themselves primarily for that reason. They would image God, not by imitating God, but in virtue of the gift to them of what remains alien to them, the very perfection of the divine image that they are not, now having become their own. Rather than being in themselves merely similar to what God is in some full and perfect fashion beyond their reach, they would share in, hold in common with God, what is and remains itself divine, the perfect divine image itself.[25]

---

[25] The distinction between this strong sense of participation and the previous weak one is implicit in David L. Balás, *METOYΣIA ΘEOY: Man's Participation in God's Perfections according to Saint Gregory of Nyssa* (Rome: Herder, 1966); and is made explicit in Verna Harrison, *Grace and Human Freedom according to St. Gregory of Nyssa*, (Lewiston, New York: Mellon, 1992), chapter 3. See Daniel A. Keating, *The Appropriation of Divine Life in Cyril of Alexandria* (Oxford University Press, 2004), chapter 4, for a similar distinction in Cyril between participation by nature and by grace.

Christ is the paradigm for this strong sort of imaging through participation. The human being, Jesus, is the image of God in a much stronger sense than any creature, human or otherwise, could ever be on its own, because Christ's humanity has the divine image for its own through the Word's assuming or uniting that humanity to itself in becoming incarnate in him. As a result of this hypostatic union of incarnation, perfect human imaging of God is achieved by way of perfect unity with what is perfectly and properly the image of God, the second person of the trinity. In short, through unity with what is not human – the second person of the trinity – the human being, Jesus, is the perfect human image of God. Despite the difference in nature that remains between humanity and the second person, the perfect hypostatic unity of the two of them in Christ makes him the perfect human image of the second person of the trinity in much the way the perfect unity of substance between first and second persons of the trinity makes the second the perfect image of the first. In both cases perfect unity makes for perfect imaging.

Ordinary human beings would be the image of God in the strongest sense too, then, not when trying to image the divine image in a created fashion all by themselves, but, instead, when drawing near to the divine image, so near as to become one with it. As Gregory of Nyssa makes the point: "Now, how can you see a beautiful image in a mirror unless it has received the appearance of a beautiful form? So it is with the mirror of human nature: it cannot become beautiful until it draws near to the beautiful."[26] Humans have the image of God only by clinging to what they are not – that divine image itself – becoming attached to it not merely physically but in every way possible for them – ideally with purity of attention, full commitment, and intense love.[27] Augustine concurs: created "imperfection or

---

[26] Gregory of Nyssa, *From Glory to Glory*, trans., Herbert Musurillo (Crestwood, New York: St. Vladimir's Seminary Press, 1995), p. 186.

[27] Gregory of Nyssa, "On Virginity," trans. William Moore and Henry Austin Wilson, in Philip Schaff and Henry Wace (eds.), *Nicene and Post-Nicene Fathers*, vol. v, Second

incompleteness does not imitate the form of this Word, being unlike that which supremely and originally is … Rather, it is when it turns, everything in the way suited to its kind, that it really imitates the form of the Word which always and unchangeably adheres to the Father."[28] "A changeable good, which is inferior to the unchangeable good, becomes a greater good when it adheres to the unchangeable good, loving and serving him with a rational and free response of the will."[29] Unceasingly and with all that they are, humans must, as Augustine affirms, keep "clinging to him and remaining turned to him of whom it is said, 'But it is good for me to adhere to God,' [Psalm 72:28] and to whom it is said, 'I will keep my strength turned toward you' [Psalm 58:10]."[30] In sum, there is only one perfect or express image of God – the second person of the trinity – and that perfect image becomes the creature's own by way of a close relationship with it, the closer the better, a closeness consummated in Christ.

Jesus Christ is more than a paradigm for what is involved here; he has become for us the very means. The humanity of Jesus has that perfect attachment or orientation to the Word in virtue of his being one with the Word, nothing apart from it; and we gain the capability of something like that through our connection to him. By the power of the Holy Spirit, the first person of the trinity sends the second person into the world so as to be incarnate in human flesh, one with the humanity of Jesus. That same power of the Spirit comes to us through the glorified humanity of Christ in order to attach us to him, make us one with him, in all the intensity of faith, hope, and love.

Series (Peabody, Massachusetts: Hendrickson, 1994), p. 356; and "On the Soul and the Resurrection," trans. William Moore and Henry Austin Wilson, in Philip Schaff and Henry Wace (eds.), *Nicene and Post-Nicene Fathers*, vol. v, Second Series (Peabody, Massachusetts: Hendrickson, 1994), p. 450.

[28] Augustine, "The Literal Meaning of Genesis," Book 1, section 9, p. 171.
[29] *Ibid.*, trans. John Hammond Taylor, in *The Literal Meaning of Genesis*, 2 vols. (New York: Newman Press, 1982), vol. ii, Book 8, chapter 14, section 31, p. 54.
[30] *Ibid.*, chapter 12, section 27, p. 51.

In virtue of such close attachment to the divine image, humans would be the images of God, not just in leading borrowed lives, but by living off God, so to speak, by drawing their very life, that is, from the divine image to which they cling, in something like the way an unborn baby lives off the life of its mother, living in, with, and through her very life.[31] Or – to use the more common biblical imagery perhaps – they would exist as images by being like branches living only off the alien sap of the vine to which they have been grafted. They would be images in the way otherwise empty mirrors enjoy brightness only by receiving from outside themselves the light of another.

Although showing off the light of the divine image itself – and in that sense good images of God themselves – they would always be doing so only by exterior illumination, by glowing with a light that remains another's, and not by some phosphorescent assimilation of that light into their own nature as an acquired created property. The human "becomes pure and luminous in contact with the true and supernal purity; in such an atmosphere it even itself emits light, and is so filled with the radiance, that it becomes itself a light ... We see this even here, in the case of a mirror, or a sheet of water, or any smooth surface that can reflect the light; when they receive the sunbeam they beam themselves."[32] But in receiving the light in this way, the human does not acquire the power to keep the light apart from the presence of God continuing to illuminate it. That light does not "take" in us, so to speak; there is no created correlate to it in our own proper powers of action. The example of light in the air makes that clear: "The air has not been given its own luminosity [when] it becomes luminous, for if it had ... and was not constantly receiving it, it would remain luminous when the light was gone. In a similar

---

[31] Panayiotis Nellas, *Deification in Christ: The Nature of the Human Person*, trans. Norman Russell (Crestwood, New York: St. Vladimir's Seminary Press, 1997), p. 118, citing Nicolas Kavasilas, *Life in Christ*, in J. P. Migne (ed.), *Patrologia Graeca* (Paris, 1958), vol. 150, columns 600CD, 601AB.

[32] Gregory of Nyssa, "On Virginity," p. 356.

way, man is illuminated when God is present to him, but when God is absent, darkness is immediately upon him."[33]

All creatures can do something like this showing off or shining back of the divine glory given to them. Even now creatures can glorify God, glow with a kind of divine penumbra by pointing to, and in that sense making manifest, the goodness of the God who made them. The wonders of the world speak of the wonders of God. In the reformation of the world to come, moreover, when death, for example, will be no more, all creatures and not just humans can image the divine in the same way we have just been talking about by living off the very eternal life of God, in virtue of a close relationship or oneness with God that makes the eternity of God's life their own.

What remains unusual about human beings – and what therefore makes them the image of God as other creatures are not – is that the character or identity of human life is remolded in the process. Humans do not simply reflect the image of God. In so doing something happens to human life itself. Its very own character is altered or transformed for the better. Humanity takes on, in short, its own perfect shape by being reworked through attachment to the divine image.

By way of this attachment, its very human character becomes an image of God in a stronger fashion than before, beyond anything possible simply by participating in God as a creature. Rather than being a poor reproduction of the divine image in a radically different medium, in the way a painting on canvas falls short of the real flesh and blood person, human nature becomes, so to speak, imprinted with the character of the divine seal itself by way of the impression that the very presence of the divine image makes upon it. The strong form of participation – participation by having the divine image for one's own – is what allows the still weak way that humans image God

[33] Augustine, *Literal Meaning of Genesis*, trans. Taylor, vol. ii, Book 8, chapter 12, section 26, p. 51; see also Augustine, *The City of God*, trans. Henry Bettenson (New York: Penguin, 1977), Book 11, chapters 9–10, pp. 440–2.

by participating in God as creatures to be strengthened as much as possible. By having the one whom they are not, the Word, for their own in Christ, they should one day be able to lead human lives that imitate God in the most perfect way possible for mere humans.

Again, the humanity of Jesus is the paradigm for this sort of reworking of the human. In virtue of being one with the Word, the humanity that the divine image assumes is itself healed and elevated, shaped and re-formed according to the character of the Word itself with which the humanity of Jesus has been united. In Christ, human nature, in short, is itself re-fashioned in the divine image so as to become humanly perfect. The man Jesus is without sin, both perfectly virtuous and perfectly pious. What marks Jesus' humanity – what makes him the "new man" – is the way he is both entirely for his human fellows and fully oriented without fail to the God he worships and serves.

This refashioning is not the divine image per se but specifically human perfection, and as such still forms only a dim analogue of divinity. Even what the humanity of Christ becomes through union with the divine image – and certainly ours re-formed through him – is a low-level image of God according to the weak sense of participation insofar as the end product is a human state – a most excellent state, indeed, but a human one, nonetheless. The divine image we possess is wholly perfect, but as possessed by us, in the form of the impression it makes on us, that image becomes something less than what it is in itself. The impression the divine image makes on human life is in this way similar to the sun's reflection in a mirror. The reflection is not at all like the sun itself in most respects – for example, it is extremely small, relatively cool, quite dim so that we can look at it without being blinded, and so on.

> Just as in a minute particle of glass, when it happens to face the light, the complete disc of the sun is often to be seen, not represented thereon in proportion to its proper size, but so far as the minuteness of the particle admits of its being represented at all. Thus do the

reflections of those ineffable qualities of deity shine forth within the narrow limits of our nature.[34]

Even in Christ the Word's own qualities are present in circumscribed human form; and the same would hold only more so for us, human beings who possess the Word without being one with it as Christ is: "Drawing from him [Christ] as from a pure and incorruptible stream, a person will show in his thoughts such a likeness to his prototype as exists between the water in the gushing spring and water taken from there in a jar."[35]

If one considers human beings in and of themselves, there is a sense, then, in which they never become a proper image of God at all no matter how well formed they may be according to the divine image. Not being God, humans can never simply become that image in and of themselves through any process of transformation, even when such improvement is predicated on the very presence of the divine image impressing itself upon them. The absence of an onto-logical continuum spanning the difference between God and crea-tures, which weakened the character of the imaging made possible through participation in God in virtue of creation, holds here too. And therefore humans cannot become the divine image, a perfect or proper image, by approximating divine qualities on the basis of the presence of the divine image to them. Simply because they remain creatures, humans are never sufficiently reformable to be made over into a good version of the divine image, its adequate reproduction in and through what they are as human beings.

Because Jesus Christ is the paradigm for what the divine image is to mean for human life – the paradigm for what it means both to have the divine image for one's own and to be transformed

[34] Gregory of Nyssa, "On the Soul and Resurrection," p. 437.
[35] Gregory of Nyssa, "On Perfection," trans. Virginia Woods Callahan, *Saint Gregory of Nyssa Ascetical Works*, The Fathers of the Church, vol. LVIII (Washington, DC: Catholic University of America Press, 1967), p. 121. See Harrison's commentary on this passage in her *Grace and Freedom*, pp. 126–7.

according to it – the Genesis discussion of human beings' creation in the image of God can be viewed in specifically Christological terms. The image that the Genesis passages discuss can be considered either the second person of the trinity or the Word incarnate. One need not choose between them since in the latter case the primary image is still the second person of the trinity and the second person of the trinity becomes an image to which human life is referred in exemplary fashion by way of the incarnation. Athanasius expresses such a Christologically-focused reading of the Genesis passages well: "For though we have been made after the image ... yet not on our own account still, but for that image ... of God inhabiting us, which is his Word, who was for us afterwards made flesh, have we this grace of designation."[36]

If the image to which Genesis refers is Christ, it might seem appropriate to give a prospective meaning to the fact that the Genesis verses do not simply say humans *are* the image but created "in," "after," or "according to" it. This phrasing would mean that we do not image the second person of the trinity in any strong way when we are created but have to wait for the divine image's incarnation. Being a strong image of God would be the destiny that awaits us in Christ, rather than our original state. The fact that humans image God strongly only when the divine image becomes their own and operates to transform their humanity might suggest the same thing – that humans do not image God in those strong ways at their creation. Such strong imaging is impossible for humans unless they are given something beyond their created nature, that is, the divine image itself; imaging of that sort requires a gift of grace, in short. Why suppose such a gift is theirs before the actual incarnation of the Word?

If humans are, nonetheless, on such a prospective reading some sort of image of God at their creation, theological attention would focus on what is properly creaturely – human nature considered on

---

[36] Athanasius, "Four Discourses," Discourse 3, chapter 25, section 10, p. 399.

its own terms. Before Christ's coming gives human nature a more genuine likeness to God, humans were on the way to it in virtue of some sort of weaker imaging of God. Using a distinction of this sort between image and likeness, Irenaeus provides a good example of a theology abiding by such a prospective interpretation of Genesis in which eventual growth into a better image takes center stage.[37]

It is true that such a prospective reading of the Genesis passages makes capacities given to humans at their creation less important than what humans are to become in Christ. But the crucial significance of Christ for human imaging of God is much more strongly emphasized by a different sort of Christ-centered reading of the Genesis passages, one in which human beings enjoyed at their creation something like the close relationship with the divine image perfectly actualized in Christ. In creating us, God would not deny us the gift of his own divine image; boundlessly generous, God would not withhold from us the best gift of all – the divine image itself. As Gregory of Nyssa suggests:

> He would not exhibit the power of his goodness in an imperfect form, but the perfect form of goodness is here to be seen by his … fully supplying him [humanity] with all good gifts … The language of scripture … expresses it concisely … in saying that man was made "in the image of God;" for this is the same as to say that he made human nature participant in … [or] filled with all good.[38]

In line with this idea, Athanasius suggests human beings at their creation were not just given their existence and the sort of

[37] Irenaeus, "Against Heresies," trans. Alexander Roberts and James Donaldson, in Alexander Roberts and James Donaldson (eds.), *Ante-Nicene Fathers*, vol. 1 (Grand Rapids, Michigan: Eerdmans, 1989), especially Books 4 and 5. For the distinction between image and likeness, see, for example, Book 5, chapter 6, section 1, p. 532. For the prospective focus and growth imagery, see, for example, Book 4, chapter 38, pp. 521–2. His motive is to shore up the value of created life per se against Gnostic challenge.
[38] Gregory of Nyssa, "On the Making of Man," trans. Henry Austin Wilson, in Philip Schaff and Henry Wace (eds.), *Nicene and Post-Nicene Fathers*, vol. v, Second Series (Peabody, Massachusetts: Hendrickson, 1994), p. 405.

participation in the Word that comes from being an intelligent creature: they also knew the very Word of God by way of its presence to them. And through that knowledge they enjoyed "a life in correspondence with God," "the true life," which, had they maintained it, would have enabled them to abide forever in blessedness.[39]

> For God ... inasmuch as he is good and exceeding noble, made, through his own Word our Savior Jesus Christ, the human race after his own image, and constituted man able to see and know realities by means of his assimilation to himself, giving him also a conception and knowledge even of his own eternity, in order that, preserving his nature intact he might not ever either depart from his idea of God nor recoil from the communion of the holy ones; but having also God's own power from the Word of the Father, he might rejoice and have fellowship with the deity, living the life of immortality unharmed and truly blessed.[40]

By partaking of the Word their natural mortality as creatures was kept at bay and they had for their own the very incorruptibility of God. "Because of the Word dwelling with them, even their natural corruption did not come near them, as Wisdom [Ws 2:23] also says; 'God made man for incorruption, and as an image of his own eternity.'"[41]

Augustine makes similar claims. The fact that humans in the Garden of Eden enjoyed goodness, wisdom, and happiness can mean only that they participated in the very goodness, wisdom, and blessedness of God at their creation. These gifts of God were theirs through the very presence of God to them. Like the angels making up the heaven of heavens (the "light" in "let there be light"),

[39] Athanasius, "On the Incarnation of the Word," trans. Archibald Robertson, in Philip Schaff and Henry Wace (eds.), *Nicene and Post-Nicene Fathers*, vol. IV, Second Series (Grand Rapids, Michigan: Eerdmans, 1957), section 3, p. 37, and section 5, p. 38. The whole of sections 3–5 is relevant.

[40] Athanasius, "Against the Heathen," section 2, p. 5; see also sections 3–8.

[41] Athanasius, "On the Incarnation," section 5, p. 38.

at their creation they were turned by God to God's own light – the Word – and gained thereby their human perfection.[42]

Here, indeed, the Word's presence to us seems necessary not just for God's creating us with extraordinary gifts of divine or near-divine character – knowledge of God himself and immortality – but simply for us to be the sort of creatures God intends us to be. A fellowship exists between human beings and angels, so that they might make up a single city, because they both are created in ways that require participation in the very light of God.[43] They are created to have within themselves something they are not. Like angels, humans can acquire the virtues that perfect them only by participating in what is other than themselves, the Word that in its simplicity is itself those things without acquiring them.[44] Thus, at their creation the angels were made "partakers of the eternal light, which is the unchanging Wisdom of God, the agent of God's whole creation … The angels, illuminated by that light by which they were created, themselves become light … by participation in the changeless light … which is the Word of God, through whom they themselves … were made. This is 'the true light, which illumines every man as he comes into the world [John 1:9];' and this light illuminates every pure angel, so that he is not light in himself but in God."[45]

As rational or intelligent creatures both humans and angels are made to cling or cleave to God.[46] Without that, they are formless. "A creature, although it has a spiritual nature endowed with intellect or reason and seems to be quite close to the Word of God, can have a formless life … Its formation consists in its turning to the changeless

[42] See his "Literal Meaning of Genesis," trans. Hill, Book 8, sections 25-7, pp. 361-2; and Book 1, sections 1-35, pp. 168-85. See also his *Confessions*, trans. R. S. Pine-Coffin (Baltimore, Maryland: Penguin, 1976), Book 12, sections 9-13, pp. 286-9; and Book 13, sections 2-4, pp. 312-4. And his *City of God*, Book 11, chapters 9-10, pp. 438-42; and Book 12, chapter 1, pp. 471-3.
[43] See Augustine, *City of God*, Book 12, chapter 1, p. 471.
[44] *Ibid.*, Book 11, chapter 10, pp. 441-2.   [45] *Ibid.*, Book 11, chapter 9, p. 440.
[46] *Ibid.*, Book 12, chapter 1, pp. 471-3.

light of Wisdom, the Word of God."[47] This formation happened at creation when "the Word had turned [spiritual creation] towards its creator and made it light by casting its own brightness upon it."[48] In an otherwise formless state, its creation was complete when it "became light, not simply by existing, but by fixing its gaze upon you and clinging to you, the light which shone upon it."[49]

Following Augustine, we could say, using my terminology, that at our creation we were images of God through participation in both strong and weak senses. We were images in the weak sense in having, for example, a rational nature, a nature formless in and of itself without illumination from the light of the divine image. In accord with this weak sense of imaging, the "light" in the Genesis verse "let there be light" (Gn 1:3) "is nothing other than intellectual life, which must be in a formless and chaotic state unless it is turned to its creator to be illumined."[50] Here "the Word is [merely] the source of whatever being and life it [a rational nature] has" in contradistinction from the wisdom and happiness such a nature gains in turning to the Word itself.[51] Simply existing with a created nature does not involve participation in God in the strong sense: God "gave existence to the creatures he made out of nothing; but it was not his own supreme existence."[52]

But we were also at our creation images of the strong sort in virtue of our attachment to the divine image itself, a divine image that in imprinting itself upon our minds and thereby making us wise produced in us a very strong image of the weak sort, human life made over according to the Word's own wisdom in imitation of it. Explicating these two senses of strong imaging, one could say with

[47] Augustine, *Literal Meaning of Genesis*, trans. Taylor, vol. I, Book 1, chapter 5, section 10, p. 24.
[48] Augustine, *Confessions*, Book 13, section 2, p. 312.   [49] *Ibid.*, section 3, p. 313.
[50] Augustine, *Literal Meaning of Genesis*, trans. Taylor, vol. I, Book 1, chapter 9, section 17, p. 29.
[51] *Ibid.*, Book 1, chapter 5, section 10, p. 24.
[52] Augustine, *City of God*, Book 12, chapter 2, p. 473.

Augustine that "when the eternal and unchangeable Wisdom ... enters into spiritual and rational creatures, as he is wont to come into holy souls, so that with his light they may shine, then in the reason which has been illumined there is a new state introduced, and this can be understood as the light that was made."[53] To be stronger images in both ways requires a stronger sense of participation, the presence in us of what we are not: all spiritual "beings receive their happiness from the same source we do, by a kind of light that is shed on them, a light apprehended by the intellect. This light ... is God. It is something other than themselves; it brings them illumination, so that they are full of light, and by participation in this light, exist in a state of perfection."[54]

If Christ is the key to understanding what humanity received at creation, the Word was present then, moreover, through the power of the Spirit. Like what happens in Christ and in us through him, the Holy Spirit, and not just the Word, must have been given to humanity at its creation as the power by which it was conformed to the image of the second person of the trinity. If one assumes that what humanity enjoys in Christ is the key to what happened then, we must at our creation have had the divine image for our own and been formed into it in something like the way the humanity of Jesus was and in much the way our own humanity is by way of him – through the Spirit.

The humanity of Christ is an image of the second person of the trinity through the power of the Spirit that is his own as the Word of God. The human being that Mary bears is the holy Son of God through the power of the Spirit that overshadows her (Luke 1:35). As the recipient of the Spirit Jesus is called the beloved son at his baptism in the Jordan. His anointing with the Spirit empowers him, moreover, for the work he does (Luke 4:18; Mt 12:18).

---

[53] Augustine, *Literal Meaning of Genesis*, trans. Taylor, vol. 1, Book 1, chapter 17, section 32, p. 38.

[54] Augustine, *City of God*, Book 10, chapter 2, p. 374; Augustine is agreeing with Plotinus here.

Theologians in the early church often interpret these verses together with John 17:19 – "I sanctify myself" – to mean that the holiness of Jesus' humanity results from the Word's gift of the Spirit, which is its own by nature, to the humanity united with it as a transformative power of new life. "If as the Lord himself has said, the Spirit is his ... it is not the Word, considered as the Word and Wisdom, who is anointed with the Spirit ... but the flesh assumed by him which is anointed ... by him; that the sanctification coming to the Lord as man, may come to all men from him."[55] The perfection of human living in Christ would be the supreme case of human capacities elevated through the gift of the Holy Spirit itself so as to conform to the image of the second person of the trinity.

Our lives are conformed to the image of Christ through the same power that conforms the humanity of Christ to the Word: through the Spirit, given to us who are not divine by nature, and therefore as a matter of grace, by Christ. Christ is in us by the Holy Spirit: "John ... thus writes; 'Hereby know we that we dwell in him and he in us, because he has given us his Spirit [1 John 4:13].' Therefore because of the grace of the Spirit which has been given to us, in him we come to be, and he in us."[56] Christ is by nature the divine Son who images the Father; human beings by the grace of the Holy Spirit become sons in the image of the divine image and thereby of the Father. Through Christ humans "receive into their hearts, as the Apostle says, 'the Spirit of his Son, crying, Abba, Father [Rom 8:15; Gal 4:6].' And these are they who, having received the Word, gained power from him to become sons of God; for they could not become sons, being by nature creatures, otherwise than by receiving the Spirit of the natural and true son."[57] By virtue of that Spirit within us, we come to lead reformed lives in imitation of him.

[55] Athanasius, "Four Discourses," Discourse 1, chapter 12, section 47, p. 334; see the whole of chapter 12. See also Cyril of Alexandria, *Commentary on John*, Book 11, chapter 10, p. 540 (John 27:18–19).

[56] Athanasius, "Four Discourses," Discourse 3, chapter 25, section 24, p. 406,

[57] *Ibid.*, Discourse 2, chapter 21, section 59, p. 380.

When, then, Christ desires us to be sanctified ... he made his
intercession for us in the words: "Holy Father, keep them in your
truth;" meaning by "truth" nothing but his own Spirit, by whom he
secures our souls, sealing them in his likeness, and edifying them ...
by his ineffable power ... exhorting us to manifest unrestrained zeal
in abundant good works.[58]

If we were in the image of the divine image in this fashion at
our creation, we must have had the gift of the Holy Spirit within
us then, too, as the power shaping our lives into the image of the
second person of the trinity. By receiving the Holy Spirit we became
at our creation a human image of that divine image like (but not
exactly like) the Word incarnate to come. The theology of Cyril of
Alexandria sees the full and explicit development of such a view,
which gives special attention to Genesis verses that could be taken to
refer to the Holy Spirit – the spirit hovering over the waters (Gn 1:2),
or the living soul breathed into Adam (Gn 2:7):

The divine scripture testifies that man was made in the image and
likeness of God who is over all ... But that through the Spirit he was
sealed unto the divine image ... saying, "And breathed into his
nostrils the breath of life [Gn 2:7]." For the Spirit at once began
both to put life into his formation and in a divine manner to impress
his own image thereon.[59]

Without any special emphasis on the gift of the Spirit at creation,
the same view is at least implicit in Athanasius. The Spirit was
dispensed by the Word before the incarnation in at least some
insecure and temporary fashion:

He [the Word] is the same; nor did he alter when he became man ...
but, as has been written, "The Word abides for ever [Is 40:8]."
Surely ... before his becoming man ... the Word, dispensed to the
saints the Spirit as his own ... He gave to Moses and the other

[58] Cyril of Alexandria, *Commentary on John*, Book 11, chapter 12, p. 560 (John 27:25).
[59] *Ibid.*, Book 2, chapter 1, p. 141 (John 1:32–3).

seventy; and through him [the Holy Spirit] David prayed to the Father, saying, "Take not your Holy Spirit from me [Psalm 51:12]."[60]

This gift of the Spirit explains how scripture can call people "sons of God" prior to the incarnation: "the Spirit is one and the same, then and now hallowing and comforting those who are his recipients; as one and the same Word and Son led even then to adoption of sons those who were worthy. For sons under the Old [Testament] were made such through no other than the Son."[61] Sons by grace were "the men who ... received the Spirit by participation, concerning whom scripture says, 'I begat and exalted children, and they rebelled against me [Is 1:2].' And of course because they were not sons by nature, therefore when they altered, the Spirit was taken away and they were disinherited; and again on their repentance that God who thus at the beginning gave them grace, will receive them again, and give light, and call them sons again."[62]

Without their making much of it, Augustine and Gregory of Nyssa also imply that the Holy Spirit was present to us at our creation, giving us the very love that attaches us to the divine image. For Augustine, what holds for the angels would hold for us: God at their creation gave them the very good will with which they turned to the divine light. "Showering grace on them at the same time he created their natures," God gave to the angels the very good will or "love with which they could adhere to him."[63]

> Therefore we must acknowledge, giving due praise to the creator, that "the love of God diffused by the Holy Spirit who has been given [Rom 5:5]" does not refer merely to holy men, but is applicable also to the holy angels; that when the scripture says, "As for me, my true good is to cling to God [Psalm 73:28]" it refers not only to the good for mankind, but first and foremost, to the good of the holy angels.[64]

---

[60] Athanasius, "Four Discourses," Discourse 1, chapter 12, section 48, p. 334.

[61] Ibid., Discourse 4, section 29, p. 445.

[62] Ibid., Discourse 1, chapter 11, section 37, p. 328.

[63] Augustine, City of God, Book 12, chapter 9, p. 482.   [64] Ibid., pp. 482–3.

Similarly for Gregory of Nyssa: "the first man ... at the moment when he first breathed ... could gaze without shrinking upon God's countenance. He did not judge what was lovely by taste or sight; he found in the Lord alone all that was sweet."[65] In the Garden we were "to enjoy the good in its purity ... and to enjoy *that*, is in my judgment nothing else than ever to be with God, and to feel cease-lessly and continually this delight, unalloyed by anything that could tear us away from it."[66] And what is that "process by which we may be actually guided" to delight in God's own beauty and goodness? "Well, the divine books are full of such instruction for our guid-ance."[67] Contrary to what Plato believes, "there is but one vehicle on which man's soul can mount into the heavens, that is, the self-made likeness in himself to the descending dove, whose wings David the prophet also longed for [Psalm 55:6]. This is the allegorical name used in scripture for the power of the Holy Spirit."[68]

If human beings were created to enjoy Word and Spirit for their own, it no longer makes sense to give isolated attention to human nature in and of itself as if that nature were properly itself in some self-contained fashion. Our faculties were made to operate as they should, to operate well, only when incorporating what remains alien to them, the very perfection of Word and Spirit themselves. By being such a prerequisite for the excellent exercise of human faculties, the presence of Word and Spirit becomes an ingredient of our very constitution in a way that makes human beings the image of God as other creatures are not.

Augustine and Cyril of Alexandria, for example, distinguish between our existing and our existing well and claim that the latter is a function of God's own entrance within us. The excellent func-tioning of our native capacities is not a self-sufficient operation in the sense of simply unrolling from our native capabilities, but requires a strong dependence on the very powers of God which have become

---

[65] Gregory of Nyssa, "On Virginity," chapter 12, p. 358.
[66] *Ibid.*, p. 359 (italics in the original).   [67] *Ibid.*, chapter 11, p. 357   [68] *Ibid.*, p. 356.

ours for the taking in some extraordinary gift of God to us of what is not ours by nature. So for Augustine, "we are [God's] work of art not only insofar as we are human beings but also insofar as we are good."[69] "Unless man turns towards the immutable good which is God, and stands firm in him, he cannot be formed so as to be just and happy."[70] "Man is not so constituted that he would be able, when once created, to perform any good deed by his own powers ... All his good action consists in his being turned to him by whom he has been made, and in his becoming, by his creator's power, just, faithful, wise and blessed always."[71] Just as when light is present in air, when "God is present to him, he is justified, illuminated, and made happy."[72]

Similarly for Cyril of Alexandria, the light that enlightens every man that comes into the world (John 1:9) is not a light that human beings have the potential to become simply in virtue of being rational creatures;[73] without it they are simply darkness (John 1:5).[74] "How should the rational creature ... need light [Is 42:6], if ... [that] very light is inherent in its nature? For God the Father gives his own Son to it as having it not already ... The Only-Begotten holds forth light to them, implanting in them the [very] own good of his essence."[75] God gives us more than our own rational natures at our creation; God also gives us the wisdom in which those rational capacities are used well, by way of Word and Spirit which are God's very presence within us. "God after the mode of creation ... implanted a root of understanding and so rendered the living creature rational ... and [sent] into the mind as it were certain luminous vapors of the unutterable brightness, in a way and mode that himself knows. Therefore our forefather Adam ... is seen to have attained the

---

[69] Augustine, *Literal Meaning of Genesis*, trans. Taylor, vol. ii, Book 8, chapter 12, section 27, p. 51.

[70] *Ibid.*, chapter 10, section 23, p. 49.   [71] *Ibid.*, chapter 12, section 25, p. 50.

[72] *Ibid.*, p. 51.

[73] Cyril of Alexandria, *Commentary on John*, Book 1, chapter 7, p. 66 (John 1:4).

[74] *Ibid.*, p. 68 (John 1:5).   [75] *Ibid.*, chapter 8, p. 82–3 (John 1:9).

being wise ... straightaway from the first beginnings of his being ... perfect in understanding, preserving in himself the illumination given of God to his nature as yet untroubled and pure."[76] "The nature of man is ennobled with *his* rather than its own excellences, when it is found to have ought (sic) that is noble ... For 'what have you that you did not receive' [1 Cor 4:7]? For together with being, the well-being, after such and such wise, is God's gift to the creature and it has nothing of its own, but becomes rich only with the munificence of him who gives it."[77] After human nature "had attained unto the propriety of its perfect nature, by means of both soul and body ... then like a stamp of his own nature the creator impressed on it the Holy Spirit, i.e., the breath of life whereby it became ... complete 'after the image of him that created it,' enabled unto every form of excellence by virtue of the Spirit given to dwell in it."[78]

The proper operation of our faculties is thought to require the presence of God for a variety of reasons. Cyril of Alexandria and Gregory of Nyssa, for example, make a distinction between what we are by nature and what we are by will. The virtue and wisdom produced through the proper operation of our faculties are properties we acquire and lose depending on the exercise of our free will. It is consequently not our nature to be virtuous or wise in the way it is our nature to be rational or alive.

> For things that pertain to any by nature have their possession inherent; things that are eligible of the will, have not that inherence: as for example ... not of one's own will does one attain to being a rational man; for one has it by nature: but one will have it of one's own will to be bad or good, and will likewise of one's own power love righteousness or the reverse.[79]

---

[76] *Ibid.*, chapter 9, pp. 86–7 (John 1:9).

[77] *Ibid.*, p. 116 (John 1:16); see also chapter 7, p. 68 (John 1:5).

[78] *Ibid.*, Book 9, chapter 1, p. 319 (John 14:20).

[79] *Ibid.*, Book 1, chapter 8, p. 79 (John 1:9).

What forms us through the exercise of choice to be virtuous or wise cannot, then, be proper to us. Something that we are not – what is alien to us in being good or wise by nature and not as we are by choice – enters within us when we become good or wise by choice. That which is good and wise by nature is goodness and wisdom itself, the divine goodness and wisdom. We therefore become wise and virtuous by way of a strong participation in God, in virtue of God's very presence in those respects within us. On a borderland between opposites – good and bad, beautiful and ugly – we choose to move in one direction or another; and therefore our nature must be one thing in itself and something else by participation in one of these opposites. "As happens with iron for example: if it [approaches] fire, it assumes the quality of heat, while remaining iron: if it is put in snow or ice, it changes its quality to the mastering influence, and lets the snow's coldness pass into [it]."[80] "Not eternally exhibiting the good," human nature is "not itself to be classed among genuine goods;" humans "become good only by sharing in … something superior to themselves."[81]

There might, moreover, be something more specific about human capabilities that makes the presence of God within them a prerequisite for their proper functioning. Augustine, for example, believes our critical faculties of judgment in moral, intellectual, and aesthetic matters must assess things against an absolute standard that the presence of the divine light within us supplies.[82] Our appreciation of the limited character of what we know or ability to put in critical perspective the degree of justice in human life or quality of created beauty that surrounds us, supposes the presence

[80] Gregory of Nyssa, "Against Eunomius," Book 1, chapter 22, p. 61; see also Book 3, chapter 6, pp. 148–9, for the application to humans.

[81] *Ibid.*, Book 1, chapter 22, p. 62.

[82] See, for example, Augustine, "On the Trinity," Book 14, chapter 15, section 21, p. 194; *City of God*, Book 8, chapter 7, p. 308; and "Of True Religion," trans. John Burleigh, in *Augustine: Early Writings* (Philadelphia: Westminster, 1953), chapters 30–2, sections 54–60, pp. 253–6.

within us of an absolute standard of goodness, truth, and beauty, against which we take the measure of all other things and perceive their failings, a standard divine in its perfection that we as finite, fallible creatures cannot therefore have given to ourselves. This position has a long and illustrious history in Christian theology with or without Augustine's controversial claim that we can have direct knowledge of the divine standard within us. While repudiating such a claim, Thomas Aquinas, for example, holds that our will is only free to choose or not to choose particular goods because we judge them to fall short of absolute goodness and therefore to be only relatively good for certain purposes or in certain respects.[83] The will is never irresistibly inclined to any particular good, and therefore retains freedom of choice with respect to it because God is the only fully satisfying good of human desire.[84]

The idea that the presence of Word and Spirit within us are necessary prerequisites for the proper operation of our faculties is hard to square with the prospective account of the way we image God: if God did not create us with the gifts of Word and Spirit it is hard to argue God intended them to be ingredients of our proper constitution. But the disagreement with a prospective interpretation is otherwise rather slight if, with the vast majority of theologians who hold the view we have been developing, we affirm humans lost both Word and Spirit almost immediately as a consequence of sin. Because there is very little difference between not having something to begin with and losing it straightaway, there might be agreement between the two views at least on the facts of the matter: apart from Christ's coming, human beings generally do not draw on the presence of Word and Spirit as they should. Despite the fact that we had Word and Spirit at our creation before the incarnation, the actual coming of

---

[83] See *Summa Theologica*, vol. II, I.II Q1 a6, pp. 587–8; Q10 a2, pp. 634–5; and Q13 a2, pp. 643–4, and a6, pp. 646–7.

[84] Karl Rahner develops this idea in a more modern idiom in his *Hearers of the Word*, trans. Joseph Donceel (New York: Continuum, 1994), pp. 84–5; see also chapter 5.

Christ would therefore be as crucial for this view as for a prospective one. Lost through sin, the gifts of Word and Spirit that made humans the image of God at their creation would need to be restored to humanity by Christ in some new way that improves upon the original situation that permitted their loss. Cyril outlines the basic shape of the narrative of creation, fall, and redemption in Christ that results:

> in the beginning … the creator of all, taking dust of the ground and having formed man, breathed upon his face the breath of life. And what is the breath of life, save surely the Spirit of Christ …? But since he, [the Spirit which is able to gather us and form us unto the divine impress] fled away from the human nature … the Savior gives us this anew bringing us again into that ancient dignity and reforming us unto his own image.[85]
>
> For since our forefather Adam being turned aside by deceit into disobedience and sin, did not preserve the grace of the Spirit, and thus in him the whole nature lost at last the God-given good … God the Word who knows not turning [needed to] become man, in order that by receiving as man he might preserve the good permanently to our nature.[86]
>
> The Only-Begotten was … made man … that in him … the good things returning and the grace of the Holy Spirit rooted might be preserved securely to our whole nature, the Only-Begotten … lending us the stability of his own nature.[87]

One might account for the loss of both Word and Spirit in my terms by saying that, although we were images of God in the strong senses of both having the divine image within us and being shaped into a human version of it through the power of the Spirit, we were not yet at our creation images through those gifts in the strongest possible fashion because of some immaturity in our reception of

---

[85] Cyril of Alexandria, *Commentary on John*, Book 5, chapter 2, p. 550 (John 7:39).

[86] *Ibid.*, p. 548.

[87] *Ibid.*, p. 549. He thinks, however, that the loss of the Spirit was a gradual process. See Book 2, chapter 1, p. 141 (John 1:32–3).

them. In contrast to Irenaeus who thinks God would not give Word and Spirit to a humanity necessarily immature at its creation – what would be the point of giving meat to babies not yet ready for it? – we might instead say that our immaturity was almost a necessary function of God's showering us all at once with them.[88] Because the gifts of God's Word and Spirit that allowed us to live well were ours from the beginning, we naturally failed to attribute them to God, seeing our well-being as a matter of our natural powers instead, thereby blurring the difference between creature and God and falling into the sin of pride so stressed by Augustine. Or, to put the matter in the way early church theologians such as Origen, Basil, and Cyril in the East would, because we already had them we naturally took those gifts for granted and failed to realize how they could be lost through our own inattention to their cultivation, for example by failing to draw upon them, turning away from them, and therefore leading lives inappropriate to them.

Such immaturity would mean that even when receiving what God was giving us – the status of being images in those two strong senses – we were not fully or properly receiving it. We were more images of both sorts from God's side – in virtue of what God was giving us – than from our own. From our own side, we took from God what our being immature allowed us to receive, becoming images of God according to such poor initial capacities that one might say with Irenaeus we were not properly likenesses of God at all.

One could even say that, in virtue of these faults of immaturity, both gifts – the gift of Word and Spirit and of their transformative effects on us – were not just imperfectly or partially received, but never in a proper way received at all: they were fundamentally distorted from the start, lost in the very process of being received. The very way in which one naturally lives according to the image of God when one has been created from the first with it and is thereby immature – with ingratitude, lassitude, and pride before God – is so

---

[88] See Irenaeus, "Against Heresies," Book 4, chapter 38, sections 1–2, p. 521.

serious a distortion of imaging through human imitation that one might as well not be said to be an image at all. However otherwise wise or good one is, in the most serious respect one is neither. To be ungrateful, unappreciative, full of oneself, is, indeed, to be turned from God and thereby to lose everything – the divine image itself and with it all the wisdom and goodness that comes by way of it. With the distortion of weak imaging through human imitation comes the loss of strong imaging by way of the presence of the divine image. The result is a human life that has turned its back on the presence of God in its meaning for human life, a human life that has made God absent to itself, for all intents and purposes, through blindness to God's presence. And such a loss of the divine image itself only makes the distortion of the weaker sort of imaging through human imitation even worse. From prideful wisdom one falls into simple stupidity. All that is left is a weak image in the weakest sense – human capacities themselves as the image of God without that divine Spirit of the Word's own good-ness and truth that allows them to be exercised excellently.

Jesus Christ, the perfect human image of God because the perfect divine image, brings human life in himself back to its perfect beginning – the perfect beginning that in a sense never was – so that it might be achieved in a way not susceptible of loss. Jesus does not just have the Spirit of God in the way a holy person might, as the gift of something that is not his own by nature; because Jesus is not just human but the Word itself become incarnate, he has the Spirit as his own. He gives to his humanity what he has by nature insofar as he is God. Jesus, insofar as he is divine, does not just *have* the divine image within himself through participation but *is* it, and therefore his humanity can neither exhibit the divine image in an imperfect way nor lose it. Because he *is* the Word, he cannot, for example, fail in any respect to live a human life in conformity with the divine image; "obedience is part of his nature."[89] And if the Spirit of God is secure

---

[89] Gregory of Nyssa, "Against Eunomius," Book 2, section 11, p. 122, discussing the obedience of the Son to the Father.

in the Word of God, it is also secure, irrevocable, in the humanity united to that Word.[90]

(Irenaeus?)

In virtue of our community of nature with the humanity of Christ – in virtue of the humanity we share with him because the Word has made our humanity its own in him – we can have the Spirit that forms Christ's humanity according to the divine image as our own too, with the same sort of consequences. Before Christ came, the divine image of the Word was simply foreign to us, even when we were being made over into it through the gift of the Spirit. Now that the Word has taken our humanity to be its own, the Word has become in a sense proper to us, for all the difference in nature that remains between divine and human. We can be knit into the Word as never before in virtue of the fact that the Word has made our humanity its own in the incarnation.[91] The Word now has *us* in a new way and that means we can have the Word too in a new way, beyond what was possible for us simply as Spirit-filled creatures. Unlike Christ's humanity, the preceding weaknesses and faults of ours will have to be purged, erased, in the process, but our humanity might some day still see the holiness of Christ's own life through attachment to him. While we may waver in our attachment to him, frail in faith and love for him, Christ nonetheless remains our unshakeable hope. In him our perfect imaging of the divine is achieved; in and with him it might confidently be ours, so that we need no longer fear its loss.

The story of creation, fall, and redemption I have just recounted emphasizes the strong sense of participation, by way of the presence of Word and Spirit within us, and the strongest form of weak participation by imitation that comes from the reformation of human life thereby. But such emphases do not make the very weakest form of imaging by participating in God through what we are as

---

[90] Athanasius, "Four Discourses," Discourse 3, chapter 27, section 38, p. 415; see also chapter 25, section 25, p. 407.
[91] *Ibid.*, chapter 26, section 33, p. 412.

creatures drop out of the picture. Those stronger forms of participation and imaging are obviously bound up with that weakest one. One cannot, for example, participate in God in the strong sense, have God for one's own, unless there is something to one apart from God, unless one is an image of God in the weakest sense by having an existence and nature of one's own as a creature. In short, one has to exist and be something oneself, participate in God in the weak sense, in order to receive what one is not – the presence of God.

But much more than this, if human beings are singled out from other creatures by imaging God in these stronger fashions, there must be something unusual about the nature with which they were created that makes sense of that fact. Certain human qualities or capacities that make up the created nature of humans and that therefore image God in the weakest sense must provide the opening for the divine image itself to become their own, present within them, in a way that reforms their humanity according to and in strong imitation of itself. Gregory of Nyssa makes the general point well: "If … man comes to his birth upon these conditions, namely to be a partaker of the good things of God, necessarily he is framed of such a kind as to be adapted to the participation of such a good."[92]

The following questions therefore remain to be addressed. What created qualities and capacities allow humans both to receive the presence of the divine image and to be transformed thereby in imitation of it? How, moreover, do those qualities and capacities themselves image the divine image through a weak form of participation in God?

First of all, human nature must be characterized by an expansive openness that allows for the presence of God within it. It must be the sort of nature that has or makes room for the divine within its basic operations. Gregory of Nyssa, for example, talks of human nature in

---

[92] Gregory of Nyssa, "The Great Catechism," trans. William Moore, in Philip Schaff and Henry Wace (eds.), *Nicene and Post-Nicene Fathers*, vol. v, Second Series (Peabody, Massachusetts: Hendrickson, 1994), chapter 5, p. 478.

this respect as an expanding receptacle or container by way of reason and will:

> Indeed, it is for this that intelligent beings came into existence; namely, that the riches of the divine blessings should not lie idle. The all-creating Wisdom fashioned these souls, these receptacles with free wills, as vessels as it were, for this very purpose, that there should be some capacities able to receive his blessings and become continually larger with the inpouring of the stream.[93]

The presence of the divine is what makes the human capacities of reason and will expand, but for this to happen these human capacities must be expandable, open-ended, that is, in their ability to grow in the good. For the infinite being and goodness of God to come within them they must have the capacity to expand in their own created goodness without end. Human operations themselves, therefore, cannot have been made by God with a fixed term for what they can reach:

> Now the spiritual is without bound or limit … Spiritual substance [that] has been brought into being by creation … is preserved in existence by a continual participation in transcendent being. Thus, in a certain sense it is always being created … for … growth in perfection; along these lines no limit can be envisaged, nor can its progressive growth in perfection be limited by any term. In this way, its present state of perfection, no matter how great and perfect it might be, is merely the beginning of a greater and superior stage.[94]

Thomas Aquinas is another theologian who distinguishes humans from other creatures on the same grounds – because the basic operations of their reason and will have no definite term of a finite, particular sort – for the same purpose – as a way of making clear the special pertinence of the divine presence for human nature. Reason and will are concerned primarily with the true and the good,

---

[93] Gregory of Nyssa, "One the Soul and Resurrection," p. 453.
[94] Gregory of Nyssa, *From Glory to Glory*, p. 197.

respectively, not with the particulars of either knowledge or choice.[95] Indeed, by considering the true and the good per se, human reason knows particulars and the human will chooses them.[96] Things without reason and will simply incline to those particular things that their equally particular natures require for their satisfaction; they incline to particulars insofar as they are particular and not, as humans do, against the background of what is generally intelligible and valuable. An animal, say, inclines through attention and impulse only to particulars that happen to meet the needs of its particular animal nature – for example, that bowl of kibble right in front of it that would satisfy its immediate hunger – without regard for the goodness or intellectual interest per se of such things, which humans take into account. This defining feature of human reason and will gives them their expansiveness, their positive inclination to the universal – that is, an interest in principle in everything that may be good or intelligible – and their negative tendency to be dissatisfied with anything short of the total and complete truth or good.[97] This unlimited openness makes them open, in turn, to the presence of God, since God is absolute truth and goodness in its fullness.

If human life is itself transformed through the presence of God to become some new human imitation of God, the simply mutability of human beings is also obviously significant. To be changed into the divine image in that way, one must have a changeable nature. As contemporary people well know, for example, human life takes culturally variable forms; and having a particular form in one time and place need not rule out another in changed circumstances. This lack of human uniformity and fixity, though it distinguishes us from

[95] See, for example, Thomas Aquinas, *Truth*, trans. Robert W. Schmidt, 3 vols. (Chicago: Henry Regnery, 1954), vol. III, Q25 a1, pp. 210–16; and *On Evil*, trans. Jean Oesterle (University of Notre Dame Press, 1995), Q6, pp. 234–47.

[96] See, for example, Thomas Aquinas, *Summa Theologica*, vol. I, Q80 a2 ad2, p. 410.

[97] For the negative tendency, see Aquinas, *Summa Theologica*, vol. II, I.II Q2 a7, p. 594; Q3 a7, pp. 600–1. See also Q1 a5, p. 587, for the characterization of the "last end," as "what fills man's appetite, [so] that nothing is left besides it for man to desire."

God, need not be lamented. Change can be for the worse; but it can also be for the better. Change indeed is one's only hope if one is not the best to begin with, but a mere creature and then one descended into sin. As Gregory of Nyssa puts this hope for mutability: "Though we are changeable by nature, the Word wants us never to change for the worse; but by constant progress in perfection, we are to make our mutability an aid in our rise to higher things, and so by the very changeability of our nature to establish it immutably in the good."[98]

Human beings must not only be changeable but susceptible to radical transformation beyond the limits of their own – or any – created nature. Human beings through divine power become what they are not and have no capacity of being by themselves: human versions of the divine image itself. They therefore must have a created nature that does put rigid bounds on what they can become. They must not be limited by their own nature in the way other things are, but must have the capacity in some strong sense to become other things. The human intellect has this very capacity, according, for example, to Aquinas:

> Intelligent beings are distinguished from non-intelligent beings in that the latter possess only their own form; whereas the intelligent being is naturally adapted to have also the form of some other thing; for the idea of the thing known is in the knower. Hence it is manifest that the nature of a non-intelligent being is more contracted and limited; whereas the nature of intelligent beings has a greater amplitude and extension; therefore the Philosopher says (*De Anima* iii) that "the soul is in a sense all things."[99]

The human intellect becomes all that it knows, since the very same forms that exist in the sensible things known come to exist in the mind in a more intelligible fashion.

If humans are to be radically reworked through attachment to God, then what is of interest about human nature is its plasticity,

[98] Gregory of Nyssa, *From Glory to Glory*, p. 216.
[99] Thomas Aquinas, *Summa Theologica*, vol. i, Q14 a1, p. 72. See also Q80 a1, p. 409.

its susceptibility to being shaped or molded by outside influences generally. Becoming a human image of God through the impress of the divine image is just an extreme case of having one's character made over by relations with what one is not – God, what is most unlike creatures generally. All creatures may be formed in relation to what they are not but humans seem to have an exaggerated capacity for this that opens them to a radical sort of re-formation from without in the divine image. In contrast to other creatures, human beings are unusually flexible, capable of adapting, of altering their behaviors in order to adjust to changing social and natural environments.[100] Irenaeus expresses especially well the importance of this essential malleability for formation by divine influence:

> Offer to him your heart in a soft and tractable state, and preserve the form in which the creator has fashioned you, having moisture in yourself, lest, by becoming hardened, you lose the impressions of his fingers. But by preserving the framework you shall ascend to that which is perfect, for the moist clay which is in you is hidden [there] by the workmanship of God. His hand fashioned your substance; he will cover you over [too] within and without with pure gold and silver, and he will adorn you to such a degree, that even "the king himself shall take pleasure in your beauty (Psalm 14:11)."[101]

Rather than leading self-sufficient lives, all living creatures become themselves, moreover, by actually taking in things from outside themselves. Their natural processes of growth require nourishment from without. Seeds, for example, will not germinate without water. All living things, in other words, are dependent upon their environments in requiring external inputs for the achievement of their proper functioning. And humans would be no exception. What is exceptional in the human case is the nature of the inputs. Because

---

[100] See Richard Joyce, *The Evolution of Morality* (Cambridge, Massachusetts: MIT Press, 2007), pp. 6–7.

[101] Irenaeus, "Against Heresies," Book 4, chapter 39, section 2, p. 523.

they are made to be in the image of God, humans require God for their nourishment. In heaven, indeed, God will be our only food and drink, as Gregory of Nyssa maintains:

> while our present life is active among a variety of multiform conditions, and the things which we have relations with are numerous, for instance, time, air, locality, food and drink, clothing, sunlight, lamplight, and other necessities of life, none of which, many though they be, are God – that blessed state which we hope for is in need of none of these things, but the divine being will become all [1 Cor 15:28], and instead of all, to us, distributing himself proportionately to every need of that existence … God [will] become … locality, and home, and clothing, and food, and drink, and light, and riches, and dominion, and everything thinkable and nameable that goes to make our life happy.[102]

What is also unusual about human dependence on environments, both social and natural, is the degree to which the character of human life is shaped by such inputs, rather than the other way around. In the case of other living things, what they take in is formed according to their own pre-established natures. For example, the natural resources assimilated by a plant for its nourishment – light, water, nutrients from the soil, and so on – are transformed to conform to the plant's nature. The plant remains what it is, becoming merely a bigger and better version of itself, where there was genuine nourishment for the plant's good. In the human case, to the contrary, the inputs have a much greater effect on the way its nature is played out; to an unusual degree, human nature takes shape in conformity with what helps it grow. Most of the innate and therefore fixed traits and dispositions of human nature underdetermine the character of actual human behaviors. These capacities, needs, and inclinations that make up human nature are designed to be culturally and environmentally sensitive in operation so as to take on a specific

---

[102] Gregory of Nyssa, "On the Soul and the Resurrection," p. 452.

form only as shaped by environmental inputs.[103] For example, the capacity to speak a language is native to human beings, but such a capacity comes to nothing, it takes no concrete form, apart from the social environment that makes one an actual speaker of a particular language.[104]

Formation through the influence of God would just be an extreme case of this sort of conformation of human character to external inputs. When human beings take in God as their proper nourishment, they are reworked according to God's image, rather than the reverse. As Augustine makes the point, "I heard your voice calling me from on high, saying 'I am the food of full-grown men. Grow and you shall feed on me. But you shall not change me into your own substance, as you do with the food of your body. Instead you shall be changed into me.'"[105] Like what happens to light, water, and soil – but now with a peculiar reversal in what are the inputs and what the results – men, women, children, Greek and Jew, free and slave – all go into the process of re-formation and come out in the form of Christ. Although Christ comes within them, Christ is nonetheless the container giving shape to them. Although Christ becomes an ingredient in their natures, they are more malleable inputs than Christ is.

> This is the purpose for us of God ... to raise our flesh and recover his image and remodel man, that we might all be made one in Christ ... that we might no longer be male and female, barbarian, Scythian, bond or free (which are badges of the flesh), but might bear in ourselves only the stamp of God, by whom and for whom we were

---

[103] For more on the way innate human characteristics are both fixed and flexible in this way, see Joyce, *Evolution of Morality*, pp. 7–8, 10, 180, 213.

[104] See *ibid.*, p. 10.

[105] Augustine, *Confessions*, Book 7, chapter 10, p. 147. A reference to the Eucharist is implied. See also his *Tractates on the Gospel of John 28–54*, trans. John W. Rettig (Washington, DC: Catholic University of America Press, 1993), Tractate 41, section 1, paragraph 3, p. 135 (John 8:31–6).

made, and [having] so far received our form and model from him, that we are recognized by it alone.[106]

One might say generally that human beings are unusually plastic because they are usually implicated in, bound up with, their external environments. Margaret Miles expresses well Augustine's stress on this character of human life. Far from being itself in sovereign isolation, the human soul for him is "a partially centered energy, initially hardly distinguishable from its cosmic, physical and spiritual environment, which comes to be cumulatively distinguished and defined by the objects of its attention and affection. For such an object-oriented or intentional entity, the pressing problem of human existence is not relationship, the building of bridges between separate entities, but differentiation, the construction of a center which defines itself and determines the direction of its investment of energy."[107]

More simply put, humans are unusually impressionable in a way that the language of image often unpacks in a quite concrete, albeit metaphorical, way: they are like soft wax that a vast variety of seals might indent to their image; they are the mirror of whatever it is upon which they gaze. They take their identities from the uses to which they put themselves, like vessels that gain their character from whatever they are made to carry. Earthenware or pure gold, what goes into them for certain purposes establishes what they are;

---

[106] Gregory Nazianzen, "Orations," trans. Charles Gordon Browne and James Edward Swallow, in Philip Schaff and Henry Wace (eds.), Nicene and Post-Nicene Fathers, vol. VII, Second Series (Grand Rapids, Michigan: Eerdmans, 1983), Oration 7, chapter 23, p. 237. I do not take him to mean that male and female characteristics are simply wiped out along with one's previous identity, but that such differences remain to be distinctively refashioned according to the same form of Christ. One is no longer identified as a man, say, rather than a woman, but what made one a man remains as the material now reworked into the image of Christ.

[107] Margaret Miles, "Vision: The Eye of the Body and the Eye of the Mind in Saint Augustine's De trinitate and Confessions," Journal of Religion 63/2 (1983), pp. 129–30.

whatever their fundamental constitution as vessels, when full of shit (for example) they can only be shit pots.[108]

This is not an entirely passive or haphazard process of openness to influence by the environment, but one that the exercise of human choice directs. Human nature may be like a mirror, but "it takes on different appearances according to the impressions of free will. If gold is held up to the mirror, the mirror assumes the appearance of gold and reflects the splendor of gold's substance. If anything abominable is held up, its ugliness is impressed in the mirror – for example, a frog, toad, centipede, or anything unpleasant to behold."[109] The entrance of free will into the process only adds to the plastic, shape-shifting character of human nature. "Human nature adapts itself to the direction of thought and it changes according to whatever form it is inclined to by the impulse of free choice."[110] Human nature is such that "whatever it may wish to be [it] becomes that very thing."[111]

In making such choices, whatever the degree of their freedom, humans manage to differentiate themselves from the complex totality of the environment that surrounds them by focusing their energies, turning their attention to specific items of special interest within that environment and engaging in a more concentrated way with them. But this very expenditure of effort produces an emotional investment that re-attaches one to these particular objects in ways not easily shaken off: one draws so close to them that one in some sense becomes them.[112] As Augustine says, "such is the strength of love, that the mind draws in with itself those things which it has

---

[108] See Basil, *On the Human Condition*, trans. Nonna Verna Harrison (Crestwood, New York: St. Vladimir's Seminary Press, 2005), p. 72.

[109] Gregory of Nyssa, *Commentary on the Song of Songs*, trans. Casimir McCambley (Brookline, Massachusetts: Hellenic College Press, 1987), Fourth Homily, p. 92.

[110] *Ibid.*, trans. Harrison in her *Grace and Freedom*, p. 181.

[111] Gregory of Nyssa, "On the Soul and Resurrection," p. 457.

[112] See Miles, "Vision," pp. 128–9.

long thought of with love, and has grown into them by the close adherence."[113] What is to hold for one's relationship with God would then hold for one's relationships with other things: "the soul ... attaches itself to [something] and blends with it by means of the movement and activity of love, fashioning itself according to that which it is continually finding and grasping."[114] "Loving relationship effects a natural commingling with that which is loved. Whatever therefore we choose through our love, that we also become." In such a relationship with external realities, those realities enter within one to turn one into them, in the way, for example, "the mouth of someone receiving a sweet-smelling spice ... becomes itself sweet smelling."[115]

The result again is exaggerated plasticity. Because of this shaping through affect-laden concern, human life takes a variety of forms depending on what it is that people care about.[116] People make a host of different fundamental decisions about what is most important to them – fancy cars, the respect of their peers, wisdom, and so on. They thereby attach themselves to these objects of desire and draw them into themselves, so to speak, as variable organizing principles of their lives.

In so doing they exercise self-reflective powers; they make an object of themselves in projects of self-fashioning and refashioning. By way of self-reflective capabilities, they are able to give the whole of the natures with which they have been created a basic moral and religious orientation, an overall character of a moral and spiritual sort. They thereby exercise husbandry on themselves, as Gregory of Nyssa would say.[117]

---

[113] Augustine, "On the Trinity," Book 10, chapter 5, section 7, p. 138.

[114] Gregory of Nyssa, "On the Soul and Resurrection," p. 450.

[115] Gregory of Nyssa, "Eighth Homily on Ecclesiastes," in Werner Jaeger (ed.), *Gregorii Nysseni Opera* (Leiden, 1960–), vol. v, pp. 422–3, translated by Harrison in her *Grace and Freedom*, p. 189.

[116] See Harry G. Frankfurt, *The Reasons of Love* (Princeton University Press, 2006).

[117] Gregory of Nyssa, "On the Soul and Resurrection," p. 467.

Such reflexive capacities of self-formation mean humans can try to reshape in a self-critical fashion even desires they cannot help having by nature. Humans have many desires reflecting fundamental needs that are part of the nature with which they have been created: desires based on the need for food, shelter, a sense of dignity or worth, human companionship, and so on. But what one makes of these desires is something else. Human beings direct themselves to the ends to which their nature also directs them, as Aquinas maintains; and therefore they remain free at least in the way they pursue those ends.[118] One may have the natural desire to eat, for example, but one need not shape one's life around the importance of food. Asceticism is an obvious case in point.

Humans have the capacity, consequently, to use the passions of their animal natures (as Gregory of Nyssa would term them) – for example, their natural attraction to what benefits them – as instruments of either virtue or vice.[119] That attraction may be the energy propelling them toward, say, profligacy – or God. In virtue of their capacity for self-oversight, humans have the power to cultivate or discourage those natural drives and tendencies that they start out with whether they like it or not, making efforts, for example, to alter their intensities through stimulation or neglect, or efforts to rework the way they figure in one's life as a whole. Indeed, these self-reflective powers account for why human lives can become so horrible, much more horrible than those of other animals. The anger, for example, that an animal might fleetingly feel when faced with an opponent can be husbanded by the human mind – dwelt upon – so as to pervade all one's dealings with others, in a host of variable forms – envy, malice, conspiracy, deceit – with the result that one's whole nature is traced anew after that design.[120]

---

[118] Thomas Aquinas, *Truth*, Q23 a1, p. 95.
[119] Gregory of Nyssa, "On the Soul and Resurrection," p. 442.
[120] Gregory of Nyssa, "On the Making of Man," chapter 18, sections 3–4, p. 408.

These self-formative capacities take humans beyond the limits of their given nature, in the sense that such capacities are not determined to one sort of thing as natural desires are.[121] Unlike the natural inclinations of inanimate forces or even animals, the rational and volitional capacities of humans do not incline in a highly canalized direction to conform to the givens of their own natural form or essential definition. Natures are particular and therefore inclinations to act on such a basis are narrowly circumscribed. Humans act, to the contrary, according to the ideas in their minds about matters they judge to be good in relevant respects for certain purposes. Their inclinations take shape depending on what the human intellect can devise and what the will can perceive to be good and therefore such inclinations show the same openness to the universal – to the true and the good per se – that characterizes those basic powers of reason and will. This accounts for the heightened variability of these inclinations in operation. People turn out in wildly different ways, for better or for worse.

Or, one might say these self-formative capacities are determined by human nature, but the peculiar nature of humans as rational agents is just to have no particular nature to be true to, in the way animals are true to their natures when acting properly for their own good. To be determined by human nature means to be determined by the open-ended nature of human reason and will, and therefore not to be determined to choose any one thing. Humans can think of a variety of things that it would be good to do in certain respects and for certain purposes, and what they decide about what is most important to them in the course of such deliberations decides in great part the character of their lives, the identity they come to exhibit in their acts – *that* is just their nature.

---

[121] For this contrast between natural desires, on the one hand, and inclinations through human cognition and comparative judgment, on the other, see Thomas Aquinas, *Summa Theologica*, vol. I, Q80 a1, p. 49; Q82 a1–2, pp. 413–14; and Q83 a1, p. 418. See also his contrast between natural and intelligent causes in, for example, Q 19 a4, p. 106; and Q47 a1 ad1, p. 246.

Humans, it is true, are determined to God: being formed in the image of God is their good by nature. But that is just *not* to be determined in any particular direction as other things are, since God is the absolute good and not a limited one. Humans have a nature that imitates God only by not having, one might say, a clearly delimited nature. Every other creature imitates God by expressing the goodness that God is in a limited form; they are good by being a definite something – a pig or a rock, indeed the best pig or rock they can be. Humans are a definite sort of creature distinct from others and in that sense of course still have a particular nature; they are not God who alone is different from others by not being a kind of thing. But humans still stand out by their failure to be clearly limited by a particular nature as other creatures are.

Inevitably when it comes to spiritual nature, and especially man ... this word "nature" will have two partially different meanings, according to whether it is applied to this particular species that we form, among other species in the universe, or to the nature of spirit in so far as this is something which goes beyond any particular species because it is innately opened to the universal and directly related to God ... This kind of infinitude is precisely what constitutes the "definition" of man and his "limit."[122]

Failure of definition by remaining ill-defined is not the primary point here. More to the point is failure of definition through excessive interest in, even love for, the unlimited. Humans seem to have an underlying concern for what is absolutely good per se – for God – for what is not merely good in certain respects but fully good in a perfectly unlimited way. They want in some sense to *be* that absolute good rather than a particular sort of thing by being formed in and through a relationship with it, for example, by knowing the absolute

---

[122] Henri de Lubac, *The Mystery of the Supernatural*, trans. Rosemary Sheed (New York: Herder and Herder, 1967), pp. 137–8; the last sentence following Karl Rahner, *Mission and Grace* (London, 1963), vol. I, p. 127.

truth that is God, the absolute good for human cognition that would come by way of God's very presence to the mind.

The early Eastern church's stress on free will as the image – or often secondarily, rule in the sense of self-rule or self-oversight – could now be taken in a new light, not as the promotion of some vaunted power in a positive sense, an imitation of divine omnipotence, but as an interest in the unusual plasticity of human lives absent of any predetermined specification by nature. Free will becomes a sign of unusual variability. Powers of self-direction mean humans can rework what they are given by nature so as to imitate almost anything along the continuum of ontological ranks, from the bottom to the top.

All the qualities of humans typically highlighted by the theologians upon whom I draw here have something to do with their rational capacities, and there is probably a good reason for this even from a more modern point of view (as I have implied) if open-ended plasticity is what these theologians are trying to highlight. Their strangely unlimited character is the fundamental reason for traditional theological preoccupation with human intelligence and rational volition when discussing the way humans image God. These faculties are of interest because of their excessive openness to what exceeds their own or any limited nature.

Especially in the early church such a focus often dovetails with a marked matter-versus-spirit dualism. It is therefore important to see the way that plastic or non-natured *bodies* are the ultimate issue even for these early church theologians. At the end of the day it is our bodies that are to be remade into Christ's body.

Mitigating any matter–spirit dualism for all these theologians (who generally hold a hylomorphic anthropology in any case) is the fact that souls are influenced as bodies are (for example, through the incorporation of nourishing outside factors and influences) and the fact that the object of self-formation includes the body. It is very easy therefore to express what they are trying to say in a more contemporary idiom not, so obviously at least, bound up with any need to distinguish spiritual from material: human beings form themselves with reference to a whole host of outside influences – people, places, animate and inanimate influences, etc. – and what is formed is their whole lives, irrespective of any division between the material and the spiritual. When our minds are therefore formed according to the divine image, so are our bodies: when the mind is "adorned by the likeness of the archetypal beauty ... the nature which is governed by it [i.e., the body] ... is adorned by the beauty that the mind gives, being, so to say, a mirror of the mirror."[123] Or as Gregory Nazianzen states: "What God is to the soul, that the soul becomes for the body, which is its servant, and adapts the fellow servant to God."[124]

When it is the plasticity of human lives before the divine that is at issue, blurring the boundary between spirit and matter is often, indeed, a primary gambit. A case in point is the seemingly oxymoronic notion of "spiritual matter" in Augustine's treatment of Genesis.[125] Rational creatures have an essential character like unformed matter (the "abyss" of Genesis 1:2) – that is, they exhibit matter's lack of form per se – when considered apart from the well-being – that knowing well – that results from their being informed by God's own image. Spiritual natures in particular are like fluid wax in need of sealing; otherwise empty mirrors to be made light by light. Even when lacking matter that gains its shape through form, they

[123] Gregory of Nyssa, "On the Making of Man," chapter 12, section 9, p. 399; the discussion continues into sections 10–11. See also his "On the Soul and Resurrection, pp. 441–2; and "On Infants' Early Deaths," trans. William Moore and Henry Austin Wilson, in Philip Schaff and Henry Wace (eds.), Nicene and Post-Nicene Fathers, vol. v, Second Series (Peabody, Massachusetts: Hendrickson, 1994), p. 375.

[124] Gregory Nazienzen, "Orations," Oration 2, section 17, following the translation of Gerhart B. Ladner, "The Philosophical Anthropology of Saint Gregory of Nyssa," Dumbarton Oaks Papers 12 (1958), p. 77.

[125] See Augustine, "Literal Meaning of Genesis," trans. Hill, vol. I., Book 1, sections 2–3, p. 169; sections 9–11, pp. 171–2; and section 17, p. 175. See the helpful discussion of such passages in Hilary Armstrong, "Spiritual or Intelligible Matter in Plotinus and St. Augustine," Etudes Augustiniennes (1954), pp. 277–83.

are like matter in being spirits that require formation by God.[126] By taking God into themselves, all that they are is turned into the matter, so to speak, for a new divine organization of what they are. Whatever the elements of their composition, it all becomes material for a new formation according to the divine image, a new formation that in its splendor renders insignificant any such underlying differences in materials: "Consider, for example, a drawing tablet. If it bears a drawing of the king's likeness [Christ], the difference in material – whether it be wood or gold or silver – does not affect the drawing. The accurate resemblance of the image to its model ... makes the difference in material pass unnoticed."[127]

Human materiality is essential, moreover, to the image of God so as to take the whole of existence, irrespective of any division between spirit and matter, to God. This is why angels or disembodied pure intelligences are not the image. Only in virtue of the fact that they have bodies can the whole world hope in humans. Humans demonstrate that, appearances to the contrary (especially in the cultural and philosophical milieu of the early church), the material world itself is plastic – by extension just as plastic to divine influence, one might hope, as human lives. God formed humans out of the dust of the earth so that when formed in the image of God humans might show that the earth too can be made over in God's image: both matter and mind are made for a single grace.[128]

How might the fact that humans are open to radical transformation – which we now see to be shared by the whole human person, body and soul – be an image of the divine image in and of itself, that is, considered apart from what happens to humans through incorporation of the divine image? One can say human

---

[126] For this sense of composition between form and what is to be formed that affects creatures irrespective of their materiality, see Balás, ΜΕΤΟΥΣΙΑ ΘΕΟΥ, p. 129.

[127] Basil, "Concerning Baptism," trans. Monica Wagner, in his *Ascetical Works*, The Fathers of the Church, vol. IX (New York: Fathers of the Church, 1950), pp. 379–80.

[128] Gregory of Nyssa, "Great Catechism," chapter 6, p. 480.

nature in this respect forms an image of that divine image by imitating God's own incomprehensibility.

God is incomprehensible, beyond human powers of positive explication through concepts and speech, because God is without limits or bounds. God is without limits of time, being framed by no beginning or end. Existing in perfect simplicity, God is without internal limits or boundaries dividing the divine nature into manageable component parts or aspects for our comprehension. The absolute fullness of being and goodness, God transcends all divisions between kinds and exceeds all bounds of a particular nature or mode of being that might allow God to be set alongside others or encompassed by anything it is not. God is in that sense formless.[129] For all these reasons, the divine cannot be comprehended or contained in any respect; it is simply not anything that we can get our heads around.

Humans imitate God's incomprehensibility by having a nature that is also in a sense unlimited, unbounded by a clearly delimited nature, in virtue, in the human case, of an expansive openness and initial indefiniteness apart from some more specific formation from without that our own self-reflective capabilities help to direct. God's own incomprehensibility is imitated here but in only a negative and prospective way. Rather than being unlimited through inclusiveness, through unbounded fullness in the way God is, our powers are unlimited through lack, through an initial failure of predetermination, by not being anything in particular in any very concrete way to start, and by an emptiness in our own nature that opens us up to everything intelligible and good.

Whatever the knowable dimensions of human nature, its apophatic ones are what count here for imaging of God. An

---

[129] See, for example, Gregory of Nyssa, "Answer to Eunomius' Second Book," trans. M. Day, in Philip Schaff and Henry Wace (eds.), *Nicene and Post-Nicene Fathers*, vol. v, Second Series (Peabody, Massachusetts: Hendrickson, 1994), p. 257. See also his "On Virginity," chapter 10, p. 355, on formless beauty.

apophatically-focused anthropology forms the natural consequence of an apophatic theology.[130] If humans are the image of God they must be, as Gregory of Nyssa affirms, an incomprehensible image of the incomprehensible: "If, while the archetype transcends comprehension, the nature of the image were comprehended, the contrary character of the attributes ... would prove the defect of the image ... Since the nature of our mind ... evades our knowledge, it has an accurate resemblance to the superior nature, figuring by its unknowableness the incomprehensible nature."[131]

This imaging of divine incomprehensibility makes them in particular the image of the divine image, the second person of the trinity. In theologies that deny the possibly subordinationalist import of talking about the second person of the trinity as the image of the first – that is, "image" does not mean any lesser degree of divinity – the second person of the trinity is not comprehensible while the first is incomprehensible, but images it in its very incomprehensibility. Athanasius following Origen can thus affirm: "If there is an image of the invisible God, it is an invisible image ... that image of the Father's ineffable and nameless and unutterable subsistence."[132] And this holds for the incarnation of the second person of the trinity too. The second person of the trinity – whether the first born of creation by being the one through and for whom the world was created, or the first born of the dead by becoming incarnate for our salvation to everlasting life – remains in a strong sense an image of the invisible.[133] Jesus is not the comprehensible stand-in or substitute for an incomprehensible divinity but the very exhibition of

---

[130] See Nellas, *Deification in Christ*, p. 22.

[131] Gregory of Nyssa, "On the Making of Man," chapter 11, section 4, p. 396; sections 2–3 are also relevant.

[132] Athanasius, "Defence of the Nicene Faith," trans. John Henry Newman and Archibald Robertson, in Philip Schaff and Henry Wace (eds.), *Nicene and Post-Nicene Fathers*, vol. IV, Second Series (Grand Rapids, Michigan: Eerdmans, 1957), chapter 6, section 27, p. 168.

[133] Col 1:15.

the incomprehensible divinity of the Word in a human form or medium.[134] Jesus displays in his life what it means to be an incomprehensible image in the flesh of an incomprehensible God. Following the paradigm of Christ, then, there would be something incomprehensible about human nature as it is shaped by a relationship with God, too, which makes it the imitation of God. We are an incomprehensible image of the incomprehensible both in those natural capacities that allow us to be radically re-formed, and in what we become in relation to the true image, the Word incarnate. Aided by God to become what we are not, we might one day come to imitate in our humanity the inclusiveness of the absolute being and goodness of God. Formed by the Word when that day comes, humans imitate the incomprehensibility of God in a positive sense, for example, by having in themselves something as incomprehensibly good as God is good. On that day we will "become ... as beautiful as the [divine] beauty which [we] have touched and entered, and ... be made as bright and luminous ... in the communion of the real light."[135] Not despairing of winning this object though it seems too high for our comprehension, we look forward to the time when we will be formlessly beautiful as the divine beauty is, when it will be possible to see in us "the beauty which is invisible and formless, which is destitute of qualities and far removed from everything which we recognize in bodies by the eye, [and which therefore] can never be made known by the traits which require nothing but the perceptions of our senses in order to be grasped."[136]

Like what happened in Christ's own human life, the new character of human lives as they are made over in him will be ultimately comprehensible according to a divine image that cannot itself be

---

[134] Even in a theology like that of Athanasius, where the stress is on the pedagogical function of the Word's incarnation in a visible form, *what* is revealed in the contest with idolatry is the incomprehensible and uncontained character of divinity in its very invisibility. See Athanasius, "On the Incarnation," chapters 14–19, pp. 43–7.

[135] Gregory of Nyssa, "On Virginity," chapter 11, p. 356.

[136] *Ibid.*, p. 355; see also his "On the Making of Man," chapter 5, section 1, p. 391.

comprehended. Becoming what we are only by way of the influence upon us of the divine image incarnate in human flesh, we become incomprehensible to ourselves in that what we have become is no longer anything explicable in simply human terms. Just as in Jesus' own life, what makes sense of our new lives – the divine image – remains mysterious in the incomprehensibility of its own full goodness.

The divine image that sets the pattern for Jesus' own human life cannot be captured in that it remains invisible in its divinity even as it surfaces as the organizing principle of now perfected human life. The divinity of Jesus' life is an inference, hidden behind the fact of a human life dedicated to our salvation, hidden behind the fact of human acts that save. All one sees is a human life with an unusual capacity to heal and forgive, unimaginable apart from divine powers, powers that one consequently must affirm by faith rather than sight. "Just as, though invisible, he is known through the works of creation; so, having become man, and being in the body unseen, it may be known from his works that he who can do these is not man, but the power and Word of God."[137] In much the same fashion, what is responsible for making our lives this way will not appear *as* itself or per se, in any part of them, but will appear invisibly, only in and through a re-formed character of human life otherwise unintelligible in merely human terms.

In leading transformed lives through Christ we will come to be more than an imitation of the incomprehensible only in virtue of our assuming or taking on the identity of what we are not, the alien identity qua divine of the Word incarnate itself. By attaching ourselves to the incomprehensible that has attached itself to us in becoming incarnate for this very purpose, we become in the strongest sense incomprehensible ourselves. One with Christ, incomprehensible in his divinity, we take on the very incomprehensibility of the divine rather than simply running after it, working to reproduce it in human terms.

---

[137] Athanasius, "On the Incarnation," chapter 18, p. 46.

This is the hidden or invisible incomprehensibility that lies behind the visible incomprehensibility of our new way of living. Christ's own life provides not just the pattern of a new human way of life for our imitation, but the cause of that pattern in us, by way of the uniting of humanity and divinity in him. The second person of the trinity not only shows forth the true image in human form by becoming incarnate but makes us like that image by uniting human nature thereby with the very incomprehensibility of the divine life. It is by being bound to the incomprehensible in and through Christ – and thereby gaining a new identity in him apart from anything we are in and of ourselves – that we will one day come to live a boundlessly full and good human life.

2 | Grace (part one)

With an eye to Christ, who is both the model for and means to our becoming the image of God, we saw in the last chapter that humans primarily image God by attachment to the divine image itself, an attachment that forms human life according to its pattern. Through the power of the Holy Spirit within them, humans are molded by the very impression of the divine image to become human versions of it. This Christ-centered treatment of the way humans image God contained implicitly an account of grace. We become images in the strongest fashion in being bound in Christ to what we are not, the second person of the trinity, and by having what we are not, the Holy Spirit, within us as the power for new life according to that divine image. The strong sense here in which we participate or share in what we are not could simply be called grace.

In this chapter (and the next) I make this account of grace explicit by developing the way it accords quite well with Protestant sensibilities while bridging the usual theological divides between Protestants and Catholics. Despite the fact that early church sources formed the underpinning for the treatment of the way humans image God in the last chapter, the Protestant resonances of what that treatment implies about grace are nevertheless very strong. Because, indeed, of those rather unusual underpinnings, the Protestant-leaning account of grace developed from it has the potential to push the usual theological differences between Protestants and Catholics in new directions.

Nature, rather than sin, is the primary reference point for understanding grace and in that respect, it is true, the position is not especially Protestant. Human beings need grace to become images of God, not because they are sunk in sin but because they cannot be images of any strong sort simply in virtue of what they are. "By grace," then, means "not by nature."

The images of God by nature, or natural images of God, that form a contrast with images by grace, are in the first place divine ones. Saying humans are images by grace and not by nature is a way of distinguishing them from both the second person of the trinity and Christ. An image of God by nature, or natural image of God, would have to be itself divine. The second person of the trinity is the natural image of the first person because of the divine nature they hold in common. Christ is the image of God by nature because as the second person of the trinity incarnate he has a divine nature in addition to a human one. If humans as mere creatures have divinity for their own only as a matter of grace, then humans cannot be images of God by nature, or natural images of God, in the way the second person of the trinity and the Word incarnate are.

Since what makes us strong images of God is the gift by grace of divinity exceeding our created nature, the image that contrasts with grace is, in the second place, human nature. To say we become images of God by grace is to say we cannot be that sort of image in virtue of the human nature with which we were created. Grace is necessary to make us strong images of God because our nature as human creatures is incapable of doing so. The image of God by nature with which the image of God by grace is contrasted is therefore simply human nature itself in whatever weak capacities for imaging God it possesses in and of itself.

God's making us images of God in a strong sense is an act of unmerited largesse or grace on God's part, not primarily because of our sin, but for much the reason creation is. In the way that we do not merit our creation as rational creatures, we also do not merit the gift of the divine light that makes us wise beyond any simple human capabilities.

Just as ... it [the spiritual creation] could make no claim on you [God], by its own deserts, to be the kind of life, which could receive your light, so, now that it existed, it could not claim to receive this gift by its own merits ... In this way it owes to your grace, and to your grace alone, both the gift of its very existence and the gift of a life [endowed with light].[1]

The problem that stands in the way of our being strong images of God and that grace remedies primarily has to do with human nature and not sin. We cannot receive the highest good that God wants to give us, the good of God's own life, while remaining mere creatures. The very created character of our existence, the fact, that is, that we are not divine, forms the major impediment to our receiving what God intends to give us in creating us, and constitutes therefore the major impetus behind the gift of God's grace. No created version of God's own goodness can ever adequately approach that goodness. If God wants to give it to humans, they have to be elevated beyond what they are themselves as creatures. In short, humans have to be given God in addition to being given themselves. Christ is the highest possible form in which the good of God's own life can be given to us: in him God and the human are one. Therefore, the grace of God in Christ becomes the highest way of addressing the impediment to God's design posed by creation, irrespective of any problem of sin.

Our created nature is inadequate not simply for the enjoyment of the good of God's own life, which is God's ultimate end in creating us, but for our own properly human fulfillment. Because we have been created to have such a close relationship with the very goodness of God, with a nature that requires attachment to God to be what it is supposed to be, grace is necessary to complete our nature, to add to it what it requires for its own excellent operations and well-being. Receiving God's grace becomes a requirement for simply being a human being fully alive and flourishing.

[1] Augustine, *Confessions*, trans. R. S. Pine-Coffin (Baltimore, Maryland: Penguin, 1976), p. 313.

Here, however, a hallmark of Catholicism – the idea that grace completes or perfects nature – has the peculiar tone of what one might call Protestant pessimism. Our created nature is no doubt good, better than nothing, an approximation of God's own goodness however weak, indeed a fuller approximation of that goodness than what is found in other sorts of creatures. But saying that grace completes or perfects nature is not a way of highlighting that fact. It is not, as in Catholic theology (which follows Thomas Aquinas in this regard) a way of emphasizing the value of creation, which the gift of God's grace respects, but a way of pointing out the inadequacies that essentially mar it and that account for God's own dissatisfaction with it. It is not a way of pointing out what is valuable about creation but what is wrong with it. Saying that grace completes nature implies human nature need not be broken for grace to be received. But this is not so much now out of respect for human nature as because in some sense human nature considered in and of itself is already in a broken condition – broken in the sense of both being inoperable by itself and broken open or emptied.

Grace completes nature not by building on what nature is positively but by remedying what it lacks. Human nature needs to be completed by grace because of a lacuna in its own operations, an absence at its heart. Grace is necessary for the perfection of the human because of how much it needs something – God – that by definition its own nature cannot provide.

Because grace is not primarily building in any positive sense on creation, on what it is as much as on what it is not, the transition between nature and grace is nothing like a continuous process of incremental improvement from good to better. It has more the disjunctive character of the either-or between sin and grace typical of Protestantism. The move from nature to grace – for example, from being rational to knowing well by way of the divine light – is a discontinuous, radical leap between qualitatively different conditions, between a condition of abject need apart from that light to a state of incredible plenty with it. The movement here is from next to nothing to everything, from unformed to formed, from having no form to being well formed.

Because it is the gift of God's own life that accounts for this movement from what we are by nature to a graced state, the movement does not as much reinforce our natural capacities as lead us in directions running contrary to them. Grace does not perfect or complete human nature by helping it to be more properly or excellently what it is in itself apart from God. Instead, we are aided by grace to live in ways that are not natural to us because in keeping with divine power. Our nature is perfected and completed, ironically, by making us act unnaturally, in a divine rather than human way. Cyril of Alexandria makes the point well:

> For not otherwise could that nature which is subject to corruption be uplifted into incorruption, but by the coming down to it of that nature which is high above all corruption and variableness, lightening the [burden] of ever sinking humanity, so that it can attain its own good; and by drawing it into fellowship and intercourse with itself ... extricating it from the limitations which suit the creature, and fashioning into conformity with itself that which is of itself contrary to it.[2]

What is prone by its own nature to fall – to die and to stray – is lifted up by a power that by nature rises without fail, the divine power of eternal life. Our natural direction is thereby reversed.

> Consider that water is cold by nature, but when it is poured into a kettle and brought to the fire, then it all but forgets its own nature, and goes away into the operation of that which has mastered it. We too then in the same way, even though we be corruptible through the nature of our flesh, yet forsaking our own infirmity by the immingling of life, are trans-elemented to its property, that is life.[3]

[2] Cyril of Alexandria, *Commentary on the Gospel according to John*, trans. P. E. Pusey (Oxford: James Parker, 1874), Book 11, chapter 12, pp. 554–5 (John 17:22–30).

[3] *Ibid.*, Book 4, chapter 2, p. 419 (John 6:53). For the Greek, along with analysis, see Marie-Odile Boulnois, "L'eucharistie mystère d'union chez Cyrille d'Alexandrie," *Revue des*

Rather than downplaying the seriousness of sin, moreover, the nature–grace dynamic as we have been developing it plays it up. If the gift of God's grace is necessary not just for the enjoyment of God's own goodness but also for the excellent operation of our own human powers, existing without it in a state of sin is an extremely dire predicament. With the loss of God's grace, we lose everything – both God and the possibility of living well. Because the means to our knowing and loving God is also the means by which we know and choose anything well, in losing the ability to know and love God, all our acts are ruined. Everything we do, even in the pursuit of penultimate created goods, is done in the wrong way, because done without the one thing necessary for every good in life, the gift of God's own goodness through Word and Spirit. The consequences here are quite in keeping with a Protestant understanding of total depravity, as expressed for instance by John Calvin:

> The gifts which the Lord left to us after the Fall are certainly worthy of praise judged in themselves. But since the contagion of sin has run riot through every part, nothing pure and free from all defilement will be found in us … All these things are polluted in us, just as wine which has been completely spoilt and tainted by the stench of its leather bottle loses the pleasantness of its flavor and has a bitter and horrible taste.[4]

Because we have been created to live by divine nourishment, the life we lead under sin is so corrupted indeed that it would be better termed a kind of death. The self-directive faculties of humans require life-nourishment from Word and Spirit and without it they in some serious sense die.

> Looking upon God is nothing less than the life-nourishment appropriate … to an intellectual nature. For just as these bodies, earthy as

Sciences Religieuses 74/2 (2000), p. 165. See also Cyril of Alexandria, *Commentary on John*, Book 4, chapter 3, p. 434 (John 6:61–2).

[4] John Calvin, *Calvin's Commentaries: The Gospel according to St. John 1–10*, trans. T. H. L. Parker (Grand Rapids, Michigan: Eerdmans, 1993), pp. 66–7 (John 3:6).

they are, are preserved by nourishment that is earthy … so … there is an intellectual nourishment as well, by which such natures are maintained in existence … To see God is … the life of the soul … When ignorance hinders this apprehension of God, the soul which thus ceases to partake of God, ceases to live … Partaking in God being no longer effected there follows at once the canceling of the soul's life, which is the worst of evils.[5]

Our bodies still have what they need to live, our mental faculties, for example, still animating their course by moving them to the acts of which they are capable according to our own self-direction – making our eyes to look in a particular direction or our feet to step according to our chosen purposes. But missing is the God-constituted vitality required for these self-directive faculties themselves, and therefore we are dead in the most important respect even as we live:

Do not the stupid and the ungodly and the unjust walk, work, see, hear, and speak? But when it elevates itself to something which it itself is not, and which is above it, and from which it itself is [God who is life itself], it receives wisdom, justice, devotion; and when it was without these, it was dead and did not have the life by which it lived itself, but that by which it made the body live. For there is one thing in the soul by which the body is made to live, another by which it itself is made to live.[6]

If our lives can still be turned around through God's help, this presumes no optimism about sin's consequences, as if something good remained of us to be the basis for simple modification. Instead, the grace that changes us has its analogue in the divine acts that created us – from nothing. The movement from our sinful state to

---

[5] Gregory of Nyssa, "On Infants' Early Deaths," trans. William Moore and Henry Austin Wilson, in Philip Schaff and Henry Wace (eds.), *Nicene and Post-Nicene Fathers*, vol. v, Second Series (Peabody, Massachusetts: Hendrickson, 1994), pp. 375–6.

[6] Augustine, *Tractates on the Gospel of John 11–27*, trans. John W. Rettig, (Washington, DC: Catholic University of America Press, 1988), Tractate 19, section 12, paragraph 3, p. 151 (John 15:19–30).

because he makes us step into nonexistence? Athanasius or Anselm?

GRACE (PART ONE)

the life we lead in Christ is like the rebirth of the dead. The starkest possible disjunction distinguishes the states between which we move from sin to grace – from death, on the one hand, to life, on the other – and therefore this movement is something like our literal recreation. Only God can help us cross from death to life, from nothing to something; we are no more responsible for this recreation through our own powers than we are for our creation.

Because what we lose through sinning is something that we are not, human nature remains as it is, however: essentially uncorrupted for all the utterly dire consequences of sin. What makes us totally corrupt is the loss of something that we are not – divinity – and therefore our human nature is not essentially changed for the worse in losing it. Since what we had – divine power – was always foreign to our nature and only externally imparted to us as a kind of accidental addition to our nature, the loss of it, while rendering our condition totally corrupt, will not make our human nature fundamentally any different. The removal of what is foreign to one's essential nature and merely adheres to it from without does not bring with it any change in one's essential nature.[7]

Divinity is an ingredient of our nature through external impartation and not because it is what human nature essentially is.[8] The divine power within us, which gives us wisdom, justice, and eternal life, is just not what our own essential nature is; our human nature is properly itself, indeed, only in virtue of a contrast with it. Human nature is one thing, equally capable of opposites, in a borderland

---

[7] See Gregory of Nyssa, "Against Eunomius," trans. H. C. Ogle, William Moore, and Henry Austin Wilson, in Philip Schaff and Henry Wace (eds.), *Nicene and Post-Nicene Fathers*, vol. v, Second Series (Peabody, Massachusetts: Hendrickson, 1994), Book 1, section 22, pp. 61–2, and Book 3, section 6, pp. 148–9. See the analysis by David Balás, *ΜΕΤΟΥΣΙΑ ΘΕΟΥ: Man's Participation in God's Perfections according to Saint Gregory of Nyssa* (Rome: Herder, 1966), pp. 147–9.

[8] See Gregory of Nyssa, "On the Soul and the Resurrection," trans. William Moore and Henry Austin Wilson, in Philip Schaff and Henry Wace (eds.), *Nicene and Post-Nicene Fathers*, vol. v, Second Series (Peabody, Massachusetts: Hendrickson, 1994), p. 440; he is discussing the passions.

between virtue and beauty and their opposites, as Gregory of Nyssa says.[9] Something else is what that nature becomes by participation in one or the other of those opposites that it is not. Humans are not by nature good as God is; human nature is one thing and the goodness it receives another, human nature coming to possess the good "by acquisition ... [of] the goodness of some good which lies above it."[10] Therefore in becoming one or the other of these opposites it retains its own nature: "as happens with iron ... if it approaches ... fire, it assumes the quality of heat while remaining iron."[11]

In much the same fashion Augustine discusses the difference between human nature and what is within it, with a similar consequence for the sort of nature humans have – a nature distinct from others in that it can lose any of the attributes that it gains in virtue of what is within it.

> None of these is what it contains; the vessel is not the liquid, nor the body the color, nor the atmosphere the light or heat; nor is the soul the same as its wisdom. Hence things of this sort may be deprived of what they have, and adopt other qualities and different attributes; the vessel may be emptied of its liquid, the body lose its color, the atmosphere become dark or cold, the soul become stupid.[12]

The elements of human nature with the capacity to receive all these different inputs – human powers of rational volition, say – would remain then essentially unaltered throughout all the changes that come by way of their reception. Stupid, unjust, dying human beings are still human in just the way wise, just, and eternally alive ones are. What makes them good images of God in a weak sense remains untouched whether dying in sin or flourishing through grace. "By reason of human nature being equally inclined to either ... virtue or vice [depending on what people choose to attach themselves to], it is

---

[9] Gregory of Nyssa, "Against Eunomius," Book 1, section 22, p. 61.

[10] Ibid.   [11] Ibid.

[12] Augustine, *City of God*, trans. Henry Bettenson (New York: Penguin, 1977), Book 11, chapter 10, p. 441.

in our power to become sons either of night or of day, while our nature yet remains."[13] The ability to lose wisdom and justice and replace them with their opposites is itself, indeed, one of the defining characteristics of human nature. God alone, being good "in a single uncompounded nature, looks ever the same way, and is never changed by the impulse of choice, but always wishes what he is, and is, assuredly, what he wishes."[14]

A Protestant stress on total depravity becomes in this way perfectly compatible with a Catholic affirmation that our good nature has been left intact. The two sides come together because the usual terms of disagreement between them have been radically shifted. The question at issue no longer concerns the degree to which human nature has been corrupted by sin, whether or not human nature has been so corrupted by sin as to be destroyed. Total corruption no longer marks the end point in the possible extent to which the essential goodness of our nature has been harmed by sin, with a difference of opinion between Protestant and Catholics amounting to how seriously to consider any good remaining to us. To the contrary, human nature need not be affected at all for total depravity to be our condition. Rather than attacking essential human capacities such as free will, sin damages the way divine power is present to us; it makes that power inaccessible to us. In contrast to the usual Protestant and Catholic disputes, human nature in and of itself is not the primary or direct focus when considering the effect of sin on us. At issue instead is the status of divine power within us, whether or not, that is, we continue to draw upon it, and the consequences for us if we do not.

The same point about human nature remaining intact under conditions of sin can be made more simply perhaps by distinguishing between the effect that the loss of divine power has on our operations and on our nature. The loss of divine power totally corrupts our operations; those operations are damaged in toto and at their root. But this total corruption of our operations need not

[13] Gregory of Nyssa, "Against Eunomius," Book 3, section 6, p. 148. [14] *Ibid.*, p. 149.

67

require any underlying damage to have been done to our essential human nature by sin. All that is required is the loss of the divine inputs necessary for the proper functioning of human capabilities. Without those inputs our nature remains as it is but our operations break down. Indeed it is just because our nature remains fundamentally the same – one requiring divine inputs for its proper functioning – that sin does our operations such harm.

Once again, the key here is to shift attention from human nature itself to our functional dependence on something outside ourselves – divine inputs – now lost to us. It is not what sin does to our nature but to our environment that matters here; our operations are corrupted because sin alters what is available in our surroundings for our proper nourishment. Without any disease or damage to our natural capabilities, we are poisoned or polluted from without, because of what we have done to the only environment suitable for us. In virtue of our sin, we are, in short, like perfectly well-formed creatures living in an environment that is not good for us. The oxygen-rich environment, in which we were made to live, has now been transformed by our sin into a high altitude one that asphyxiates and enervates us. Sin forces us therefore to make do with external inputs to which our nature does not suit us. Missing what we need, we substitute other things for it: created inputs replace a divine one as our central formative principle. But this means we are forced to work in ways we are not designed to. Nothing we do, consequently, is satisfying for us. Made to be ever-expanding containers for divine good, we repeatedly take within ourselves created goods with the expectation that they will be similarly satisfying; but rather than filling us up those created goods merely run through us leaving us empty and hungry for more.[15]

[15] See the discussion of Gregory of Nyssa's "Life of Moses " and "Fourth Beatitude" by Verna Harrison, *Grace and Freedom according to St. Gregory of Nyssa* (Lewiston, New York: Mellon, 1992), pp. 185–7.

Of course sin does not make for an unhealthy environment without our cooperation. Sin means that we have chosen an environment for ourselves that is not suitable for our nature; it means we seek of ourselves nourishment that is not good for us. This seems a function of the odd openness of human faculties that we discussed in the last chapter: human faculties seem open to what is both good and bad, even for themselves. But it also suggests our fundamental desires and inclinations are slightly askew, not properly attuned to our own good, frail or even damaged in their orientation to what is naturally good for us. Such damage is not the consequence of sin but its precondition. A perversity of our fundamental desires precedes any loss of divine powers corrupting our operations; that perversity indeed is responsible for the loss, turning us away from our true good so that we no longer draw upon it for our nourishment.

Besides this natural precondition, sin also has certain natural consequences. Because it is our nature to be bound up with our environments, what we become through sin forms a kind of second nature. What we become is knit into us in a way we cannot remove. Taking within us what is not good for us as our constant diet, we have so incorporated this material over time as to become inseparable from it.

The transition between sin and a graced state therefore involves a painful disarticulation of our true nature from what we have become. Though an act of God's loving mercy, the transition is not sweet and congenial but a violent one that seems to be doing us harm. "The foreign matter, which has somehow grown into its substance, has to be scraped from it by ... force, and so occasions ... anguish."[16] We have become attached to what is bad for us like earthquake victims under the weight of rubble that has pierced through our flesh; God's drawing us to himself mangles us all the more in ripping us out from under it.[17]

---

[16] Gregory of Nyssa, "On the Soul and Resurrection," p. 451.   [17] Ibid.

Indeed, all that we have become has to be melted down so that we can be made over. Sinful through our hardening to divine influence, we must be re-spun or refashioned, in a way that brings us back to the fundamental plasticity of our nature, broken down in order to become ourselves anew. The transition from sin to grace is therefore not simply the starkest one possible, from death to life, but itself a kind of death, a passage by way of our dying. We must die to what we have become through sin, in order to begin again, reborn. Our sinful nature has to become, against itself and through God's great mercy, like a seed of grain dissolved in the earth, leaving behind its own bulk and shape to germinate into the enjoyment of God's own life.[18]

Because sin has both this natural precondition – wayward desires or inclinations – and this natural consequence – a second nature contrary to what God intended us to be – the problem of sin cannot be addressed simply by returning us to our original situation at creation. Returning Word and Spirit to us in the way we had them at creation will not do us any good if the problem was that we were not sufficiently interested in them to begin with. Even if we happen to cling this time to the Word through the power of the Spirit offered to us anew, nothing, moreover, would seem to stop us from turning away again. And something new has to be done to rid us of what we have become over lifetimes of nourishment through the wrong inputs. The simple return of the presence of the power of the Spirit and re-attachment thereby to the Word would leave us too much as we are. These are mere external aids when the corruption of human life requires an internal cure. Unlike our circumstances at creation, we are now inextricably bound up with what has harmed us. It is this bondage that needs to be broken; and the mere return of Word and Spirit does not seem adequate to address the problem.

The solution to all these difficulties is the new way Word and Spirit are ours in Christ. The attachment of humanity to the divine in Christ is of a much closer and stronger sort than anything human beings

---

[18] *Ibid.*, p. 466.

enjoy at their creation. Jesus is not simply a human being conforming in his human dispositions and actions to the second person of the trinity through the divine power of the Spirit within him – a Spirit-filled human, in short, of the sort we had the capacity to be at our creation. The humanity of Jesus is instead assumed into unity with the second person of the trinity to form a single person, a hypostatic unity.

This hypostatic unity is what is responsible for the fact that the humanity of Jesus is perfectly oriented to the Word in his dispositions and acts – rather than the other way around. Were a simple human being to exhibit the perfect conformity in affection and will to the divine image to be found in Christ this would not make such a person one with the Word in the way Jesus is. Instead, the hypostatic unity between the human and the Word – the fact that this human being is the Word – precedes as its cause the perfect way humanity mirrors the divine image in Christ. Hypostatic unity, in short, is the precondition for humanity's attachment in will and deed to the divine in Christ; it is not the product of that sort of attachment and thereby dependent upon its character.

The same hypostatic unity is what makes the Spirit the sure possession of the humanity of Christ: the humanity of Jesus cannot lose the Spirit because he is the Word. One with the Word, the humanity of Christ receives what is the Word's very own – the Word's own Spirit. The Spirit is therefore securely lodged within Christ's humanity, despite the Spirit's remaining by nature foreign to it and on that account something that humanity in general might have otherwise been capable of losing: "nothing which he … received, did he receive as not possessing before; for the Word, as being God, had them always; but … he is said humanly to receive, that, whereas the flesh received in him, henceforth from it the gift might abide surely for us."[19]

---

[19] Athanasius, "Four Discourses against the Arians," trans. John Henry Newman and Archibald Robertson, in Philip Schaff and Henry Wace (eds.), *Nicene and Post-Nicene Fathers*, vol. IV, Second Series (Grand Rapids, Michigan: Eerdmans, 1957), Discourse 3, chapter 27, section 40, pp. 415–16.

grave dove *

One with Christ in and through the humanity we share with him, our unity with the divine should be established and secured in much the same way – independently of our wayward dispositions. The Word has united itself with our humanity by way of the hypostatic unity of the incarnation before any change in our own attitudes and dispositions comes to reflect that fact. The sort of relationship that holds between the hypostatic union and Christ's own perfect human life therefore also holds for the relationship between the unity we have with Christ, in virtue of the humanity we share with him, and our imperfect human conformity to the divine image. Our unity with Christ by way of the humanity we share with him precedes any change in our wayward dispositions that re-orients us to God; this unity is indeed what brings about our changed dispositions. For the same reason, moreover, once changed, those dispositions do not have the capacity by their frailty to alter this unity we have with Christ. To the extent it did not come about to begin with by way of our dispositions, our unity with Christ is not affected by any fall back into sin by us. The Word's making itself one with us in Christ remains, however much we might backslide. Christ is one with us in virtue of our humanity whatever we might do.

Finally, the way corruption is knit into human lives finds its antidote here in a comparably close binding into unity of humanity with divine life and goodness in and through Christ. We are not simply given back Word and Spirit and told to turn to them without addressing the corrupted creatures we have become. Instead what we are given in Christ so adheres to us as to amount to a kind of redone internal constitution. Via the hypostatic union, we are wrapped around with something we cannot get rid of, something that therefore inevitably makes itself felt in all that we go on to become. We are bound so tightly to what is opposed to the harm we have done ourselves that it breaks the hold of those things on us. We are given a new sufficiently strong tie, a new bondage, if you will, to what is life-giving and nourishing, to counter our old bondage to what harms us. The clothing of the Spirit that we had at our creation and lost through sin is returned to us as more than the mere exterior garment it seemed to have been then; it is now knit into the fabric of our humanity by way of the incarnation in much the way the created inputs that do us harm have been. It works its way in and through our humanity to drive out what has become part of it, rather than merely working from the outside on what would therefore remain itself of a thoroughly corrupted character.

The divine is no longer foreign and external to us in the way it was at our creation, but so properly and inseparably ours in Christ as to imitate a connection by nature. In Christ we do not simply receive the divine again as a gift of grace but have the greater grace "conferred on [us] of gathering as it were into kinness of nature that which was alien from God."[20] Being children of God through Christ, we have something like a natural kinship with God, in virtue of the natural connections that hold between him and God and between him and us: "The Word ... conjoined to himself things human through the flesh which was united to him, [and he was] conjoined of nature to the Father, in that he is by nature God ... [Thus we were] so to say raised up to the dignity which is in him by nature."[21]

By being in a hypostatic unity with it, by being one with the second person of the trinity, humanity gains a sort of natural connection to the divine comparable to the natural connection that the Word enjoys with other members of the trinity. The unity between Word and Spirit that comes by way of a shared nature is, for

[20] Cyril of Alexandria, *Commentary on John*, Book 1, chapter 9, p. 106 (John 1:13).

[21] *Ibid.* I am suggesting the point of all this "one nature or unity of nature" language for talking about Christ is not to oppose the idea of hypostatic unity by blurring the difference between human and divine natures but to clarify the advance in grace made by the hypostatic union itself. See John McGuckin, *Saint Cyril of Alexandria and the Christological Controversy* (Crestwood, New York: St. Vladimir's Seminary Press, 2004), pp. 207–16; and Steven A. McKinnon, *Words, Imagery and the Mystery of Christ: A Reconstruction of Cyril of Alexandria's Christology* (Leiden: Brill, 2000), pp. 59–79.

example, transferred to the humanity of Christ: despite the fact that humanity and divinity remain distinct in Christ, the humanity of Christ has the Spirit in the way the Word has the Spirit. And what the humanity of Christ has is transferred to us in virtue of the connection by nature we have with him, in virtue of our shared humanity. Through a natural connection with his humanity, other human beings enjoy something like the natural connection, then, between Word and Spirit that Christ enjoys. Cyril of Alexandria summarizes in compressed fashion the reasoning behind our kinship by nature with God in Christ this way:

> For the Word of God is a divine nature even when in the flesh, and we are his kindred, notwithstanding that he is by nature God, because of his taking the same flesh as ours. Therefore the manner of the friendly relationship is similar. For as he is closely related to the Father, and through the sameness of their nature the Father is closely related to him; so also are we to him and he to us, is so far as he was made man.[22]

Because of the natural connections that underpin it, our relationship with God in Christ no longer has proper human dispositions for its precondition and is more stable than anything with that sort of basis. The problem of our wayward dispositions is solved by giving us a form of natural attachment to God in Christ more fundamental than those dispositions.[23] We are joined to God before our actions and attitudes are oriented to him, joined to God indeed whether we like it or not, in much the way we are children of our parents before

---

[22] Cyril of Alexandria, *Commentary on John*, Book 6, chapter 1, p. 84 (John 10:15).

[23] For the priority of natural connections over bonds of "love, concord, and peace" see *ibid.*, Book 11, chapter 40, pp. 544–52 (John 17:20–1); the highest connection between us and God and between human beings and Christ is clearly here a natural connection like that among members of the trinity. For the same idea that natural union is a higher form of union than union of wills, see also Hilary of Poitiers, "On the Trinity," trans. E. W. Watson and L. Pullan, in Philip Schaff and Henry Wace (eds.), *Nicene and Post-Nicene Fathers*, vol. IX, Second Series (Peabody, Massachusetts: Hendrickson, 1994), Book 8, sections 16–18, p. 142.

and whether or not we ever consistently develop the habit of feeling or acting in ways that respect that fact. Natural relationships cannot be withdrawn or forfeited, moreover, in the way relationships of affection can be. A likeness rooted by nature is secure and cannot be changed for the worse in the way a likeness of operations without such a basis can. It is because indeed we lacked that root in virtue of our creation that we slipped away from any orientation by action and affection to God: because we were not by nature God it was only a matter of time before our operations fell out of conformity with God.[24] If we now turn back to God, this turning consequently has a stability beneath it beyond anything that the strength of our own willful and affectionate attachment to it would warrant. And finally, we are given here a new form of natural connection with what is life-giving and nourishing by nature to counter our second nature of sin. Naturally one with the humanity of Christ who is naturally one with God in being divine, we are children of God, however corrupt our second nature may be, in a way that disrupts the apparent finality of the sorry state we find ourselves in. A mere relationship with Christ by way of will and affection would not be enough to make what is corruptible by nature itself any different. To overcome that corruption at its root requires a comparable natural participation in what is essentially life-giving and good that comes to us by way of Christ's humanity. With that humanity our own might be physically intertwined so as to make it inconceivable that life and goodness should be finally vanquished by death and sin.[25]

As Protestants stress, then, the grace of Christ specifically addresses sin and not merely a problem with our nature. A mere gift of the Spirit conforming us to the divine image – being merely Spirit-filled human beings, in other words – is insufficient after sin.

---

[24] Cyril of Alexandria, *Commentary on John*, Book 1, chapter 5, pp. 351–2 (John 6:27).
[25] See *ibid.*, Book 10, chapter 2, p 370; and pp. 371–2 (John 15:1). Cyril is talking specifically here about our humanity coming to be physically entwined with Christ's through the offer of his body and blood in the Eucharist.

Christ must come and we must be joined to him, in order to conquer sin, in order for us to have the Spirit that conforms us to the divine image in a new way that rectifies our sinful failure. Apart from sin, what Christ achieves in his humanity might merely represent the goal of human life, what we could conceivably achieve apart from him by the mere presence of the Spirit within us; with sin, Christ must also be the means, the ideal pattern become fact to change the human situation fundamentally.

Such a sin-centered treatment of the importance of Christ does nothing however to interrupt the nature–grace problematic upon which this account of grace primarily rests. Indeed, any either-or between a nature–grace problematic and a sin–grace one is avoided here, since what finally resolves the problem of nature is exactly what also remedies sin. The best way to solve the problem with our nature is through the grace of God that comes to us in Christ; the greatest good of God's own life is ours in the highest possible fashion in virtue of the fact that divinity and humanity are one in him. But the same grace of Christ, as we have seen, provides the only effective remedy for sin.

The manner in which humanity is elevated here to address both sorts of problem has, moreover, a distinctly Protestant ring to it. Despite the fact that this account of grace makes nature the primary reference point for understanding the importance of grace, the shift from nature to grace does not shine a spotlight on human nature itself, on changes made to it by way of the grace of God in Christ. At issue instead is the shift of humanity's fundamental circumstance before God. Our relationship with God changes. The way Word and Spirit can be ours in virtue of our creation is what the grace of Christ improves, and not the character of human nature per se.

This account of grace makes clear that our proper posture toward God is the one stressed by Protestants: utter humility. Grace knocks us flat, preventing any form of self-congratulation. All the good we achieve is to be attributed to God rather than to ourselves. What makes our lives good is not anything we are ourselves but the presence within us of what we are not, a divine presence never ours by right because never ours by nature. All the glory for the good we exhibit in our lives should therefore be reserved for God.

While our proper posture is the one Protestants emphasize, the primary reasons for that humility are not the usual Protestant ones: sin and a devaluation of any good achieved by us. Sin may make us horribly corrupt, as we have said. And the grace of Christ that allows us to conquer it may for that reason make slow headway within us: in this life one may never be finally rid of it. But humility would be our proper posture toward God even if sin were totally removed by the grace of Christ or we had not fallen into it to begin with. The propriety of humility before God therefore need not be a reason for insisting upon the seriousness of sin either before or after Christ's coming. While likely given the fact of our totally corrupt condition under sin, the continued existence of sin among the redeemed, for example, can become a mere empirical matter now that our feeling humble before God does not depend on it.

The value of what human beings achieve before or after the grace of Christ also need not be downplayed relative to God's own full and pure goodness in order to make humility seem our appropriate posture. One is not primarily humble because the inevitable imperfections of the best human works stand out and all human achievements seem comparatively puny and small when in the presence of God – say, when brought before a righteous God's judgment seat. The account I have offered of grace does downplay the value of created goods relative to God's: that is the problem of nature that grace addresses. But the value of the human achievements that become possible with the grace of God is hardly minimized. And in any case – with or without grace – the limited value of human achievement is not the primary reason for humility: what lies behind the goodness we achieve is what makes us humble.

The primary reason for humility simply stems from the strong sense of participation in God that we have stressed throughout. We are good not in virtue of what we are but in virtue of what we are not, like darkness lit up by a light that enters into it from without. We are not light in ourselves but in virtue of having within us what is light in itself. The light that is in us is one thing; what it enlightens – our nature – is another. That distinction is what underlies the humility proper to our situation, the reason why we must turn so completely away from ourselves in giving thanks for anything good we have become. In our pride we might think that we could carry the light away with us in turning from it; but that is just to lose it and to fall back into the darkness that is our nature in and of itself.[26]

If it has this source, the humility upon which Protestants insist can be a constant of human life in any circumstance, whatever the extremes between which it swings. In a state of extreme poverty absent the gift of God's own life, one can only of course plead to God like a beggar. But even in an extreme state of well-being that comes from having the gift of God's own Spirit in the strongest possible way through Christ, one must still humbly thank God for divine powers not one's own and for what they have wrought in one. Following Augustine, one must see "beneath this diversity of state … [the same] complete powerlessness without God. Beneath this difference one duty … the avowal of this powerlessness, the avowal that all comes to man from God, even what he has not had to ask for; it is the acceptance of total dependence. Beneath the difference in the manner of prayer there remains one and the same fundamental attitude, the humble attitude of prayer."[27] Because we are to be elevated beyond ourselves through divine powers not our own, what Protestants view as the typical posture of the sinner becomes just as appropriate for those renewed in Christ. No matter how spiritually renewed we may be, no matter how thoroughly we

---

[26] See the association of humility with participation in what is life and light itself by Augustine, *Tractates on John 11–27*, Tractate 14, section 6, paragraph 2, p. 69 (John 3:29–36); Tractate 22, sections 8–12, pp. 205–9 (John 5:24–30); and Tractate 23, section 3, pp. 213–14 (John 5:19–40).

[27] Henri de Lubac, *Augustinianism and Modern Theology*, trans. Lancelot Sheppard (New York: Crossroad Herder, 2000), p. 91.

may have repudiated our past lives and been reborn in Christ's image, we remain as beholden to God as before.

There is no possible trade off, as Protestants seem to suggest there is, between glorying in our achievements and glorifying God, when what we achieve involves our elevation beyond ourselves, our constant employment of strictly divine powers. It is not the case that the more we have to glory in the less likely we are to glorify God. The situation, as Catholics typically affirm, is rather the reverse: the more of value we achieve the more we should glorify God since what we achieve has God's grace for its source.[28]

Glorifying God by denying glory to creatures, by insisting there is nothing of value to them in which they might glory, is a bad strategy. Putting artificial restrictions on the good effects that God's grace can have on us is no way to make us glorify God more. If God could give us more, say, perfectly holy lives by the grace of Christ, but chooses not to do so simply to keep us in our place, we have less reason to glorify God rather than more. God seems, to just that degree, less good and great, less worthy of our praise.

The stress on a strong rather than weak form of participation in God, nevertheless, distinguishes the position here from a Catholic one. God is the source of the good one does in a different way than the usual Catholic complaint about a Protestant either-or supposes. Or at least the distinction between the strong and weak forms of participation clears up an ambiguity in the usual Catholic reasoning.

One might not be able to glory in oneself without glorifying God simply because what one is in oneself is the creation of God. This is the weak sense of participation in God in virtue of what one is. And it would hold for both human nature and what humans become through grace. God does not give less to those whom God raises to his own life than God gives to those God creates. When God gives human beings the gift of God's own life God therefore acts as a

---

[28] For a good discussion of the Catholic position, see Etienne Gilson, *The Spirit of Medieval Philosophy*, trans. A. H. C. Downes (University of Notre Dame Press, 1991), chapter 7.

creator here too, bestowing on humans certain forms and powers, which are the principles of acts, in order that they may be of themselves inclined to the renovation of their lives that comes to them by way of grace.[29]

Human beings nonetheless cannot glory in what they achieve because the powers by which they do so are gifts of grace, gifts, that is, that exceed both their natural powers and the sinful character of the lives they led before.[30] Because the first gift of these new powers is a gracious one, God is only crowning God's own gifts rather than our merits when we gain further good things by way of those powers. The whole sequence is a gracious one in which one receives by way of one's own powers what is merely grace for grace.[31]

This sort of explanation for why self-congratulation is inappropriate allows for the possibility that the powers we are given by grace are sufficient in and of themselves to bring about what they effect. Even if those powers were so capable in and of themselves, we would not be able to glory in what we achieve. Indeed, this sort of reason for humility is usually found together with a strong suggestion of

---

[29] Thomas Aquinas, *Summa Theologica [Theologicae]*, trans. Fathers of the English Dominican Province, 5 vols. (Westminster, Maryland: Christian Classics, 1948), vol. II, I.II, Q110 a2, p. 1133.

[30] See *ibid.*, Q114 a5, p. 1157.

[31] See Augustine, *Tractates on the Gospel of John 1–10*, trans. John W. Rettig (Washington, DC: Catholic University of America Press, 1988), Tractate 3, section 10, paragraph 1, p. 84 (John 1:15–18); "On Grace and Free Will," trans. Peter Holmes, Robert Ernest Wallis, and Benjamin Warfield, in Philip Schaff (ed.), *Nicene and Post-Nicene Fathers*, vol. V (Grand Rapids, Michigan: Eerdmans, 1980), chapter 15, p. 450; chapters 20–1, pp. 451–2; and "Enchiridion," trans. J. F. Shaw, in Philip Schaff (ed.), *Nicene and Post-Nicene Fathers*, vol. III (Grand Rapids, Michigan: Eerdmans, 1956), chapter 107, p. 272. See the comparable reasoning of Thomas Aquinas, *Summa Theologica*, vol. II, I.II, Q114 a1, p. 1154: "Now the manner and measure of human virtue is in man from God. Hence man's merit with God only exists on the presupposition of the divine ordination, so that man obtains from God, as a reward of his operation, what God gave him the power of operation for, even as natural things by their proper movements and operations obtain that to which they were ordained by God." As Thomas adds in ad3: "It does not follow that God is made our debtor simply, but his own, inasmuch as it is right that his will should be carried out."

that: the new powers that are ours by God's grace in Christ – say, the power to love God in a new way – seem sufficient of themselves to enable the achievement of further goods, culminating in the final good of eternal life. A parallel is made with what is assumed to hold for the case of created gifts: the powers of action that are ours by nature are sufficient for the achievement of natural ends; so the powers we are given by grace are sufficient for ends that exceed our nature such as eternal life. In neither case is there reason for self-glorification. One cannot congratulate oneself for doing what created powers enable since we are not responsible for the fact that we have those powers to begin with. The whole sequence from natural powers to natural ends, moreover, is one for which God is responsible as its creator: God is the creator not just of the powers, but of what they achieve. The same would hold for one's creation with new powers by God's grace: self-congratulation is ruled out because the whole progress from initial gifts to later ones under grace is entirely the result of what God acting as creator chooses to give us, both initially and at the end.

The Protestant complaint about these suggestions is this: self-sufficient capacities allow what happens by way of them to be considered apart from any reference to their divine giver. Because there are sufficient created causes for what one becomes, one can easily lose sight of God behind it all. One may know that what happens does not really take place apart from God's creative action, but the sufficiency of the created causes gives the whole sequence a self-contained quality that allows one to consider it as if it did. Even though none of this exists without being sustained in existence by God's creative power, it is possible to consider it independently of that fact with no loss of intelligibility. Thereby one might claim for created causes self-sufficiency in the achievement of the good.

The usual Protestant way of preventing a hubristic claim of self-sufficiency here is to deny altogether that new human powers are given to us by grace, or to claim that sin vitiates them. Sin, for example, may corrupt the initial gifts by which we are to be empowered to do the good works that earn eternal life. We never really love God as we should. No strictly causal connection ever exists, therefore, between good works done on that basis and God's further gift of eternal life. Our works are never sufficiently good to merit that gift even when operating on the basis of God's grace in Christ. Our deeds as Christians are counted perfectly good in a way that would really merit eternal life only when their faults are continually covered over by Christ's own perfect obedience. We have nothing to glory in when enjoying God's grace in Christ because we remain poor sinners.

This Protestant solution to the problem reflects badly, Catholics point out, on the efficacy of God grace: God's grace does not seem capable of fundamentally transforming us; what God wants to do for us in Christ seems continually stymied by sin. A better solution would be one compatible with a stress on the new human powers and achievements that are ours through grace. Those powers and capacities can achieve as much as one likes; we can become fundamentally different people by way of them, for example. All that need be true to avoid prideful self-congratulation is that nothing is achieved by them apart from the gift of properly divine power. New powers and capacities are ours; they are just insufficient of themselves to do anything. They are capable of bringing about the ends that God intends only by working with what they are not – the Holy Spirit. The Protestant worry is addressed by bringing in the strong sort of participation to supplement the Catholic stress on the weak sort.

What renders the created powers we receive through grace ineffective is not sin. It is just not possible for them to be sufficient of themselves to bring about ends that are themselves divine. What God wants to give us through the grace of Christ is itself divine – for example, eternal life – and as such exceeds the capacity of any possible created powers to reach, even those new created powers given to us by grace.[32] The primary power by which we achieve such

[32] See Thomas Aquinas, *Summa Theologica*, vol. II, I.II Q110 a2 ad2, p. 1133; and Q114 a2, pp. 1154–5.

ends must for this reason be a properly divine power, the Holy Spirit itself. The fact that God does not give us sufficient powers to gain such ends does not, then, reflect badly on God. It simply indicates God's great love for us, the fact that God wants to give us more than created goods.

e.g.

(infused virtue)

The gift of the Holy Spirit to us does give rise to new powers and capacities in us; there are certain created correlates of the gift of the Holy Spirit in us – new human dispositions, for example, of faith and love – by way of which our whole life is eventually renovated in Christ's image. But there is no adequate created correlate for the power of the Holy Spirit itself. That power cannot be made our own in the way the created powers proper to our human nature are our own. Like any power of one nature that resides in another nature quite different from itself, divine power, because it surpasses human nature, can be in us only improperly and imperfectly. Divine power is in us only as light is in the air or the way heat from a flame is in iron.[33]

Imperfectly possessed powers remain dependent on the power of the Holy Spirit itself for anything they might achieve. The effects of divine power can amount themselves to powers with the capacity to bring about their own effects but only in close cooperation therefore with the divine power that continues to make its own power felt in them. The heat in iron for example can heat up other things but only in virtue of the flame whose own heat continues to be applied to it.

> Anything that has a nature or a form or a virtue perfectly, can of itself work according to them; not, however, excluding the operation of God who works inwardly in every nature and in every will [by giving

---

[33] See *ibid.*, Q 62 a1 ad1, p. 851; Q68 a1, p. 879; Q110, a2 ad2, p. 1133; and vol. III, II.II Q4 a4 ad3, p. 1187, although this specifically concerns the act by which God justifies. See also *Summa Contra Gentiles*, trans. Vernon J. Bourke (University of Notre Dame Press, 1975), Book 3, Part 1, chapter 53, section 5, p. 181; chapter 54, sections 8–9, pp. 184–5; and chapter 65, section 7, p. 216.

such things to it]. [But] that which has a nature, or form, or virtue imperfectly, cannot of itself work, unless it be moved by another. Thus the sun that possesses light perfectly can shine by itself; whereas the moon which has the nature of light imperfectly, sheds only a borrowed light. Again, a physician, who knows the medical art perfectly, can work by himself; but his pupil, who is not yet fully instructed, cannot work by himself, but needs to receive instructions from him.[34]

The Holy Spirit is in this way the irreplaceable motor for everything we achieve by way of the new dispositions we receive from it. It does not simply effect new dispositions in us and let them go, to work on their own with the usual creative support of God sustaining them in existence and moving them to their own acts for the achievement of ends of which their own powers are capable. Nothing unrolls in this way simply from a first created gift of grace, as if what comes later finds its sufficient cause there. Once received through the power of the Holy Spirit, new dispositions, like faith and love, do not come to replace the Spirit as the sufficient motor of subsequent good works. The Holy Spirit remains instead the motor of all that we become, of both our new dispositions and what follows from them.

The effects of the new powers we receive through grace are therefore never explicable simply with reference to those powers themselves. Even if we do lead holy human lives of love and service to God through the power of the Spirit that is ours in Christ, it is not possible to consider our abilities to do so independently of the Spirit, as if leading such lives were intelligible simply on the new human basis given to us by grace. In abstraction from the gift of the Holy Spirit, the connection between our new powers and their effects becomes inexplicable: a gap looms between those effects and what any created power is capable of.

Indeed, because we never act independently of the Spirit, when considering the new lives we lead by Christ's grace one should never

---

[34] Thomas Aquinas, *Summa Theologica*, vol. II, I.II Q68 a2, p. 879.

split off human acts intelligible in merely human terms from what the Holy Spirit does to or with them. It is not that we do a little bit on our own, or something that remains inadequate because of sin, with the Holy Spirit coming onto the scene to make up the difference; the Holy Spirit does not improve the acts we take on our own and therefore make more fitting the gift of eternal life that would otherwise be more than our acts deserve. It is simply with the grace of the Holy Spirit that all our actions become at all efficacious of divine ends; given the fact that the Holy Spirit is at work in them, it makes sense that eternal life results from powers that do not have the capacity in and of themselves to produce that result. To consider merely the human character of the powers that become efficacious with the help of the Spirit is to reveal human incapacity, a gap between our own powers and what they achieve.[35]

The fundamental reason, in short, why we cannot glory in our achievements is that the power by which we do them remains God's.

> Is not a crown given as the reward of good deeds? It is, however, only because [God] works good works in men, of whom it is said, "It is God that works in you both to will and to do of his good pleasure [Phil 2:13]" ... They are warned against boasting of their good deeds as if they were their own, by attributing to themselves the performance of anything good ... You do not boast of your good works – as if they were your own, since it is God who works within you.[36]

Glorying in their achievements, "they wrongfully retain the credit for grace that passes through them, as if a wall should say that it gave birth to a sunbeam that it received through a window."[37]

---

[35] See Thomas on condign merit, *ibid.*, Q114, aa2, 3, 6, 9, pp. 1154–60.

[36] Augustine, "On Grace and Free Will," chapter 21, p. 452. See also chapter 16, p. 450; and his "On the Spirit and the Letter," trans. Peter Holmes, Robert Ernest Wallis, and Benjamin Warfield, in Philip Schaff (ed.), *Nicene and Post-Nicene Fathers*, vol. v (Grand Rapids, Michigan: Eerdmans, 1980), chapter 13, p. 88; and chapter 50, p. 105.

[37] John Calvin, *Institutes of the Christian Faith*, trans. Lewis Battles, ed. John T. McNeill (Philadelphia: Westminster, 1960), Book 3, chapter 12, section 8, p. 762.

The same stress on strong participation in God, through attachment to what one is not, encourages a very sharp, typically Protestant distinction between justification and sanctification. We are not justified in virtue of the righteousness we possess in and of ourselves by leading renovated lives under God's grace. This would make justification a matter of sanctification, a consequence of our own holiness. Instead, we are justified through our attachment to Christ, who is righteous as we are not. We are justified in being attached to him because of what he is and not what we are in ourselves.

What about us that accounts for our being justified is simply the change of state we undergo in relationship to him. What justification refers to in us is the fact of our unity with him, our incorporation within his own life, which brings about our being born again to a new identity in him. Nothing about us, in and of ourselves, therefore has to change in order for us to be justified; it is the fact of our attachment to Christ, irrespective of anything else that might be going on with us, that accounts for God's declaring us just.

Justification here has the usual meaning stressed by Protestants. To be justified means to be found favorable in God's sight, offered God's free forgiveness and succor as God's beloved children, despite our sins, apart from and without regard for the degree to which the virtues of our own lives would merit such consideration. We are justified in this way through attachment to Christ. Christ's attachment to us through the humanity he shares with us is itself an act of God's free and loving mercy on us; neither our human nature, nor certainly our sin, makes us worthy of the divine favor expressed in and through the fact that God has chosen to be attached to humanity via the hypostatic union for our benefit. And our attachment to Christ brings along with it God's forgiveness of us as sinners and approval of us despite our sins. Joined to Christ, we receive God's free mercy and approval for Christ's sake, because of what Christ already is and has achieved. "To the extent that Christ is pleasing to God and that we cling to him, to that extent we, too, are pleasing to God and holy."[38] Attending, not to what we are in ourselves but to Christ with whom we are robed or covered, God no longer accuses us as we deserve but approves us for Christ's sake. "The Father embraces us in Christ when he clothes us with the innocence of Christ and accepts it as ours that by the benefit of it he may hold us as holy, pure, and innocent."[39] As Protestants would have it, we continue to be justified in this way, however long sin remains in us. "Furnished with this righteousness, we obtain continual forgiveness of sins."[40]

> We always have recourse to this doctrine, that our sins are covered and that God does not want to hold us accountable for them (Rom 4). This does not mean that there is no sin in us ... But it is ignored and hidden in the sight of God, because Christ the Mediator stands between ... Where Christ ... [is] not present there is no forgiveness or hiding of sins.[41]

Sanctification refers to the good changes in us that attachment to Christ brings about. Sanctification is a matter of what happens in and to our humanity, what is different about the way we live, as a consequence of attachment to Christ. That attachment itself is one thing; its effect on our human lives something else. Christ can be attached to us, and we to him in virtue of his attachment to us, whether or not that attachment shows itself in the changed human dispositions and actions that are its effects.

In being attached to Christ, we gain the power of the Spirit to renovate our lives. Actual renovation of our lives on that basis is what one means by sanctification: the leading of a new way of life made possible through unity with Christ and the gift of his Spirit. Drawing on the power of the Word – Christ's Spirit – our own human lives come to be sanctified: we begin to draw upon the power

---

[38] Martin Luther, "Lectures on Galatians" (1535), in Jaroslav Pelikan and William Hansen (eds.), *Luther's Works*, vol. XXVI (Saint Louis, Missouri: Concordia, 1963), p. 378 (Gal 4:6).

[39] Calvin, *Institutes*, Book 3, chapter 14, section 12, p. 779.

[40] *Ibid.* [41] Luther, "Lectures on Galatians," p. 133 (Gal 2:16).

of the Spirit of the one to whom we are attached, so that we lead
fundamentally transformed lives. Molded according to Christ's
atoning work by his Spirit within us, our sins are crucified, put to
death, in the purging of remorse and renunciation of our past ways.
Our sins are cut away from us through the new circumcision of the
Spirit (Rom 2:29): "by receiving the most sharp working of the divine
Word in our hearts, and admitting into our mind the sword of the
Spirit, we drive away lusts after all the basest things, never doing after
our own wills ... but persuaded only to love and do the will of
God."[42] Molded according to Christ's own life of holiness by that
same Spirit, we begin to do good to our fellow creatures, following
God's own love for the world displayed humanly in Christ. On the
one hand, when Christ is present he drives out "lust, sadness of heart,
fear of death and the like."[43] On the other hand, through the gift of
his Spirit Christ "creates a new life and new impulses in us."[44] In
both these ways, our sanctification is a progressive matter: "we have
the first fruits of the Spirit and have thus begun to be leavened," only
to be "completely leavened when this sinful body is destroyed and we
arise anew with Christ."[45]

Attachment to Christ, in virtue of which one is justified, and the
gift of the Holy Spirit, through which one comes to be sanctified,
are very closely associated in this account of justification and
sanctification. The one indeed cannot exist without the other. If we
are genuinely attached to Christ, Christ's Spirit becomes our own.
Attachment to Christ has as its immediate obverse or flip side the gift
of the Holy Spirit to us: this is just the same act of attachment
between the two considered on its human side, in terms of what
we receive thereby. When a seal is brought together with wax it
immediately makes a mark or impression in that to which it is
attached. That immediate impression is formed by the gift of the

[42] Cyril of Alexandria, *Commentary on John*, Book 4, chapter 7, pp. 500–1 (John 7:24).
[43] Luther, "Lectures on Galatians," p. 350 (Gal 3:26).
[44] *Ibid.*, p. 260 (Gal 3:10).   [45] *Ibid.*, p. 351 (Gal 3:26).

88

Holy Spirit within us, as an available power to draw upon.[46] The gift of the divine power to live differently can therefore be considered part of what it means to be justified: God's free mercy and loving regard for us despite our sin are expressed in both Christ's attachment to us and the immediate gift of the Holy Spirit to us thereby.

The fact that the gift of the Holy Spirit is part of what it means for us to be justified does not, however, make justification part of sanctification, as if we are justified to the extent we are made just. Nothing has necessarily happened to change our human character. The immediate impression made on us is a divine rather than human one: it amounts to the presence of the Holy Spirit itself.[47] The impression itself is constituted by what we are not. The human consequences of this divine impression are not similarly immediate but unroll over time in a constant struggle against a sinful past and against the sinful impulses that always seem to remain within us despite the gift of God's grace. The presence of the Holy Spirit might be the simple obverse of attachment to Christ, but the human consequences are not. The Holy Spirit may be genuinely given to us, present within us, even when that fact is not made visible in our changed dispositions and deeds. We can have the Spirit for our own in virtue of our attachment to Christ without drawing upon it. We are justified in virtue of our attachment to Christ before that Spirit has done its work on us. We are justified in this same sense whether or not, and whatever the degree to which, our lives have been made over through the power of the Spirit to conform to the pattern of the human life that Jesus lived.

It is true that, because we have the gift of Christ's Spirit, in being justified we are made holy in a certain sense, not just declared righteous. There is a holiness in us and not simply a holiness outside

---

[46] See by way of comparison John Henry Newman, *Lectures on the Doctrine of Justification* (London: Longmans, Green and Co., 1914), pp. 170–8.

[47] Again, see by way of comparison Newman, *ibid.*, who considers the impression to be primarily a human one.

ourselves that can be considered ours through attachment to it. But, again, this holiness within us is not what we ourselves are, and remains ours in the same way whatever the degree to which our human lives have been, or fail to be, reformed by way of it. One must carefully distinguish the holiness of the divine Spirit itself from any holiness of ours that is its consequence. Making such a distinction allows one to see how one can be wholly righteous and wholly a sinner at the same time, *simul justus et peccator*, even when in a sense made righteous and not just deemed so with reference to Christ. One gains the entire righteousness of Christ through possession of his Spirit, while remaining simply a sinner in and of oneself.

Besides a seal in wax, several other biblically associated images can help clarify the way that our justification, through attachment to Christ and the gift of the Holy Spirit thereby, is to be distinguished from sanctification, our drawing on that Spirit to reform our lives. Consider the difference between a tree and its fruit, or how an example to be imitated is different from a gift to be received, or the way a foreign branch's grafting onto a vine can be distinguished from that vine's being in the branch through its sap. Justification, for example, makes us the new tree capable of bearing the fruit of sanctification – the fruit of all those new dispositions and habits that make us imitators of Christ's human example.[48] But becoming this new tree is not equivalent to its bearing fruit. We have Christ for our example as we are able to imitate Christ's own virtuous dispositions and acts by the power of his Spirit – that is what it means for us to be sanctified. But we have Christ as gift when we receive Christ himself – his innocence, righteousness, wisdom, and so on – for our justification, so as to find the favor and forgiveness of God as sinners. Receiving Christ by being incorporated into him, by putting Christ on as our new clothing or covering, we are born again, a new creation, forged with a new

---

[48] See by way of comparison Luther's claim that faith makes us a new tree – for example, in "Lectures on Galatians," p. 255 (Gal 3:10).

identity or constitution.[49] We are *in Christ* by being grafted onto
his life like a foreign branch on a vine. In virtue of being so grafted
we have the Holy Spirit as the sap for new life upon which we can
draw. Christ lives *in us* through that Spirit when we do continually
draw upon it to lead a life according to Christ's own pattern.[50]
Calvin expresses the major point succinctly: "we are said to be in
him because, grafted into his body, we are partakers of all his
righteousness and all his blessings. He is said to be in us because
he plainly shows by the efficacy of his Spirit that he is the author
and cause of our life."[51] As the imagery of a foreign graft helps one
to see, being in Christ is inseparably connected with Christ's being
in us through his Spirit. These are logically distinct ways of talking
about the same thing – what it means to become one with Christ.
One is not genuinely grafted if the new sap for a different life has
not become available to one. But the imagery also makes clear the
difference between that grafting itself and the foreign branch's
growth and flourishing, through the actual employment of the
life-giving sap that comes to it thereby.

Because it is a matter of attachment to Christ, this account of
justification focuses attention on those human dispositions and
deeds that might themselves, from our side, be considered acts of
attachment to Christ. Faith, for example, is one. As heartfelt trust in
what God has done for us in Christ, faith is a human act of turning
away from self toward Christ in order to cling only to him. Faith
breaks us out of that self-enclosure in which we remain preoccupied
with our own acts and what they deserve, so as to focus all our
attention on him and what he has done for us. "Faith in its proper

[49] See *ibid.*, pp. 352–3 (Gal 3:27); see also p. 90 (Gal 2:4–5), and p. 140 (Gal 6:15).
[50] See Augustine, *Tractates on the Gospel of John 55–111*, trans. John W. Rettig
(Washington, DC: Catholic University of America Press, 1994), Tractate 81, section 1,
paragraph 1, p. 120 (John 15:4–7).
[51] Calvin, *Calvin's Commentaries: The Gospel according to St. John 11–21 and First
Epistle of John*, trans. T. H. L. Parker (Grand Rapids, Michigan: Eerdmans, 1961), p. 84
(John 14:20).

function has no other object than Jesus Christ ... It does not ... say: 'What have I done? Where have I sinned? What have I deserved?' But it says: 'What has Christ done? What has he deserved?'"[52] "We must form the habit of leaving ourselves behind, as well as the law and all our works, which force us to pay attention to ourselves. We must turn our eyes completely to ... Christ."[53] "Faith is a constant gaze that looks at nothing except Christ, the victor over sin and death and the dispenser of righteousness, salvation, and eternal life."[54]

This turning of one's whole attention to Christ in faith constitutes a form of attachment to him and for that reason might be closely associated with our being justified in virtue of his own righteousness. By way of faith in him, Christ is in and with us and thereby we are justified. Luther suggests as much: "Christ who is grasped by faith and who lives in the heart is the true Christian righteousness on account of which God counts us righteous and grants us eternal life."[55] "Faith takes hold of Christ and has him present, enclosing him as the ring encloses the gem. And whosoever is found having this faith in the Christ who is grasped in the heart, him God counts as righteous. This is the means and merit by which we obtain the forgiveness of sins and righteousness."[56]

Indeed, faith might be too closely associated with justification in this way. In contrast to what the importance of faith might imply, attachment to Christ does not come about because of our own dispositions of attachment to him such as faith. Christ instead attaches himself to us in order to give us those new dispositions of attachment to him. Without our doing anything on our side to bring about that attachment, Christ is first of all attached to us in virtue of the humanity he shares with us. The incarnation of the Word in human flesh, in other words, is the primary form of God's own attachment to us by which we are justified. The action of Christ's

[52] Luther, "Lectures on Galatians," p. 88 (Gal 2:4–5).   [53] Ibid., p. 166 (Gal 2:20).
[54] Ibid., p. 356 (Gal 3:29).   [55] Ibid., p. 130 (Gal 2:16).   [56] Ibid., p. 132.

own Spirit, sent to us from that glorified humanity, attaches us, moreover, to him by effecting in us our own inclinations to cling to him in faith. Faith is a gift of the Holy Spirit, and as such, is part of our sanctification to new life. It should be placed on the side of sanctification rather than justification in that it is one human consequence of the latter. Faith is something that is going on in us as a result of our being justified through attachment to Christ and the gift of the Spirit thereby.

As a form of attachment to Christ, faith, moreover, has no special privilege. There are other human dispositions – for example, love and gratitude for what God has done for us in Christ – that might equally well be considered acts of simple clinging to what we are not. This is indeed why, one can easily argue, love figures so centrally in accounts of justification that make it a matter of sanctification. Love becomes a pure form of clinging to the divine powers required for new life.

> The human will is so divinely aided in the pursuit of righteousness that … in addition to free-will and [instruction] in how he ought to live … there is formed in his mind [through the Holy Spirit] a delight in, and love of, that supreme and unchangeable good which is God … in order that … he might conceive an ardent desire to cling to his maker, and may burn to enter upon the participation in that true light, that it may go well with him from him to whom he owes his existence.[57]

Love represents simply the intense desire to embrace for one's own what is necessary to renovate one's whole life for the better.

If faith and love have any privilege over other human dispositions and acts it is not because of their human character, but because of the divinity they enclose or contain. Lacking the opacity that would draw attention to themselves, they are transparent media of the object of

---

[57] Augustine, "On the Spirit and the Letter," chapter 5, p. 84; see his *City of God*, Book 12, chapter 9, pp. 481–3.

their concern. Faith, for example, "is colorless, like air or water; it is but the medium through which the soul sees Christ; and the soul as little rests upon it and contemplates it, as the eye can see the air."[58]

Love might have peculiar dangers, as Protestants allege, to suggest otherwise. Love can easily be considered that particular human aspect of our acts under the influence of grace that makes them especially praiseworthy or that accounts for our continued progress in good works. It is the intensity of our love for God, for example, that keeps us on the straight and narrow in the latter regard. In this way love would turn attention to itself and its own relative merits in human terms. But faith is a human act too and therefore care must equally well be taken here too to avoid making its human character into some kind of work by which we are justified. What is important about it in that case becomes its own strength and sincerity. One begins to worry about, or congratulate oneself for, the character of one's own conversion experience as if that were responsible for one's salvation independently of Christ.

If there is any privilege to faith and love over other human dispositions and inclinations it is a matter of their own empty receptiveness to what comes to them from without. Faith and love are privileged because they suggest simple openness to what God offers us in drawing near to us in Christ. They are privileged in virtue of the way they refer to God and therefore not because their own psychological character establishes their greater importance over other human acts and dispositions. Faith and love are not privileged moments in Christian life, for example, because their psychological character makes them the motor of everything else that happens in Christian life: faith in Christ produces gratitude for what God has done; love then gives one the desire to act in God's service as one should, selflessly and without fear.[59] Faith and love are instead

---

[58] Newman, *Lectures on Justification*, p. 336.

[59] For the way love and good deeds follow from faith, see Luther, "Lectures on Galatians," pp. 133, 138 (Gal 3:16).

privileged over the rest of Christian life as entry points for the reception of the divine power that remakes human lives; in their openness to it they allow that divine power to be an active force in human life. What makes love the principle of all other Christian virtues is not, then, its psychological quality but the fact that love "approaches nearer to its object."[60] The reception of divine power is necessary for everything we do; and therefore faith and love are required in all that we do. They become of principal importance for every other aspect of the new lives we lead under grace, because divine power is.

More important than any difference between faith and love is the difference between what we do and what God does. Focusing controversy on the relative merits of different sorts of human acts, such as faith and love, as Protestants sometimes do, is therefore likely to prove unproductive, by distracting attention from the real matter for concern. Indeed, the point of privileging some human dispositions over others in justification – or sanctification – is that in so doing the importance of the difference between our acts and God's stands out more clearly. This, one might argue, is the very reason faith is held up for special attention in the Protestant claim of justification by faith alone: "Faith … has this peculiarity, that it signifies, in its very nature, that nothing of ours justifies us."[61] It is a way of magnifying the grace of God, of pointing out our inability to do any good thing of ourselves, of saying that God alone justifies us, that we are justified solely by what God does in Christ rather than by our own works.[62]

Being able to distinguish between what is in our own power and what is not is crucial to getting beyond our sinful predicament, as Protestants often understand: a predicament in which we veer from unwarranted hubris in our own powers to utter desperation

---

[60] Thomas Aquinas, *Summa Theologica*, vol. II, I.II, Q66 a6, p. 871.
[61] Newman, *Lectures on Justification*, p. 246.   [62] *Ibid.*, pp. 243–4, 283.

over our incapacity to act as we should.[63] In either case we act as if our lives were in our own hands: as if we were independently responsible for everything about us that is good, or in our need we could find no help from beyond ourselves that was not simply a response to our own prior deeds. In line with this Protestant preoccupation, indeed, the account of sin I offered earlier made confusing what we do with what God does our primary fault: we lost the Spirit to begin with because we thought of it as a given of our nature and not an alien gift; we took it for a natural property and not a merciful, free gift of what is beyond us, and therefore took it for granted.

Sharply distinguishing justification from sanctification is itself a way of cleanly separating divine from human, in order to give the clear priority to God's own action for our sakes. Making justification part of sanctification threatens to submerge the gift of divine powers under our renovated human capacities, and to suggest that God's own action for our sake follows in response to ours. Indeed the two sets of distinctions are closely connected to one another, and therefore that connection is apparent from the other side as well: the distinction between divine and human acts is what helps make clear that justification is distinct from our sanctification. We are justified insofar as Christ's Spirit – something divine – is given to us sinners; sanctified insofar as we commit human deeds of a holy character on that basis. The priority of God's act over our own establishes the priority of justification over sanctification. Justification as the free act of divine mercy that binds us to Christ and gives us his Spirit, makes clear our elevation beyond human powers for more than human ends; sanctification, the mere living of a holy human life, requires even in this life powers not our own in virtue of their divinity.

At stake in properly distinguishing and ordering justification and sanctification is the humility before God so stressed by Protestants.

---

[63] For Protestant concern with that topic, see, for example, Luther, *Bondage of the Will*, trans. J. I. Packer and O. R. Johnston (Fleming H. Revell, 1957).

The constant dependence of our sanctification on the free gift of justification through Christ – the fact that it is only in virtue of our justification that we have the divine power necessary for the performance of good works – supports the humility proper to saints over the whole course of Christian life:

> the saints, when it is a question of the founding and establishing of their own salvation, without regard for works turn their eyes solely to God's goodness. Not only do they betake themselves to it before all things as to the beginning of blessedness but they repose in it as in the fulfillment of this. A conscience so founded, erected, and established, is established also in the consideration of works, so far, that is, as these are testimonies of God dwelling and ruling in us.[64]

The priority of justification in Christ, as the free gift of God that makes our sanctification possible, must be kept in mind if the good that is part of our lives by way of sanctification is still to seem to reside in Christ. "What sort of foundation have we in Christ? Was he the beginning of our salvation in order that its fulfillment might follow from ourselves? Did he only open the way by which we might proceed under our own power? Certainly not."[65] We are righteous only in virtue of Christ's own righteousness in us. Christ himself *is* our righteousness, and only by his remaining such will our own humanity exhibit any of the good works proper to human life. By looking to our justification in Christ, "we preserve the credit for good works whole, complete, and unimpaired for the Lord,"[66] as Calvin would like, because to him is to be ascribed the power by which they are ever done.

Making a primary distinction between faith and works seems counterproductive on all these fronts, at odds with fundamental Protestant intentions to distinguish clearly both justification from sanctification and God's doing from our own. If love, for example, is

---

[64] Calvin, *Institutes*, Book 3, chapter 14, section 18, p. 785.
[65] *Ibid.*, chapter 15, section 5, p. 793.   [66] *Ibid.*, section 3, p. 790.

considered a work and distinguished from faith on that basis, what is in fact a human work – faith as a function of our own efforts to believe and trust – is easily blurred with God's own act to justify us in Christ. It becomes all the more difficult, as a result, to keep what God is responsible for doing distinct from what we are responsible for. Justification and sanctification are similarly blurred, for the same reason. If justification is closely associated with faith, our justification tends to become, as faith is, the first moment in a series of human acts on the way to greater holiness and eventual eternal life, the first step in a chain including all the rest of those new dispositions and forms of action that make up our sanctification. If one wants to distinguish justification and sanctification quite clearly, it is really not the best idea to associate justification so closely with that faith in Christ that naturally gives rise to love and gratitude to God and on that basis to good deeds, to associate it so closely, in other words, with the human act of conversion that turns us from a life of sin to a life of faith and thereby sets us upon a path of new life. For justification as a result of the process of being sanctified, one would in this way simply substitute justification as the first stage of being sanctified. For the idea that when our lives have been made over we can be considered just, one would simply substitute faith as the human cause of our becoming just.

Christ is at the center of the account of justification and sanctification that I am offering here, for a variety of different reasons and in a number of different respects, in much the way Protestants would like. For one, Christ is at the center because what is to be achieved in us is achieved first in him: in his own humanity is found realized both our justification and sanctification. Before us and for the sake of us, the humanity of Jesus, suffering like us under the sins of the world, is itself joined to the Word as an act of God's free favor for the purpose of giving to it what neither by nature it deserves nor in its sinful circumstances should expect: the greatest good of God's own life. As the divine Word, the human being Jesus has the power of the Holy Spirit; it is by way of this divine power possessed by his humanity that over the course of his life and death his own humanity is gradually healed and glorified until his final resurrection from the dead.

Justification and sanctification are therefore already clearly distinct in him; the account of their distinction in us has its basis in what happens in him. The humanity of Christ is justified in that it is one with the Word, and has the Spirit for its own thereby, in order to benefit humanity. Justification, in short, is a matter of incarnation, and of the divine powers possessed by the humanity of Christ in virtue of that unity with the Word. Sanctification refers to what happens to the humanity of Christ on that basis over the course of his life and death. The character that Christ's own humanity comes to display by drawing upon that power of the Spirit is the sanctification of his humanity, a sanctification extended to us through it once thoroughly glorified in this way. For example, the trials and infirmities he underwent over the course of his life in struggle with a sinful world are finally overcome in his own life through the power of the Spirit by the end of it; victorious over them he lays them aside in his own resurrected life, so that, through that thoroughly sanctified humanity of his own, our lives might be sanctified as well.

The distinction that underlay our treatment of the way we are *simul justus et peccator* – the distinction between, on the one hand, having divine powers through attachment to what is itself divine, and, on the other hand, drawing upon them – also therefore has its roots in Christ. Like the *simul justus et peccator* that is true of us in virtue of a justice that is wholly ours independently of our sin, Christ is perfect and holy at once in virtue of his divinity, whatever the character of his own life – as much before he displays that holiness in his ministry as after it, as much when suffering under temptation as when conquering it, as much in facing the agonies of suffering and death on the cross as in being victorious over them. His humanity is always holy in a manner that does not vary in degree insofar as he is divine, one with the Word and thereby in immediate possession of the divine Spirit. But the perfection and holiness of

Christ's human life as that takes shape over time, by way of his active drawing on the powers of the Holy Spirit, is something else again: that is the sanctification appropriate to his humanity rather than his divinity, the sanctification of his humanity properly speaking, for example, the leading of a perfectly good human life and the healing of a body, broken by the sin of others, to new life.[67]

Because our justification and sanctification are found in him, Christ is central to the certainty of our salvation, as Protestants commonly affirm. By looking to Christ we come to know that our salvation is sure. "With our gaze fastened firmly to him we must declare with assurance that he is our righteousness and life and care nothing about the threats and terrors of the law, sin, death, wrath, and the judgment of God ... In him a sure comfort has been set forth for us, and victory has been granted."[68] Our salvation is sure in him because what we need is found already achieved in him, indeed to the utmost degree and in a way that cannot be broken. Our own clinging to Christ by way of faith in and love for him may be weak; but his humanity is inseparably bound to the Word, and turned thereby to the one he calls Father in perfect trust and self-dedication. We may struggle constantly against sin but his humanity has already been perfectly renovated, through a gift he cannot lose: the Spirit that he has for his own as the Word of God. In him is the gift of God's own life as a secure possession in virtue of the Word's assumption of that human nature as its very own in a unity of person with it. In him, we see perfectly achieved what the divine Spirit is to mean for human life when made over in the image of the second person of the trinity. However far our lives remain from being what his is, we need not despair if we hope in him. "Whenever our sins press hard on us, whenever Satan would drive us to despair, we must hold up this shield, that God does not want us to be overwhelmed in everlasting destruction, for he has ordained his Son to be the salvation of the

[67] See Newman, *Lectures on Justification*, p. 390.
[68] Luther, "Lectures on Galatians," pp. 166–7 (Gal 2:20).

world."[69] We have Christ as the rock upon which we stand. "This is our foundation: The Gospel commands us to look, not at our own good deeds or perfection, but at God himself as he promises, and at Christ himself, the mediator."[70]

Christ achieves all this for us without us and in our stead in that he achieves what we would not and could not do for ourselves. Christ becomes central for us in this sense because of our incapacity to effect our own salvation. While we remained sinners standing apart from God in repudiation of him, Christ took our place as the one in whom God is well pleased, the one, though crucified as a sinner, whose life God vindicates, pronounces acceptable, in raising from the dead.[71] When we were still wallowing in sin absent the Spirit, Christ's humanity was the one sanctified in virtue of the holiness of his divinity so as to lead a human life fully righteous in God's sight. Christ "has put on our flesh and consecrated it as a temple to God the Father and has sanctified himself in it to make atonement of our sins."[72] Thoroughly repudiating righteousness by works in the way Protestans typically do, one must recognize that Christ does for us all that we cannot: "The whole substance of our salvation is not to be sought anywhere else than in Christ."[73]

Everything for us has therefore already been done without us; there is nothing more we need to do, as if some deficiency remained in what Christ has done for us, to be remedied by our own worried attention to the character of our deeds. All we need do is draw upon what has been achieved without us, grasp it with empty hands, open our hungry mouths to it, which is just to recognize that everything

---

[69] Calvin, *Commentary on John 1–10*, p. 75 (John 3:17).

[70] Luther, "Lectures on Galatians," p. 387 (Gal 4:6).

[71] Newman, *Lectures on Justification*, pp. 77, 207.

[72] Calvin, *Commentary on Hebrews* 9:12 (Oliver and Boyd: Edinburgh, 1963), cited by Trevor Hart, "Humankind in Christ and Christ in Humankind: Salvation as Participation in our Substitute in the Theology of John Calvin," *Scottish Journal of Theology* 42 (1989), p. 71.

[73] Calvin, *Commentary on John 1–10*, p. 73 (John 3:16).

CHRIST THE KEY

necessary has already been done for us to remedy our own utter incapacity.[74] As Luther expresses the sentiment: "Here we are not obliged to do anything at all. The only thing necessary is that we accept the treasure that is Christ, grasped by faith in our hearts, even though we feel that we are completely filled with sins."[75]

What Christ has achieved apart from us does not, however, remain outside us at a distance, but is imparted to us. By doing for us what we could not do for ourselves, Christ substitutes himself for us in a way that implicates us in, rather than excluding us from, what he has achieved in himself.[76] What Christ has achieved in his own humanity is also to be achieved in us by way of him. "Christ, having been made ours, makes us sharers with him in the gifts with which he has been endowed."[77] In this way Christ becomes central to the character and achievement of our own Christian lives.

We are justified, then, not simply because what has happened independently of us is imputed to us but because what he has achieved becomes ours through him. Through him we participate, indeed, in both the justification and sanctification of humanity that have taken place in him. "By partaking of him, we ... receive a double grace: namely, that being reconciled to God through Christ's blamelessness, we may have in heaven instead of a judge a gracious Father; and secondly, that sanctified by Christ's spirit we may cultivate blamelessness and purity of life."[78]

Through unity with him we are to have what he has, to participate in all the benefits his own humanity enjoys. What Christ has already accomplished in himself becomes ours in being joined with him. The righteousness proper to him thereby becomes ours. "We do not ... contemplate Christ outside ourselves from afar in order that his righteousness may be imputed to us, but because we put on Christ

[74] For the last image, see Calvin, *Institutes*, Book 3, chapter 12, section 8, p. 762.
[75] Luther, "Lectures on Galatians," p. 139 (Gal 2:16).
[76] Hart, "Humankind in Christ and Christ in Humankind," p. 79.
[77] Calvin, *Institutes*, Book 3, chapter 11, section 10, p. 737.   [78] *Ibid.*, section 1, p. 725.

and are engrafted into his body – in short because he deigns to make us one with him."[79] We are already one with him in the achievements of his own life in that our humanity is his: "Indeed, there is an important sense in which ... we were in him when he wrought our salvation for us. Thus Calvin writes, 'mankind was united with God in the person of one man, because all men are made up of the same flesh and the same nature.'"[80] To whatever extent we are members of his human body, what Christ has in his own humanity – the Spirit of holiness – should flow down to cover ours, like ointment flowing over the head to the rest of the body of someone consecrated.[81] Fellowship with his own humanity gives us "fellowship of righteousness with him."[82]

> We are watered with the graces which were poured out on Christ. For not only as God does Christ bestow upon us what we receive from him, but the Father conferred upon him what would flow to us as through a channel. This is the anointing which was liberally poured upon him that he might anoint us all along with him.[83]

Christ's being alien to us – what we are not – does not require him to be kept at a distance, far off from us. Christ retains his righteousness for his own even as that righteousness exists within us, if it becomes ours simply through attachment to him. "Because he lives in me, whatever grace, righteousness, life, peace, and salvation there is in me is all Christ's; nevertheless, it is mine as well, by the cementing and attachment that are through faith, by which we become as one body in the Spirit."[84] Christ is foreign to us even when imparted to us; while existing within us Christ is something

[79] *Ibid.*, section 10, p. 737.
[80] Trevor Hart, "Humankind in Christ and Christ in Humankind," p. 79, citing Calvin, *Commentary on Hebrews* 5:2.
[81] Ronald S. Wallace, *Calvin's Doctrine of the Christian Life* (Grand Rapids, Michigan: Eerdmans, 1961), p. 16.
[82] Calvin, *Institutes*, Book 3, chapter 11, section 10, p. 737.
[83] Calvin, *Commentary on John 1–11*, p. 24 (John 1:16).
[84] Luther, "Lectures on Galatians," pp. 167–8 (Gal 2:20).

other than ourselves. Commenting on Galatians 2:20 – "It is no longer I who live, but Christ who lives in me" – Luther makes the point: "There is a double life: my own ... and an alien life, that of Christ in me."[85]

The righteousness that we possess in Christ remains alien to us in that Christ is what we can never be: the unity of divine and human in a single divine person; a human being who can be identified with God. Christ's humanity has divinity for its own in that the Word has become incarnate in him. We never have divinity in and of ourselves in that way, by being what Christ is. We have what is his – the divine power for new life – only in dependence upon him.

The source of all the righteousness we possess by way of his humanity remains, moreover, alien to us in its divinity. In much the way the heat of the sun that warms the earth remains the sun's and not the earth's, the Spirit as a specifically divine power does not become our own.[86] Divine power may be possessed by us but it is never proper to us. It may no longer reside outside ourselves but it remains beyond anything that we have the power to produce ourselves; it remains ours as a gift to us of what is not ours by right.[87] Divine power in being given to us never becomes some kind of "inherent form," some odd but still human quality of a supernaturally elevated sort, but remains the power of divinity itself, made ours only by clinging to what we are not.[88] Rather than being inherent in us, this power merely adheres to us in virtue of that clinging: "What seems to be inherent, may be more properly termed adherent, depending, as it does, wholly and absolutely upon the divine indwelling, not ours to keep, but as heat in a sickly person, sustained by a cause distinct from itself."[89]

---

[85] *Ibid.*, p. 170.

[86] Calvin, *Institutes*, Book 3, chapter 11, section 6, p. 732.

[87] Heiko A. Oberman, *The Dawn of the Reformation: Essays in Late Medieval and Early Reformation Thought* (Grand Rapids, Michigan: Eerdmans, 1992), pp. 121–2.

[88] See Luther, "Lectures on Galatians," p. 127 (Gal 2:16).

[89] Newman, *Lectures on Justification*, p. 187.

This is a quite Christologically focused account of justification and sanctification, finally, in that the benefits of justification and sanctification which we receive cannot be considered apart from Christ.[90] As Calvin affirms, "we possess [the righteousness that we have in Christ] only because we are partakers of Christ."[91] Christ is not the mere condition of or prerequisite for the benefits received through him, a mere means or instrument of our attaining them. The gifts of our own justification and sanctification are, to the contrary, inseparably bound up with their giver. Rather than merely gaining them by way of him, we have such benefits only *in* him.[92] We therefore must not ask "'what do I gain from grace?' as if the latter were some independent quality, but 'who am I in Christ?'"[93] In him we tend, moreover, only toward him, to what he already is as our own end; we never move beyond Christ's humanity as the goal for our own reformed lives.

[90] See Hart, "Humankind in Christ and Christ in Humankind," pp. 70, 72.

[91] Calvin, *Institutes*, Book 3, chapter 11, section 23, p. 753.

[92] See Wallace, *Calvin's Doctrine of the Christian Life*, p. 18. He is making reference here to Calvin, *Commentary on Romans* 6.11.

[93] Hart, "Humankind in Christ and Christ in Humankind," p. 70; see also pp. 69, 81.

3 | Grace (part two)

The final issue about grace is one that I would like to discuss in some detail. It concerns how to resolve a set of problems that often arises in contemporary Catholic thinking about the relationship between nature and grace when human nature is taken to be itself directed or oriented to grace. Because my own account makes grace central to human life, it raises these same problems. They concern the free character of grace and the integrity of human nature.

If God had created humans in a way that allowed them to exist entirely apart from grace by giving them a nature that made no reference to it, there would be no trouble recognizing the free or gratuitous character of God's grace. God's grace in that case offers something over and above what we are by nature, a whole new layer or tier of gifts that our nature neither requires nor gives us any particular reason to expect. For the same reason, the integrity of human life, its dignity and value, would also be easy to see apart from the gift of grace. However wonderful, grace would come as a supplement to a nature complete on its own terms and esteemed in unqualified fashion for its created goodness.

Indeed, in order to show that God's grace is not owed to us and that human life without it is still something to be appreciated, Catholic theologians in the early modern period increasingly posited a "pure" human nature, meaning by that human nature with a self-contained and self-sufficient character apart from God's grace. Humans do not require God's grace to be themselves and to live a decent life. The essential characteristics of human nature are self-contained in that they make no reference to God's grace and specify a set of ends that human powers are sufficient to achieve apart from special divine help.[1]

The worry about making pure nature the basis for the integrity of human nature, especially from a Protestant point of view, is that it suggests we are properly ourselves, and exist as we should, when left on our own without God's grace. The dignity of our nature seems essentially unaffected by the prospect of the gift of God's own life to us that is God's primary intent in creating us. The fact that we are created to be the recipients of God's grace does not seem to lie at the root of our dignity as creatures; that dignity has an independent basis in what our created nature is simply for itself. It is thereby possible to downplay significantly the seriousness of sin's consequences. If we had God's grace and lost it, that loss need not do us any real harm; it simply leaves us in the state of pure nature. Absent grace, human nature is left to itself in its original goodness. Regaining grace therefore becomes unnecessary for the repair of anything. It merely adds something good to what remains good.[2]

The other worry about the idea of pure nature is that it makes grace seem gratuitous to the point of near irrelevance. God's grace appears extrinsic to human life, an external disruption to human life properly preoccupied with more mundane matters, something we could very well do without and seem to have no need for. Grace becomes an optional, even superfluous addendum to human life lived quite well on its own terms. Here and now for all intents and purposes one has no reason to concern oneself with it. Its importance recedes behind the importance of what human beings are

[1] For this historical argument, see Henri de Lubac, *Surnaturel* (Paris: Aubier, 1946), Part 1, published in English as *Augustinianism and Modern Theology*, trans. Lancelot Sheppard (New York: Crossroad Herder, 2000).

[2] This understanding of the relationship between pure nature and sin can be found in Luis de Molina and Francisco de Suarez. See de Lubac, *Augustinianism*, pp. 220–8; and Henri Rondet, *The Grace of Christ*, trans. Tad W. Guzie (Westminster, Maryland: Newman Press, 1967), p. 333. Especially after the papal condemnation of Baianism in 1576, it worked to counter Protestant pessimism about the dire consequences of sin.

clearly capable of achieving on their own terms and by way of their own powers. Pure nature as the basis of God's free grace becomes in this way indistinguishable from a modern naturalism, from a simple affirmation of the self-sufficiency and self-containment of the natural, and easily colludes with the vaunted elevation of human powers in modern thought after the Enlightenment.

Contemporary Catholic theologians who share the above two worries – because, for example, they are Augustinians – affirm to the contrary that human nature brings with it some essential reference to God's grace; human nature is itself fulfilled, for that reason, by the gift of grace, which can be no mere extrinsic add-on to our natural state. These theologians often support such an idea by claiming – with Thomas Aquinas, the primary theological authority for Catholics in modern times – that humans have a natural desire, that is, a desire that is a fundamental part of their created constitutions, for a supernatural end – communion with God – they cannot achieve by their own powers. Because they have a natural inclination or tendency to something that only God can provide, the very nature of humans refers them to God's grace. The account of nature and grace I offer also affirms that a reference to grace is part of human nature: humans are created to operate with the gift of God's grace; human nature requires the grace of God for the excellent operation of its own powers and general well-being.

The difficulty for any idea that human nature is essentially bound up with God's grace is that it seems to conflict with the free or gratuitous quality of that grace and with the integrity of human nature: grace appears to be a requirement of human life and human life nothing apart from it. My own account raises both problems in a very strong fashion. In the first place, my account of the nature with which we are created does not allow one to imagine humans properly existing without the actual gift of grace in the way a Thomistic account of our created nature in terms of a simple desire for grace might. To be created as a human being means to be created with grace and not simply with a desire for what grace supplies. Human life therefore seems utterly wrecked apart from the actual gift of grace. In the second place, grace, understood as a strong form of participation in God, is necessary for the excellent exercise of our ordinary functions as human beings, and not merely for the achievement of distinctly super-natural ends such as eternal life. Because grace is required for human life to be properly itself, God, it seems, must give it to us; God is required to give us grace by God's intent to create us as the sort of creatures we are.

But the same problems also make themselves strongly felt in a Thomistic account of a natural desire for God. A life of dissatisfaction and unhappiness seems the only lot of humans missing what by nature is the object of their desire. Human life without the gift of grace is therefore fundamentally incomplete. And here too the essential nature of humanity seems to demand the gifts that only God can give to it, say, the beatific vision of God face to face. God has created human beings with the sort of constitution that makes seeing God face to face their natural end; this is what they are naturally attracted to, what their nature requires them to be attracted to. Unless God is willing to frustrate God's own intentions, it seems that the actual gift of grace follows necessarily from God's gift to humans of such a nature. Given the fact that God has created creatures with such a nature, God is obligated to give them the grace that fulfills them. The only real gratuity here would be reducible to the freedom with which God decides to create humans of that sort to begin with. The grace of Christ would be no more gratuitous than creation. Which is just another way of saying that such grace is owed to them as creatures; once created, it is their right.

Catholic theologians have tried in various ways to resolve these problems. In what follows I focus especially on the way they try to avoid the apparent conflict with free grace, and argue that none of their efforts is adequate for reasons having to do with a Thomistic understanding of a natural desire for God. Besides being generally less than compelling, most of the proposed solutions sidestep the original problem by either weakening the claim of gratuity or by going back on the effort to avoid naturalism and proposing something like pure nature.[3] If, as I recommend instead, the essential dependence of human life on a strong sense of participation in God takes the place of a Thomistic natural desire for God, the problem of gratuity – at least – is better addressed and without any alteration of its initial terms. Both the graciousness of grace and the anti-naturalistic attack on the sufficiency of human power remain quite strongly affirmed in keeping with a Protestant emphasis on God's free mercy in Christ and thoroughgoing repudiation of anything that might suggest we save ourselves.

A common way to defend the gratuity of grace in the face of a natural desire for it is to draw a distinction between desire and attainment. If, like the desire for love, the achievement of one's desires depends here on the cooperation of someone outside one's own power to control, simply having a desire for grace does not mean one will get what one desires as a matter of course. The gratuity of grace is thereby assured: the gift of God's grace remains a free act of love because that is just what the desire for love is a desire for – an uncompelled act of personal regard for oneself by someone else.

Complicating such a defense, however, is the fact that it is God who has created us with a desire that can be fulfilled only through the further action of God's grace. Unlike the case of human love, here the one who can fulfill the desire is also the one producing the desire for it in another. The actual gift of that fulfillment by God seems, then, a necessary consequence of God's having made us creatures who need it. Karl Rahner asks the pertinent question: "Can that person, who himself created such an ordination to the personal and intimate communion of love between two persons (in our case man and God), once this has been presupposed still simultaneously refuse

---

[3] For criticism of the Catholic view of a natural ordination to God generally on both these grounds, see Karl Barth, *Church Dogmatics 2/2*, ed. G. W. Bromiley and T. F. Torrance (Edinburgh: T & T Clark, 1978), pp. 530–4.

this communion without offending against the meaning of this creation and his very creative act itself?"[4]

The gratuity of the gift of grace therefore requires that the distinction between desire and attainment be more sharply drawn. It is not simply that desire does not bring about its own fulfillment where personal relationships are concerned; it now seems such a desire need not be fulfilled at all. The desire per se for God constitutes human nature and that desire has some kind of intelligibility and meaningfulness considered on its own. In other words, that desire would constitute a sustainable mode of existence of some significant worth and value irrespective of whether it is ever satisfied through the gift of God's grace.[5] God could therefore deny us the gift of grace without absurdity. Even if God does give us the gift of grace, as Christians believe, God did not have to.

What ensures the gratuity of grace here also ensures the dignity of human life apart from grace. The desire itself for God is sufficient to establish the peculiar dignity of human life even were such a desire to be frustrated. Though its value pales in comparison with the beatific vision, the desire for God that is naturally part of the human spirit is "neither meaningless nor harsh but can always be seen as a positive, though finite, good which God could bestow even when he has not called man immediately before his face."[6] Whether or not humans attain the object of their desire that only the actual gift of God's grace can deliver, they would have the dignity of a life devoted to such an end.

If a desire, however, is by definition a desire for something, it is hard to see the way in which it can be intelligible and meaningful

[4] Karl Rahner, "Concerning the Relationship between Nature and Grace," trans. Cornelius Ernst, in his *Theological Investigations* (New York: Crossroad, 1982), vol. I, p. 306.

[5] See, for example, the terms in which Rahner characterizes the desire for God that is part of our natural constitution as that is determined by abstracting from the supernatural existential that is itself the gift of grace. *Ibid.*, pp. 314–16.

[6] *Ibid.*, p. 316.

on its own apart from a concern about some end or other one has the real hope of attaining – if not the end of God's grace, then something else. More proximate ends, one might suppose, would have to step into the place of the ultimate end of God's grace for the latter to be a genuinely optional matter; only with reference to those more proximate ends would the desire for God remain fully intelligible and meaningful irrespective of the achievement of its primary object. In short, there must be some way of living out a desire for an end that may very well never come in terms of ends that are achievable. Especially when also offered as a defense of the integrity of human nature, the response we have been looking at strongly implies as much: God's grace may never come but something else that approximates it might very well be likely to; a focus on the latter would make human life worthwhile even were the desire for God's grace to remain unfulfilled. Indeed, one might go so far as to say that human life could be led in some satisfying way without God's grace, in virtue of the pursuit of ends that, while in some way ordered to that ultimate end by being analogous to or approximations of it, would be more in keeping with human nature per se and therefore achievable by its own powers.[7]

The desire for God itself is often thought to bring with it such powers for more proximate ends and thereby the hypothetical character of all this speculation – about what could have or would have been the case if God had not chosen to give us grace – is to that extent removed. The desire for God that constitutes our created nature has the power to move us to ends approximating the final one that only God can give us, irrespective of the way that desire may be affected by any gifts of grace. This is because the desire for God itself has an

---

[7] See de Lubac's discussion of the logical progression of Bellermine's views, *Augustinianism*, pp. 153–7. De Lubac seems to approve of this logical progression as long as such a state is not proposed as our normal one but what could have happened, as long as it is not our actual state but a hypothetical one. It comes to be affirmed as our normal state after Suarez. See *Augustinianism*, pp. 157–9.

active dynamic quality.[8] The desire for God as the absolute truth, for example, has the power to drive us forward in constant dissatisfaction with any form of knowledge short of absolute truth and in this way our knowledge progressively improves in a never-ending approach to what only God can give. By one's natural powers of reason, one might proceed from knowledge of the universe to know something about God's own existence and nature, even if the trinity remains beyond one's grasp and requires revelation from God. Because it brings about a movement of its own toward God, the desire for God, simply insofar as it constitutes a part of our created nature and might thereby operate apart from grace, has the power of itself actually to get us somewhere.

All that keeps this account of what we can get to on our own from being an account of pure nature is the fact that such achievements are subordinated to what grace alone can give and placed on a single historical trajectory with it. Everything that we are capable of achieving without it is on the way to that one end that requires the help of God's grace in order to be achieved; that final end thereby puts in proper perspective all that comes before it. But humans still seem capable of significant achievement independent of the grace God gives in Christ, so that the actual gift of that grace retains the flavor of an appendage for all its abilities to rectify and elevate what comes before it. No matter how provisional and ultimately inadequate when viewed from the standpoint of the grace that brings the beatific vision of God, the knowledge of God that one can get to on one's own, for example, might very well seem a kind of natural completion of the human desire to know, satisfying in its own terms. At least when abstractly considered, some provisional form of self-containment approximates a naturalistic self-sufficiency of the human here. Naturalism of a weakened sort in this way returns as

---

[8] Karl Rahner, for example, in his *Hearers of the Word*, trans. Joseph Donceel (New York: Continuum, 1994) follows Joseph Maréchal in talking about the desire for God – the *Vorgriff ad esse* – as such an active dynamism.

the prerequisite for both the gratuitous character of grace and the integrity of the human.

An alternative strategy for getting around the problem of gratuity focuses not on the character of our desire for God but on the character of God's decisions, more specifically, on what does or does not interfere with the freedom of those decisions. One might try to argue that God's decision to create us with a particular nature does nothing to constrain God's decision to give us grace.[9] The one decision is just as free as the other. Nothing about us obligates God to create us since before God's creation of us there is literally nothing to us; and the same would hold for God's decision to give us a supernatural end, the enjoyment of God's own life. "No more than creation itself is the necessary consequence of something that preceded it ... is the supernatural gift a simple *sequela creationis* [a necessary consequence of creation]."[10]

It is true that God's free decision to create us with a particular sort of nature does not adversely affect the free character of God's decision to give us additional gifts. This is simply a consequence of the fact that God's decisions are not sequential as ours are. We find ourselves constrained by decisions we have already made because we will one thing after another with some ignorance of what our initial decisions might imply. Rather than willing one thing and then being constrained to will whatever else turns out to follow from a decision to create something of that sort, God, to the contrary, wills at once the whole of what God wants to happen: both creatures with certain natures and what follows from their having those natures.[11]

[9] See Henri de Lubac, "The Mystery of the Supernatural," trans. Anne Englund Nash, in his *Theology in History* (San Francisco: Ignatius Press, 1996), pp. 299–303.

[10] *Ibid.*, p. 302.

[11] See Thomas Aquinas, *Summa Theologica [Theologiae]*, trans. Fathers of the English Dominican Province, 5 vols. (Westminster, Maryland: Christian Classics, 1981), vol. I, Q14 a7, pp. 77–8; Q19 a5, pp. 106–7; a8; pp. 109–10, and Q22 a4, pp. 124–5. For analysis, see Kathryn Tanner, *God and Creation in Christian Theology* (Oxford: Blackwell, 1988 / Minneapolis, Minnesota: Fortress, 2005[reprint]), chapters 2 and 3.

The issue of gratuity concerns, however, not whether one divine decision constrains another but the strength of the connection between the different things God wills, specifically here whether the fact of our creation with a desire to see God face to face does not in some sense imply the fulfillment of that desire in the actual vision of God by God's grace. Because its freedom is a function simply of its non-sequential character, God's decision to give further gifts to us remains free in any case, however strong the connection between those further gifts and the human nature that God has created us with. The connection indeed could be a necessary one without God's decision being constrained in any way, since God freely wills at once both the one and the other and the connection between them.[12]

Because this free God is also wise, bringing about an internally ordered world in which, for example, some things exist for the sake of others, connections of a strong sort among the things that exist within the world are in fact a common occurrence. In the strongest case of connection, the things that follow from the nature one is created with are simply gifts of creation, because they are essential constituents or ineluctable implications of it. There is no gap, no additional grace here, unless the natural course of things is somehow interrupted – say, by God or by sin's disturbance.

The question to be addressed is whether the relationship between the desire to see God and the vision of God approaches a strong connection like this, whether the vision of God is anything more than the gift of creation, a simple implication of the nature with which we have been created, owed to it by right, or whether it is something over and above it. The mere fact that God's decision remains free tells us nothing one way or the other about that, since, whatever the case might be, the freedom of God's decisions is never jeopardized. If the problem is that our natural desires seem

---

[12] See Thomas Aquinas, *Summa Theologica*, vol. I, Q19 a8, pp. 109–10; and Q22 a4, pp. 124–5.

to point of themselves ineluctably to the graced state that would complete them, the simple fact that God's decision all along the way remains free does nothing to address it; divine freedom in and of itself will not suggest otherwise.

A similar gambit suggests that proper attention to the gracious character of God's whole intent for us is sufficient to avoid any problem of grace's gratuity.[13] The proper starting point for considering the question of the relationship between our created nature and grace is God's gracious intent to give us God's own life as our own end. A single divine intent to give us the grace of God's own life underlies the whole of what happens to and for us, from our beginning in creation to our end in salvation; this intent is entirely gracious in that it has its basis in nothing but God's free love for us. The proper starting point for considering our created nature is therefore grace. Starting from grace, from the top-down perspective of God's own gracious intent to give us God's own life, the question of human nature is simply what a creature created for this purpose must be like. Because this question presumes to begin with the absolute graciousness of God's intent for us, the answer poses no problem for that presumption. What we are by nature cannot make God's act to give us God's own life anything less than gracious, if we only have a nature like that to begin with because of God's gracious intent to make us the beneficiaries of God's own life.

The problem of gratuity is therefore only an apparent one, caused by not following through on the change of perspective represented by a grace-centered account of the creature. The problem is produced by a distorted bottom-up view, one that starts from the character of the creature, independently of any question of grace,

[13] For this line of argument, see Leopold Malevez, "La gratuité du surnaturel," Parts 1 and 2, *Nouvelle Revue Théologique* 75 (1953), pp. 561–86, 673–89; Hans Urs von Balthasar, *The Theology of Karl Barth*, trans. Edward T. Oakes (San Francisco: Ignatius Press, 1992), p. 297, citing P. Delaye in *Orientierung* (Zurich, June 30, 1950), p. 138; and S. Dockx, "Du desir naturel de voir l'essence divine d'après Saint Thomas," *Archives de Philosophie* 27/1 (1964), pp. 80–3.

and then asks about the character of the grace to come – is it really free? The distance between what we are by nature and what we become by grace seems, from this point of view, the only guarantor of grace's gratuity. One thereby overlooks the fact that the whole is a matter of God's grace. The order in which God's intent is realized in the world, an order that moves from nature to grace, mistakenly comes to substitute for the order of God's own intent, one where grace, God's decision to give us God's own life, has absolute priority in a way that is completely free and unconstrained by anything else.

This solution to the problem of gratuity is basically the same one offered to explain the gratuity of further gifts of grace after a first one, which we looked at earlier in connection with questions of humility and self-glorification, and found wanting. The fact that the whole sequence is the product of God's grace is supposed to support the claim that what comes later is not required by what came earlier. But as we saw in our prior discussion, this way of arguing for gratuity does not rule out the idea that human powers, given to us through God's grace, are sufficient created causes of what comes next, of further gifts of grace. And something similar is allowed for here: the priority of grace in God's intent does not rule out a realization of God's gracious intent in which grace is required by our nature; the order of that realization of God's gracious intent might still be one in which grace is demanded by the sort of creatures we are.

The central issue, therefore, remains to be addressed. If humans have a natural desire for an end that God supplies, then an apparent continuity or connection exists between our created nature and that end in virtue of our nature's own fundamental orientation or inclination to it. God did not make us creatures for whom the vision of God would mean nothing, but creatures for whom that vision means everything; and therefore our nature demands it, yearns for it, tends to it, as if our very life depended on it. There seems, in short, to be some fairly strong continuity on the created plane between the desire to see God face to face and that vision itself, even if God's grace is also required for us to achieve that vision. That is just what a natural inclination or tendency to such a vision essentially implies.

Sin might very well be the interrupting factor that makes our final end gracious in a stronger sense. The corruption of our natures that results from sin might be so extreme as to break any continuity on the created plane between our present condition and our future destiny. We are so corrupted that we might as well be rocks, as far as appreciating what God originally intended to give us goes. But this is more a gratuity from our side than God's and for that reason of a superficial sort. Sin has no power to break God's faithfulness to God's own original intentions for us; we are still in God's eyes at least the creatures God created us to be. In virtue of that fact, it could still be the case that the grace of Christ is no more gratuitous than God's gift of creation.

Rather than appealing to sin, the common Catholic response simply weakens the strength of our natural desire for God in order to break any continuity between the desire itself and its own end. Our desire for God becomes a yearning, demanding, and uncondi- tional desire for the vision of God only under the influence of God's grace and not before. Before the influence of grace that strengthens it, it does not of itself place any requirements on grace. Simply as a desire of our natures it is a mere openness to grace, a simple receptiveness to being affected by the action of another upon us, what is usually called in Thomistic terms an obediential potency.[14]

The capacity for grace represented by our natural desire need not be reduced here to the simple non-repugnance of any creature before the power of God. Our reception of the beatific vision is not a miracle in the way the reception of the beatific vision by a stone would be. There is something about humans, in contrast to other creatures, that makes them genuinely open to God's grace. But we are opened to God by our nature in no more than the way in which the essential

---

[14] See, for example, Rahner, "Nature and Grace," pp. 315–16.

properties of large bodies of water make them in particular open to the pull of the moon. At issue here is a purely passive capacity and not an active orientation toward anything. Although it makes a very big difference to us when its effects are felt, we do not seek out God's grace of ourselves any more than the ocean seeks out the moon that produces its tides.

The more the desire for God is weakened in this way the more it approximates, however, the idea of pure nature. That is, the more the desire is weakened the greater its potential to close in on itself in simple self-satisfaction. Human beings might make do with a simple posture of openness to divine action in much the way large bodies of fresh water such as Lake Michigan seem to make do without the upheaval of ocean tides.

One might avoid the appearance of naturalism here by suggesting that what is described is a mere hypothetical state. The universal condition of human beings is in fact one in which our natural desire for God has always already been transformed by grace so as to become an intensely felt yearning or demand. The description of our natural desire for God as an obediential potency is produced by subtracting the influence of grace from the concrete desires we actually feel under the influence of grace, so as to leave a "remainder concept."[15] Our natural desire for God is the desire for God we would have had if our nature had been left to itself, which is not in fact ever the case.

The problems, however, with such a hypothetical description are many. Even if it were possible to know what to subtract and one could arrive at some conclusions about what our natural desire is like, it seems very strange for a theology that makes grace primary in God's creative intent to define the natural apart from grace, as if grace were not as central to human life as it in fact is.[16] A hypothetical description does not, moreover, address the question at issue, which has to do with the connection between the desires we

---

[15] *Ibid.*, pp. 302, 313–14.   [16] von Balthasar, *Theology of Karl Barth*, pp. 300–1.

actually have and their fulfillment.[17] "It is necessary for the super-natural to appear gratuitous not only in relation to a generic, abstract and unrealized nature but in relation to the concrete nature in which I participate here and now."[18] In some other world human life might exhibit a mere openness to grace and grace might for that reason appear to be a free gift, but this is not the world we live in. Finally, the position admits that the actual desires we have are very strong ones, because they already feel the force of God's grace; and with respect to these real desires the very same gratuity problem simply reappears. The gap between desire and fulfillment closes the stronger our own desires are: desires elevated by a first gift of grace require the further gifts of grace that would fulfill them.

Short of a simple naturalism, moreover, the natural desire for God can never be made sufficiently weak to make the gift of grace purely gratuitous. No matter how wide the gap between desire and fulfill-ment some continuity remains in virtue of the very desire itself. The more openness to God represents a genuine desire for some satis-faction beyond human capacity, a genuine tendency or orientation of itself, that is, to something that would fulfill it, the more human nature itself closes the gap.

Weakening the natural desire for God to show the free character of grace in this way trades on, rather than fundamentally questions, the presumption of pure nature as the guarantor of gratuity. It simply enforces the same direct relationship between the two, while making it a matter of degree. The more naturalistically self-enclosed the desire is, because its orientation to God is weak, the more gratuitous grace appears to be; the less self-enclosed human nature is, because the natural desire for God is strong, the less gratuitous grace seems. This solution simply admits defeat on the question of whether a strong anti-naturalism and the gratuity of grace can be combined with one another, as Protestants would like.

---

[17] de Lubac, "Mystery of the Supernatural," pp. 292–5.   [18] Ibid., p. 294.

Another way that some Catholic theologians break the appearance of continuity between our natural desire and its fulfillment involves no weakening of that desire for God, and this might suggest a more fundamental questioning of the presuppositions behind a claim of pure nature. Instead of weakening the natural desire for God one considers it a negative rather than a positive one. Desire on this way of looking at it is just as incapacitated as any weak desire but naturalism is ruled out by making the situation of mere desire an intensely unattractive one.[19]

Before its elevation by grace our natural desire for God does not yet have the slightest positive ordering to its end in the way an ordinary appetite has.[20] If it were an ordinary appetite, it would bring with it some real advance or effective movement forward that presupposes at least the beginnings of possession of what it seeks.[21] The natural desire for God, to the contrary, is not the positive seed of anything, participating in what is to come, "even initially or distantly in a way which needs but to be developed and enriched."[22] It is not the source of any sufficient activity that would make it, however minimally, of itself a certain inchoate possession of what it seeks.[23]

"Before the transformation which it must undergo in order to attain its goal, [it] is different in kind from all the desires of our common human experience" by lacking, one might say, all positive significance.[24] Lacking any forward movement or progress it has nothing in which to delight. It faces instead only the agony of an endless pursuit that fails to satisfy because it never gets anywhere

---

[19] De Lubac himself comes close to this following Maurice Blondel; see the more specific references below to *The Mystery of the Supernatural*.

[20] Henri de Lubac, *The Mystery of the Supernatural*, trans. Rosemary Sheed (New York: Herder and Herder, 1967), p. 111.

[21] *Ibid.*, p. 263.

[22] *Ibid.*, p. 109; citing Maurice Blondel, *La philosophie et l'esprit chrétien* (Paris: Presses Universitaires de France, 1944), vol. 1, p. 261.

[23] *Ibid.*, p. 111; citing Thomas all along the way on this page concerning the effects of sanctifying grace.

[24] *Ibid.*, p. 301.

at all.[25] This is desire as purely negative hunger, as starved lack rather than positive appetite for anything, one might say. Or desire incited by something like the salt that makes one thirsty rather than the water that makes one want to drink.[26] Desire that is a mere confused fumbling in the dark before grace. Or, desire as exasperated anguish in light of something one wants so badly but has utterly no chance of reaching through one's own power.[27]

In this way a gap looms between going nowhere by way of our natural desires and somewhere with grace, between despair and the vain dissipation of our energies without the gifts of grace, on the one hand, and joy and a real sense of achievement with those gifts, on the other. Ruled out is any sense of progress toward a supernatural goal through natural tendencies that are simply to be completed by grace, as talk of desire as an active dynamism suggests. But this strategy of changing a positive inclination into a negative one leans, once again, in a naturalistic direction in order to increase the gap between our natural and graced states. To make clear the gap between the two, one imagines a natural desire left entirely on its own, self-contained at least in the sense of being locked up within its own misery and confusion apart from grace.

The negative character of our desire, moreover, threatens to close up the very gap it was supposed to open. Indeed, the weaker our desire becomes in a positive sense the stronger it becomes in its very negativity. We have now a complete gap of achievement between going nowhere and getting somewhere through grace, it is true. But the very strength of the negative desire, of the hunger for what would relieve one's utter frustration and confusion, is as strong an orientation to grace as any positive one. A positive inclination in which one is propelled by desire to the asymptotic limit of all one's achievement, in which one seems to be going somewhere – for example, gaining a better understanding of God – at the same time as the vision of God's essence remains always beyond one's grasp, clearly

---

[25] *Ibid.*, p. 263.   [26] *Ibid.*, p. 41.   [27] *Ibid.*, p. 269.

implies grace as the next step if one's desires for God are ever to be satisfied. But only a sadist would deny grace to a creature as thoroughly miserable and at a complete loss without it as a purely negative desire for God suggests. Surely someone in a complete state of starvation is more strongly oriented to a good meal than someone making do for the moment with bread and water. Avoiding the continuity that comes from some partial possession of what one desires, one merely replaces it with the stronger orientation that comes from not having anything of what one desires. A seemingly strong continuity between partial and complete achievement is gone, only to be replaced by an even stronger continuity between utter lack and fulfillment.

One might try to avoid this impression of strong continuity between lack and fulfillment by saying our actual situation is never one of mere negative desire: grace in some degree or other is always present to provide us with a desire more properly oriented in a positive way to grace.[28] But if the actual historical state of humans, short of the beatific vision, is one in which an otherwise negative desire has been transformed into a rightly ordered desire by grace, then the gratuity problem as originally posed returns. A desire for God properly ordered to further gifts of grace by an initial one has grace in some degree; and in virtue of that very prior possession anticipates in itself what is to come. At first, as properly desirous of grace, one has some grace; with the satisfaction of that desire, one merely has more of what one's own desires in some incipient way already possess.

The underlying difficulty, I suggest, with all these Catholic efforts to show the gratuity of grace apart from some recourse to naturalism is this: the fact that our nature is essentially referred to grace by way of an internally generated desire for God, one, in other words, that our own nature generates of itself and that is in that sense natural to us. It is the self-generated character of desire for God – following, for

---

[28] For this suggestion of grace as a universal gift in some degree, see *ibid.*, p. 266.

example, an Aristotelian account of nature-based finalities or innate tendencies toward some end – that produces the problem of gratuity in the first place, and then prevents Catholic resolution of it without a fall back into naturalism.

A self-initiated inclination toward grace on the part of human nature lies behind the problem of gratuity: it is what suggests that the essential nature of humanity demands the gifts that only God can give. Tending or oriented of itself to something, a natural desire brings with it a capacity or power of its own, be it active or passive, negative or positive, toward an end; and thereby inevitably implies some inherent connection between desire, on the one hand, and its fulfillment, on the other. The idea of a nature-based desire for God suggests as a matter of course some more-or-less continuous trajectory from our created nature to grace, something like a mere transition from potentiality to actuality in the movement from nature to grace, whatever the means – divine or human – that prove necessary to get from the one to the other. No matter how far one modifies the idea of a self-prompted inclination, if one continues to assume it, the same problems of gratuity, as we have seen, only thereby return.

By affirming the idea of a nature-based desire for God, one cannot, moreover, avoid in any thoroughgoing way the naturalism associated with a two-tier account of nature and grace – nature as a self-enclosed substructure with grace an added superstructure – because the idea of such a desire is itself implicitly naturalistic. It makes a naturalistic presumption by leading one to account for human nature's reference to God apart from grace – in terms of a desire for which human nature itself is responsible. And it has a naturalistic implication. A self-generated natural desire always brings with it the suggestion of a self-initiated dynamism or movement, some forward-looking drive or impetus. Whether or not the final end of such a natural drive requires the outside help of God and exceeds created human powers, naturalism is always broached just to the extent humans are moving on their own toward God, in some degree of fashion, in virtue of it.

One might think that the naturalism of pure nature could be countered by stressing the way humans are oriented of themselves to God as their end: the problem with pure nature is that human nature is no longer ordered to anything but itself. But the problem lies deeper: with the very idea of a natural orientation in the usual Aristotelian-influenced Thomistic terms favored by Catholic theology. A position that tries to counter the idea of a self-enclosed nature by stressing our natural orientation to God in this sense shares with modern naturalism the idea of internally self-generated desires or inclinations, arising of their own accord in virtue of one's fundamental nature apart from any consideration of grace. With naturalism, it concentrates on the creature's own powers and capacities, inclinations and tendencies, and what they demand of themselves. Naturalism assumes those desires, in so far as they are natural, should be able to be satisfied by natural powers; an anti-naturalistic theological position assumes that they cannot. But the underlying picture is disconcertingly similar – one of self-generated trajectories of human nature – with the only difference of opinion being about means – whether something beyond human power is necessary to complete them.

Finally, if one thinks about the relationship between nature and grace in terms of natural human desires in an Aristotelian sense and what would fulfill them, human states become the focus for discussion in ways that hamstring efforts to show the gratuity of grace. The natural desire for God, when understood along Aristotelian lines as a nature-based tendency, carries the discussion of nature and grace along a trajectory of varying human states, those without or with the help that only God can give if such a trajectory is to come to its end. One pictures an unrolling sequence of human states, whether they be temporally or merely logically distinct: first, human nature in its natural state of desire for God, then that desire elevated by grace into something more properly ordered to God as its end, and finally the desire fulfilled by the actual gift of grace. The gratuity of grace has to be demonstrated along this axis of varying human states, by some sort of gap or discontinuity between the human character we were created with and the human state we will enjoy when saved. One is thereby pushed to increase the gap between our natural and graced states, to pull them apart as much as possible, by imagining what life might be like without the gift of grace and considering that to be a state in which human beings could actually live. This is the internal push toward naturalism in the position. But it can only go so far. If a simple naturalistic description of that first state is to be avoided, humans must still be oriented to grace while in an actual state of existence without grace, by way of desires that are therefore purely natural, purely a function of their created natures. But these very desires close the gap; the gap between our created and graced states is bridged by the natural orientation itself to the human fulfillment that a graced state brings.

Problems of gratuity arise all along this axis of different human states because continuity among them is guaranteed by the natural desire presupposed throughout; the differences in the steps or stages are simply differences in that same underlying desire's own states of, say, non-fulfillment, partial, and then total fulfillment. It becomes hard to see the radical character of the gap between what we are by nature and what we are given by grace since the human presuppositions and consequences of that grace in terms of human nature's own desire for it are being pressed in this way to the fore.

The importance that the strong form of participation in God has in my account of both human nature and grace shifts attention away from a natural desire for God altogether if that means a desire that human nature itself generates. If a natural desire for God in that sense is what creates all the problems, my account of the relationship between nature and grace allows one to say one does not have one. An alternative explanation for our desire for God lies readily at hand. Rather than being generated by our nature per se, desire for God results from the presence of God that forms an essential ingredient of our constitution as the prerequisite of human well-being. Desire for God is the product, in short, not of our nature but of grace, understood as a strong form of participation in God. One need not say, then, that human nature itself generates a desire for God because, for example, it so needs the divinity it lacks in and of itself as a mere created nature, or because something about its own created nature is itself some form of participation in God requiring completion by grace. Rather than arising from either what we are or lack as creatures, desire for God, one can say instead, arises from what we have that is not our nature – the divinity in which we participate.

The presence of God to us elicits our desire for God: God, as Gregory of Nyssa affirms, "is essentially capable of attracting in a certain way every being that looks towards it."[29] The presence of God to us gives rise to our desire for God because the divine is in and of itself attractive – good and beautiful – and because it has beneficial effects on us. We desire God as a matter of course because God remains superior to us and the source of our own good. "As long as a nature is in defect as regards the good, the superior existence exerts upon this inferior one a ceaseless attraction towards itself."[30] As the infinite or unbounded good, God is always superior to us and therefore always an object that attracts us in being present to us; "the true sight of God consists in this, that the one who looks up to God never ceases in that desire."[31]

Given what prompts it, desire for God as a form of inclination or tendency toward God is therefore not self-moved. It is the presence of God that instead gives us our desires and draws us toward God by way of them: "The fountain of grace constantly draws to itself all

[29] Gregory of Nyssa, "On the Soul and the Resurrection," trans. William Moore and Henry Austin Wilson, in Philip Schaff and Henry Wace (eds.), *Nicene and Post-Nicene Fathers*, vol. v, Second Series (Peabody, Massachusetts: Hendrickson, 1994), p. 449; and *The Life of Moses*, trans. Abraham Malherbe and Everett Ferguson (New York: Paulist Press, 1978), paragraph 225, p. 113.

[30] Gregory of Nyssa, "Against Eunomius," trans. H. C. Ogle, William Moore, Henry Austin Wilson, in Philip Schaff and Henry Wace (eds.), *Nicene and Post-Nicene Fathers*, vol. v, Second Series (Peabody, Massachusetts: Hendrickson, 1994), Book 1, section 22, p. 62.

[31] Gregory of Nyssa, *Life of Moses*, paragraph 233; p. 115; and paragraph 239, p. 116.

those who thirst."[32] We do not, in virtue of our desire for God, move toward God on our own apart from the gift of God's own presence as the spur to such movement. Our desire for God therefore never gets us anywhere on our own steam – even to proximate ends on the way to God – apart from the gift of God's own presence pulling us along the chain.

If desire for God implies some impetus or inclination to what one does not yet have of God, the explanation for this is no self-generated movement of the desire itself toward what it lacks. Movement prompted by a desire for more is powered instead by divine presence already enjoyed. "To those who have tasted and seen by experience 'that the Lord is sweet' (Psalm 33:9), this taste becomes a kind of invitation to further enjoyment. And thus the one who is rising towards God constantly experiences this continual incitement towards further progress."[33] God's presence makes one want more of the boundless good of God that always lies ahead: "since this good has no limit, the participant's desire itself ... has no stopping place."[34] Fueled by the unlimited character of the divine beauty and goodness it enjoys, "the soul which looks to God and conceives that desire for incorruptible beauty always has a new desire for the transcendent, and it is never dulled by satiety. Such a soul never ceases to stretch forth to what lies before, going out from her present stage to what lies ahead."[35] The satisfaction of desire that comes from the presence of God, indeed, only makes one want more by expanding one's capacities to receive what God has to give. Our capacities "become continually larger with the inpouring of the stream ... The fountain of blessings wells up unceasingly, and the partaker's nature ... becomes at once more wishful to imbibe the nobler nourishment and more capable of containing it; each grows along

---

[32] Gregory of Nyssa, *From Glory to Glory*, trans. Herbert Musurillo (Crestwood, New York: St. Vladimir's Seminary Press, 1995), p. 213.

[33] *Ibid.*   [34] Gregory of Nyssa, *Life of Moses*, paragraph 7, p. 31.

[35] Gregory of Nyssa, *Commentary on the Song of Songs*, trans. Casimir McCambley (Brookline, Massachusetts: Hellenic College Press, 1987), Twelfth Homily, p. 223.

with each, both the capacity which is nursed ... and the nursing supply which comes on in a flood."[36]

The character of grace, centering on a strong form of participation in God, helps make sense of the way in which this desire for God is not a natural desire. The desire for divine presence is not based on our created nature, strictly speaking, not generated out of it apart from any consideration of grace, just to the extent what we desire remains foreign in its divinity to our created nature. What we desire, a share in God's life, is not something properly ours by nature, if one considers the character of human nature in and of itself; our nature gives us no claim to it in the way a natural desire seems to suggest.

If not ours by nature, the gift of God's own life is still, however, naturally ours or natural to us; and in this way any naturalistic claim of self-containment for the human creature apart from grace is countered.[37] Despite the fact that desire for it is not solicited by our nature independently of grace, grace in the form of God's presence to us remains natural to us in that our nature has not been made to exist on its own apart from it. The grace of strong participation in God is natural to us because our nature is such that we exist well only with it. The gift of strong participation in God shows itself to be natural to us in this sense in that its loss does us fundamental harm; in some significant sense we lose ourselves in losing God. Life without it must be an unnatural condition, a condition contrary to the character of our created nature, given the wretchedness and suffering that ensue.[38]

[36] Gregory of Nyssa, "On the Soul and the Resurrection," p. 453.
[37] For the distinction between what is ours by nature and what is natural to us, see David Balás, ΜΕΤΟΥΣΙΑ ΘΕΟΥ: Man's Participation in God's Perfections according to Saint Gregory of Nyssa (Rome: Herder, 1966), p. 149.
[38] Augustine, City of God, trans. Henry Bettenson (New York: Penguin, 1977), Book 11, chapter 17, p. 448; Book 12, chapter 1, pp. 472–3. See the similar argument of Gregory of Nyssa, "On Virginity," trans. William Moore and Henry Austin Wilson, in Philip Schaff and Henry Wace (eds.), Nicene and Post-Nicene Fathers, vol. v, Second Series (Peabody, Massachusetts: Hendrickson, 1994), chapter 12, pp. 357–8;

"Adherence to God belongs to our nature" in much the way that seeing and hearing what exists outside them belongs to the eyes and ears.[39] In keeping with the nature God gave us, God intended us to exist in the state of clinging to God whose essential character exceeds our own nature. That was to be our normal state, in the sense of being both our regular and proper one. As the ordinary condition in which we were supposed to exist according to God's intentions for us, enjoying God's own life is natural to us even if what we enjoy remains foreign to our nature in its divinity.[40]

Because our nature is not one that can properly exist on its own apart from grace, what is natural is not human nature per se, but the concrete state in which we actually exist together with grace. Human nature per se, considered apart from the gift of grace, is not natural, and in this sense the natural is not primarily contrasted with grace. It is natural, instead, for us to have grace; grace is to be part of the ordinary and proper state of human life.[41]

In this sense of natural, existing with the grace of God was the natural state in which we were created. "Adam found [the help of God] naturally, as something normally at his disposal, and always as it were within his reach, without having to ask for it first. He did not have to seek God, because God was already near him."[42] "The first man on earth ... had for choice the [divine] good and the [divine] beautiful lying all around him in the very nature of things."[43] In this

"On Infants' Early Deaths," trans. William Moore and Henry Austin Wilson, in Philip Schaff and Henry Wace (eds.), *Nicene and Post-Nicene Fathers*, vol. v, Second Series (Peabody, Massachusetts: Hendrickson, 1994), pp. 376–7; and "One the Soul and the Resurrection," p. 457.

[39] Augustine, *City of God*, Book 12, chapter 1, pp. 472–3.
[40] For the way Thomas Aquinas follows Augustine here, see William R. O'Connor, "The Natural Desire for God in St. Thomas," *New Scholasticism* 14/3 (1940), pp. 27–9.
[41] Etienne Gilson, *The Spirit of Medieval Philosophy*, trans. A. H. C. Downes (University of Notre Dame Press, 1991), pp. 291–2.
[42] de Lubac, *Augustinianism*, p. 90, recounting Augustine's position.
[43] Gregory of Nyssa, "On Virginity," chapter 12, p. 357.

sense of natural, sin is unnatural, and grace, at the very least, restores us to a natural condition.[44]

The desire for God is itself natural to us in the same sense. It is what we would ordinarily and properly display in virtue of a strong form of participation in God granted to us as our normal state. We would not, then, acquire such a desire as an addition to our natural state, for example, by being taught it by another: "Instruction in yearning for the divine does not come from outside; but simultaneously with the fashioning of the living creature," as Basil says.[45] Though requiring cultivation and capable of falling into neglect, such a desire is not learned but natural to us in the same sense that love of one's benefactors – love, for example, of children for their parents – is natural to us.[46] Desire in the form of an affectionate inclination toward God naturally arises as a response to the love already shown to us by God in and through, for example, God's gift of God's own life to us as our normal condition.

Because existing with the grace of God is the normal condition that God created us to be in, this understanding of the relationship between nature and grace gives one no reason to imagine what human nature would be like apart from the gift of grace and then to identify that with our original created state. One might speculate, as we did in the first chapter, about what human nature must be like in and of itself given the fact that grace is our normal condition. But it makes no sense to speculate, as much contemporary Catholic thinking about nature and grace does, about what human beings would have been like if they had not been given grace. Imagining human nature apart from the gift of grace that is its normal condition is tantamount to asking whether humans might not have been

---

[44] For another case of this understanding of the natural, see Etienne Gilson's treatment of William of Thierry in his *The Mystical Theology of Saint Bernard*, trans. A. H. C. Downes (New York: Sheed and Ward, 1940), p. 202.

[45] Basil, "Long Rules," trans. Nonna Verna Harrison, in his *On the Human Condition* (Crestwood, New York: St. Vladimir's Seminary Press, 2005), question 2, answer 1, p. 112.

[46] *Ibid.*, answers 1–2, pp. 112–15.

created as the sort of creatures they are, but with a more self-contained nature somehow capable of making do without the actual gift of God's grace. Naturalism is therefore more thoroughly repudiated here than in the Catholic treatments of nature and grace previously discussed.

More specifically, my account gives one no reason, first of all, to imagine human life without the gift of grace in an effort to show the gratuity of grace. One is tempted to imagine humans in a purely natural state in which grace does not seem strictly necessary or required for human well-being, if the gap between natural and graced human states is what makes clear the gap between nature and grace. But my account of grace does not make gratuity a function of what happens to the human in this way.

There are, it is true, rather marked differences in the human condition with and without grace on my account. We are miserable and fundamentally incapacitated without it, and excellently exercising one's capacities and enjoying the divine life with it. Differences in the human states that are ours through grace also exist before and after Christ's coming. With the grace of Christ, as we have seen, we gain a remedy for sin, have God's presence in a more stable way than before, and come to enjoy something like the Word's own relationships with the other members of the trinity (as will be discussed more fully in Chapter 4). But what accounts for such differences deflects attention from any direct comparison of these human states themselves on a purely human level; and therefore will not be further clarified simply by fuller treatment of the human itself in these various states, in particular its condition apart from grace. What accounts for all such differences is whether or not the presence of God is available as a formative power in human life, and the way it is before and after Christ.

Because the gift of God's presence is what accounts for them, differences between human states themselves are not the primary guarantors of the gratuity of grace. What assures gratuity, instead, is the very difference between that gift of God's presence and any and all human preconditions and consequences of it. In virtue of the gap that exists between the divine and the human, the grace of God's very presence is as gratuitous, un-owed and freely given as anything can be.

There can exist some mediating continuum between human states, no matter how low the one and how elevated the other. The natural desire for God would, as we have seen, itself act as such a mediating continuum between naturally lowly and graciously elevated human states. But there cannot be any such continuum between God and creatures. Grace that takes the form of the gift of God's own presence is for this reason never anything less than unexacted.

The difference between the divine and human allows one, indeed, to bypass consideration of any gap in human states when affirming the gratuity of grace. Even if our existing with grace is preceded by no merely "natural" human state of desire without fulfillment, even if grace is therefore always in fact enjoyed by us as our normal condition, the difference between the divine and the human remains and is sufficient to show that grace is gratuitous. As Augustine makes the point: "the soul itself, even though it may be always wise – as it will be, when set free from all eternity – will be wise through participation in the changeless Wisdom, which is other than itself. For even if the atmosphere were never bereft of the light which is shed on it, there would still be the difference between its being and the light by which it is illuminated."[47]

Second of all, my account does not prompt one to imagine human nature without the gift of grace but still somehow ordered to it, in order to avoid the impression that grace is a mere supplement to human life lived properly on its own terms. That way of countering the idea of grace as an extrinsic addendum only brings with it, we have argued, the problem of gratuity. On my account, there is no way, to begin with, for the gift of grace to appear a superfluous

---

[47] Augustine, *City of God*, Book 11, chapter 10, pp. 441–2.

addition to human life; grace is hardly an irrelevant add-on if human nature does not properly exist at all without it. The recourse to a natural desire for God in a Thomistic sense becomes necessary to prevent the extrinsic character of grace only if one imagines that human life can be lived in some adequate fashion without God's grace. But that is just what my account does not permit.

It is true that sin brings the loss of grace as a sort of historical stage to which grace must then be added. Such a loss might be thought to prompt once again (in Catholic circles worried about an extrinsic grace) a consideration of how humans without the gift of God are still ordered to it, in virtue of whatever purely natural desires remain under conditions of sin. But according to my account retention of a desire for God in a state of sin might be better understood as the product of the continuing influence of divine presence. That gift is still being offered even as we turn away from it in sin. When we shut our eyes to the light of God, it is we who produce the barrier to the light without the light of God itself retiring or withdrawing from us.[48] God is not absent from us while we are absent from God; in much this way the sun continues to shine on the face of the one who is blind to it.[49] Even if one is not *with* the light by attending to it and drawing upon it for one's good, one remains *where* it is and must thereby be feeling some effects of its own presence on one.[50] It is only because of this ongoing influence of the presence of God on us despite our refusal that we retain any desire for God at all, some attraction to God as our good, even as we lead lives of sin.

---

[48] Gregory of Nyssa, "On Virginity," chapter 12, p. 357.

[49] Augustine, *Tractates on the Gospel of John 1–10*, trans. John W. Rettig (Washington, DC: Catholic University of America Press, 1988), Tractate 1, section 19, paragraph 1, p. 58 (John 1:1–5); Tractate 3, section 5, paragraph 1, p. 79 (John 1:15–18); and *Tractates on the Gospel of John 28–54*, trans. John W. Rettig (Washington, DC: Catholic University of America Press, 1993), Tractate 35, section 4, paragraph 2, p. 74 (John 8:13–14).

[50] For this distinction between being where Christ is and being with him, see Augustine, *Tractates on the Gospel of John 55–111*, trans. John W. Rettig (Washington, DC: Catholic University of America Press, 1994), Tractate 111, section 2, paragraph 4, pp. 302–3 (John 17:24–6).

Finally, in fully repudiating naturalism my account of the relationship between nature and grace need not render the problem of human integrity more acute. It might seem as if our natural dependence on properly divine powers violates the integrity of human nature. But the natural integrity of the human here simply does not require self-containment or completion on its own terms. Because existing with grace is natural to us, because that is the very state that human nature has been made for, human nature certainly need not itself be broken open or violated in any way in receiving it. In receiving grace, human nature exists in just that state it was created to be in, the state appropriate to its own nature as a nature not properly existing apart from grace.

Grace respects the integrity of our nature, indeed, by not requiring it to be in any way fundamentally reconstituted. Even for God to be present within us in the highest possible fashion through Christ, nothing about our essential constitution has to change. To receive God, our own natural powers of intellect do not need to be elevated beyond the human, as Thomas, otherwise a champion of human integrity, claims.[51] Those powers are already properly disposed, as much as they can be, to such reception, because that is what they have been created for. Nor, as Thomas also affirms, do the normal operations of our intellect have to be interrupted, intellectual powers made for knowledge of the world through sensible means now bypassed in some exceptional fashion by the divine essence itself coming to replace any sensibly derived phantasm or image.[52] Instead, the proper object of our intellectual operations was always God, even as sensible creatures made to exist in a sensible world. An intellect like ours, bound up with the material world through our bodily-based senses, nonetheless naturally has God for its object.[53]

[51] See, for example, *Summa Theologica*, vol. I, Q12, pp. 48–59.   [52] *Ibid.*

[53] See for purposes of comparison Thomas' position as summarized by Gilson, *Spirit of Medieval Philosophy*, pp. 248–50: While God is the adequate object of the intellect per se, God cannot be the natural object of the specific sort of intellect we have which has been made to know everything that it knows through sense impressions.

All that has to change at the highest reaches of grace is the character of our relationship to God through Christ; our nature as originally created is already perfectly suited to that new relationship. Although our relationship with God has been altered in ways that perfect it, *what* is brought into new relationship to God through Christ is the very same human nature we had to begin with, operating excellently as usual by way of divine presence and power just as it was created to. In this sense, "the glory of the resurrected saints is a glory fitted to our nature."[54]

The integrity of human nature follows here, as the gratuity of grace does, from the gift to us of what is foreign to us – God. As we have seen, it is simply part of what it means to acquire something alien from outside oneself that its being given or taken away does not affect one's essential character.[55] Although the excellence of our operations requires the presence of God, the reception of divinity foreign to our nature leaves that nature itself intact.

Having the divine for our own does not lead to any confusion of divine and human; no blurring of the divine into the human occurs thereby to compromise the integrity of our nature. Although the presence of God is an essential ingredient of our constitution, it does not form any sort of composite with us. The divine nature is perfect and complete in itself and therefore cannot inform the nature of anything else so as to make up one nature with it, in the way, say, the soul informs the body to produce a composite human nature of body and soul.[56] When God perfects our operations God does not then become any part of our nature, some proper component of that nature itself. Because God's nature is already complete in the way no

---

[54] Daniel A. Keating, *The Appropriation of Divine Life in Cyril of Alexandria* (Oxford University Press, 2004), p. 176.

[55] See, as another example, Cyril of Alexandria, *Commentary on the Gospel according to John*, trans. P. E. Pusey (Oxford: James Parker, 1874), Book 11, chapter 7, section 6, p. 503 (John 17:6). He is discussing kingly power as a human attribute.

[56] Thomas Aquinas, *Summa contra Gentiles*, trans. Vernon J. Bourke (University of Notre Dame Press, 1975), Book 3, Part 1, chapter 51, section 4, p. 176.

created form or informing principle is, our nature also remains complete in its own essential definition as a created nature even while being formed according to a divine pattern by divine power.

When divine power perfects our operations, it is therefore not our nature that is fundamentally affected but at most our state. Leaving an unnatural condition behind, our state becomes one in which, for example, we are genuinely able to avail ourselves of what is unlike our nature in its divinity. But human nature itself remains essentially as it was, its created integrity respected. "A change of form ... will not carry us away to some other nature, for we will be the very thing we are, that is, human beings except incomparably greater; for we will be incorruptible and indestructible" through intimate attachment to God's own powers of life.[57]

Nothing of our nature is subtracted or replaced in the process; instead, something properly divine is added to a human nature that remains complete in its created character. Grace does not supply some missing part of our nature comparable to its other parts; and therefore one should not think of grace as providing some alternative or substitute for an aspect of our nature. One should not think of grace, for example, as supplying some power that could have been ours by nature but was not, a power therefore necessary to complete the exercise of our natural power for natural ends.[58] Nor should one think grace provides us with some new supernatural version of a human capability, beyond those possible for us as creatures and therefore required for the achievement of supernatural ends.[59] Instead, the whole of what we are by nature achieves a new state by God's grace; grace raises our full human nature, complete on its own

---

[57] Cyril of Alexandria, *In 1 Cor* 15:50–6 (Pusey iii, 317), cited by Keating, *Appropriation of Divine Life*, p. 176. See also Leo the Great, *Sermons*, trans. Jane Patricia Freeland and Agnes Josephine Conway (Washington, DC: Catholic University of America Press, 1996), Sermon 71, section 4, p. 313, cited by Keating, *Appropriation of Divine Life*, p. 285.

[58] See de Lubac on Baius' reduction of the supernatural to the natural in *Augustinianism*, pp. 15, 29.

[59] This is the worry about any Thomistic account of infused theological virtues.

terms, up to another divine level of existence and functioning. In just this way, the Holy Spirit at our creation was something over and above our human soul rather than some divine replacement for it; the Holy Spirit could thereby be the organizing principle for the complete human person in all its aspects. As Cyril of Alexandria makes the point:

> No one ... would suppose that the breath which proceeded from the divine essence became the creature's soul, but that after the creature ... had attained ... the propriety of its perfect nature by means of both body and soul ... then like a stamp of his own nature the creator impressed on it the Holy Spirit, i.e., the breath of life, whereby it became molded unto the archetypal beauty.[60]

In the same way, the grace that we are given to change our hearts as sinners should not be identified with some new supernatural human disposition bringing us to will as we ought. Instead, the gift of grace underlies a whole reworked manner of behaving with nothing but our original fundamental dispositions and capacities. The usual complement of our ordinary created human dispositions and acts of will now work well through God's grace; grace is what brings them to be themselves victorious over sinful impulses.[61]

Furthermore, although our nature considered in and of itself does not approach the goodness that is ours through close relationship with God, it remains of irreplaceable value. For example, while our character is unformed as rational creatures apart from the light of God's own presence, our being rational can nonetheless be considered the first stage of a wholly good creation. There exists a human nature made for grace to be properly respected in its created qualities.

Indeed, compared to other creatures, our nature has an unusual nobility, a nobility that comes from not being, as others are, the sort

---

[60] Cyril of Alexandria, *Commentary on John*, Book 9, chapter 1, p. 319 (John 14:20).
[61] See de Lubac's discussion of problems with the theology of Jansenius in *Augustinianism*, pp. 64, 68–9, 72–4.

of creature that can properly exist without the grace of God's very presence to them. Contrary to appearances, our very incapacity of ourselves to achieve what is good for us therefore demonstrates that nobility. "The nature capable of attaining a perfect good with help is of a more noble condition than that which attains an imperfect good without help."[62]

Of greater value than any creature that simply exists in and of itself is the creature that adheres to the goodness of God for its own well-being. While our need for that relationship means that the ultimate value of our lives depends on something outside us and that our lives are made miserable without it, yet other things in the created universe are not in a better condition for that reason. Even in a state of misery our lives are more valuable than theirs; in just this way "the other members of our body are not to be called better than our eyes because they cannot be blind."[63]

[62] *Ibid.*, pp. 117–18, citing John Versor's commentary on Aristotle's *Nicomachaean Ethics*, Book 10, question 14 (Alfaro, pp. 237–8), following Aquinas.

[63] Augustine, *City of God*, Book 12, chapter 1, p. 472. See also his *Confessions*, trans. R. S. Pine-Coffin (Baltimore, Maryland: Penguin, 1976), p. 316.

— Understanding trinitarian relationship involves integrating contrasting Scriptural perspectives

— Some of the grounds of Filioque controversy

— Our life follows a trinitarian pattern of ascent (justification) and descent filled with the Spirit (sanctificate). Paul? Baptism + Eucharist

— The role of Son + Spirit is to manifest each other, the Son "gives shape" to the working of the Spirit

4 | Trinitarian life

Christ is the key, we have seen, to human nature, and to the sort of grace human nature was made to enjoy. But Christ is also the key, I want to show now, to the trinity and its significance for us. Christ is the key to understanding this second set of topics because of the peculiar character of the human life he leads. Because he is the Word, Jesus Christ displays in his human life the relationships that the Word has to the other members of the trinity; as a human being he leads, in short, a trinitarian way of life.

The life of the Word is constituted by its dynamic relationships with the other members of the trinity from which it is inseparable; the Word has no life apart from the other two. In becoming incarnate the Word therefore extends this same pattern of trinitarian relationships into its own human life so as to give it shape according to that pattern. The description of Jesus' human life, which the New Testament offers, becomes in this way the basis for understanding both what the relationships within the trinity are like and what they are to mean for us as new organizing principles of human living.

This meaning of the trinity for us brings the discussion of previous chapters to its appropriate next step. Although the preoccupations of earlier chapters might seem to have nothing to do with the present one, they lead into it. We concentrated in the first chapter on the way we are strong images of God by close association with the perfect divine image through Christ. But we have not yet talked about what is to happen to human life in being so identified with that divine image, the character that human life is to assume thereby. We have developed an account of the grace we gain through a strong form of participation in God that is ours in Christ. But we have yet to discuss what it means to live a human life with that grace. What happens to our lives, I now argue, is that they take on a trinitarian shape. In keeping with the emphasis of previous chapters, human lives do not have that trinitarian shape in and of themselves, as any kind of separable by-product of the grace of strong participation, but in and through it. In being one with the Word, Jesus achieves this new way of life before us; and we gain it through close connection with him.

Indeed, our previous discussion of human beings as the image of God leads directly to the present topic, the trinitarian character of human life. If human beings image the second person of the trinity, they also for that reason image the trinity – specifically the relations of the second person to the other two. When human life is in the divine image of the second person of the trinity, human life also images that person's relations to the other members of the trinity, and in that way the trinity as a whole.

Because we are created in its image, the second person of the trinity is our place within the life of the trinity, the position with which we are to be identified in relations with the other two. Formed from the dust according to this divine image, we are to be some sort of version or counterpart of the second person – a created one, refracted through the nothingness that distinguishes us from God.[1] Though merely adopted and not natural offspring of the Father because of our created status, we are to be "sons" alongside the one divine Son of the Father; that is one traditional way of making this trinitarian point about human life, following a common scriptural idiom or manner of speaking.[2] As adopted sons we are to enjoy the

[1] Louis Bouyer, *The Eternal Son: A Theology of the Word of God and Christology*, trans. Simone Inkel (Huntington, Indiana: Our Sunday Visitor, 1978), p. 401.

[2] Note that I will often use very traditional Father/Son/Spirit language in what follows. This is not because I am especially wedded to these terms. It is mainly a function of my use of early church biblical commentary to make the arguments of this chapter. Substituting other terms would require me to show that the same theological points

true divine Son's prerogatives, through relations with the other persons of the trinity in some sense comparable to the ones that the second person of the trinity has. The very love, for example, of the Father for the Son, poured out upon him through the Spirit, is what we as adopted children of the Father are to feel.

We hold this special place in trinitarian life in the hope that the whole world will approximate it. The entire world is created by the first person of the trinity, in and through the Word by the power of the Spirit, to be an expression or manifestation like the Word of all the good things the first contains. The Word is the perfect reproduction, spreading forth, or laying out of all the good things of the first person in inseparable counterpoint to it, as that becomes possible through and is brought to completion in the power of the Spirit. Something similar is to hold for the whole world as the divine image's created counterpart; the first and third persons of the trinity thereby relate to the world in something like the way they relate to the second. The exceptional character of human beings would be as placeholders, then, for creation generally, focal points for a worldwide imaging of the second person's relations with the other two.

But the second person of the trinity is not just the prototype for our relations with the first and third persons of the trinity, a divine exemplification of the sort of position we are to take up vis-à-vis the other two. The second person of the trinity is, as well, our entryway, our point of access into those relations. We are to take up the very position of the second person of the trinity as that person joins our life to its own through the incarnation.

In keeping with the conclusions of Chapter 1, if we image the relations among members of the trinity, we do not do so in and of ourselves, because, for example, the relations among our own created

could be made using them, which would require more of a defense than I can muster here. For an argument for such substitution see Kathryn Tanner, "Gender," in Mark Chapman, Sathianathan Clarke, Ian Douglas, and Martyn Percy (eds.), *Oxford Handbook of Anglican Studies* (Oxford University Press, forthcoming).

capacities imitate those of the persons of the trinity. We image them instead by way of an actual close attachment to them. Through the power of the Spirit humans are to be joined to the second person of the trinity in Christ, and in virtue of that attachment human lives are to be given a shape that images the first person of the trinity in something like the way the second person of the trinity images it.

This imaging of trinitarian relations through attachment is the achievement of the incarnation for human life. As the divine image, the second person of the trinity is the primary form or pattern, which human life is to be patterned after by way of a close relationship with it. The principle and perfect human realization of a trinitarian form of life is therefore to be looked for in the Word's own incarnation in human life. In the incarnation one finds human life worked over into the image of the second person of the trinity in unity with it, as that becomes evident in the way this human life exhibits over its course the relations of the second person of the trinity to the other two. What Jesus achieves perfectly and primarily, we will then enjoy through him imperfectly and derivatively.

Jesus' human life displays the relationships among the persons of the trinity simply because he is the Word incarnate. By way of the incarnation humanity is united to, bound up with, the Word. Relationships among the persons of the trinity thereby come to include the human, come to take along the human as they move together for the benefit of the world. The Word of God assumes or attaches the humanity of Jesus to itself in becoming incarnate, so as to give its own life and form to Jesus' human existence, so as to carry it up into its own dynamic manner of trinitarian existence. This human being, Jesus, is now to enjoy what the Word enjoys – the relations that the Word has with the other members of the trinity, which bring with them all the goods of divine life.

Jesus is not an already existing human being who, in being tied to the Word subsequently, is dragged along, so to speak, by association with the Word into relationships not of his ken. As mere human beings, our access to the life of the trinity through him has that character. The humanity of Jesus, to the contrary, is bound up so tightly to the Word that he is the Word; this is so close a relationship between humanity and the Word as to bring about a relationship of identity between Jesus and the Word. Therefore humanity enters into the life of the trinity in the most complete and transparent fashion in him.

To say that the Word is incarnate in Christ is to say that the humanity of this one Jesus exists only insofar as it has been united with the Word, only insofar as it has been taken to the Word to be the Word's very own in the closest possible relationship of unity with it. One with that Word from the start, as the very condition of its existence, the humanity of Christ has no other life, then, than the life it lives in and with the Word. Bound to it, tied up with it quite literally, the humanity of Jesus never exists apart from the Word in its relationships with the two other persons of the trinity as they all act together for the life of the world; this is the only shape or organizing principle that Jesus' human life has.

The incarnation is for the purpose of humanity's entrance into trinitarian relations. In enabling that entrance, the Word's becoming incarnate is for our sake rather than its own. In general, the point of the incarnation is not what happens to the Word but what happens to us. We are the ones who gain thereby, not the Word.

Contrary to the common associations of the term "become," the Word is not fundamentally altered in becoming incarnate. It undergoes no basic transformation of character or change of location. The Word does not become a man in the way, for example, a character in a Kafka short story might become a roach, feeding off the refuse of life, for a change, in some darkened corner. The Word is not going somewhere in becoming incarnate with the intent, say, of gaining a new set of experiences to offset its previous ignorance of the sufferings we have brought upon ourselves through sin. What is new in the Word's becoming incarnate is our relation to the Word, our placement, so to speak, with respect to it. The important changes here are to humanity, by way of the closest possible relationship of identity with the Word now gained for it in Christ.

One can make the same point in trinitarian terms. There are no new movements of the trinity represented by the mission on which the one Jesus calls Father sends the Son and Spirit. The persons of the trinity just keep doing what they are always doing, but now with humanity along for the ride. The usual movements among the persons of the trinity continue; it is just their relations with humanity that are now different.[3] The alterations of primary importance are therefore to the human: a changed relationship for us with the trinity in virtue of Christ, whose humanity is bound to the second person of the trinity, and all that follows from that new relationship for human life – moral righteousness, human fulfillment, eternal life, and so on.

We are given access in Christ to the trinity as it already exists, in short. Room is carved out for us within it by him; we are taken along with him into the space that has opened up for us within it by his side. In virtue of the incarnation, one should picture humanity going where the Word already is, permitted in Christ to take up the very position of the Word within the life of the trinity. In Christ humanity is slotted into its place alongside the Word. One with the Word, humanity now shares in what the Word eternally undergoes and does, in the course of its relationships with the other members of the trinity.

This sharing in trinitarian life from the first in Jesus' life by way of the incarnation is what brings about the redemption of the human as

---

[3] See Thomas Aquinas, *Summa Theologica [Theologiae]*, trans. Fathers of the Dominican Province, 5 vols. (Westminster, Maryland, Christian Classics, 1948), vol. I, Q43, a2, ad3, p. 220: "Mission signifies not only procession from the principle [which is eternal], but also determines the temporal term of the procession ... Or we may say that it includes the eternal procession, with the addition of a temporal effect ... Hence the procession may be called a twin procession, eternal and temporal, not that there is a double relation to the principle, but a double term, temporal and eternal." Such a temporal effect or term is that "a divine person be possessed by any creature, or exist in it in a new mode" (*ibid.*, corpus).

his life proceeds. The humanity of Christ shares in these relations from the start but they come to better expression over the course of his struggle with a world of sin and death, so as to be made fully manifest upon that world's defeat, in Christ's own life first and one day in ours. Over the course of Jesus' life, death, and resurrection, the character of human life suffering under the weight of sin and death is being made over, in order better to reflect the trinitarian relations with which it has been bound, so as to exhibit perfectly, in the end, what it has already entered into in virtue of the incarnation.[4] At the ascension and glorification of the humanity of Christ, the Word, with that humanity which is its very own, retakes, so to speak, its rightful seat in the life of the trinity, regains, that is, the clear exhibition of its divine mode of life distorted through sin and refracted by death. Jesus returns to the one that he calls Father and, because of what has been achieved in his own life, there is now room enough in the divine household – many rooms, many mansions – not just for his own humanity but for the whole human family to occupy. "In my Father's house there are many dwelling places ... I go to prepare a place for you ... so that where I am, there you may be also" (John 14:2–3). When Christ ascends to the Father at the glorification of his own humanity to regain the position rightfully his as the Word, he takes us with him.[5]

---

[4] This is how the change of form, from lowly to exalted, in Phil 2:7–9 might be interpreted. See Hilary of Poitiers, "On the Trinity," trans. E. W. Watson and L. Pullan, in Philip Schaff and Henry Wace (eds.), *Nicene and Post-Nicene Fathers*, vol. IX, Second Series (Peabody, Massachusetts: Hendrickson, 1994), Book 9, section 14, pp. 159–60; sections 38–41, pp. 167–9; sections 55–6, p. 175; Book 10, section 7, pp. 183–4, and Book 11, sections 34–49, pp. 213–17. See also Gregory of Nyssa, "Against Eunomius," trans. H. C. Ogle, William Moore, and Henry Austin Wilson, in Philip Schaff and Henry Wace (eds.), *Nicene and Post-Nicene Fathers*, vol. V, Second Series (Peabody, Massachusetts, 1994), Book 5, sections 2–4, pp. 174–8.

[5] Athanasius, "Four Discourses against the Arians," trans. John Henry Newman and Archibald Robertson, in Philip Schaff and Henry Wace (eds.), *Nicene and Post-Nicene Fathers*, vol. IV, Second Series (Grand Rapids, Michigan: Eerdmans, 1957), Discourse 2, chapter 21, section 69, p. 386; and Discourse 3, chapter 26, section 33, p. 412.

In Christ one finds the definitive translation of the Word's own existence into a human form for the purpose of making over human life into the form of the Word.[6] Incarnation is for the sake of human redemption, in other words. The ultimate point of the incarnation is not to give the Word a human shape but to bring about an altered manner of human existence, one realizing on a human plane the very mode of existence of the second person of the trinity. In Christ human life is to be given shape by the Word, to find its organizing principle in the Word, through unity with it; here humanity is to take on the very manner of existence of the Word as that is displayed in the Word's relations with the other members of the trinity.

Because Jesus' human life exhibits the Word's relationships with the other members of the trinity, one can use it, as I do in this chapter, to uncover their general pattern. My primary intent, indeed, is just to interpret the New Testament story of Jesus' life and death in trinitarian terms, as an account of the basic shape of the relationships that the persons of the trinity have with one another.[7] The trinity in this way becomes, not a matter for arcane theological speculation beyond the biblical witness, but a central feature of the way Christians tell the story of his life and its consequences for us.

There are also theological advantages to interpreting the story of Jesus' life and death this way, as an account of trinitarian relationships. The complexity of the story of Jesus' life and death holds the key, I argue, to a theology of the trinity that does justice to both Eastern and Western theological concerns about how the persons of the trinity are related to one another. A trinitarian narration of Jesus' life and death, following the biblical witness, has the potential to

---

[6] Again a reference to Phil 2:7–8, in particular to the way the changes of form, from lowly to exalted, are logically ordered to one another. See, for example, Gregory of Nyssa, "Against Eunomius," Book 2, section 10, p. 117; see also in this connection Book 10, section 4, p. 227.

[7] For a similar project, see William Placher, *Narratives of a Vulnerable God: Christ, Theology, and Scripture* (Louisville, Kentucky: Westminster John Knox, 1994), p. 53; and the whole of chapter 3.

resolve controversies between East and West that hinge, in particular, on the place of the Spirit within the life of the trinity.

The same general pattern, we shall see, captures not only how the persons of the trinity relate to one another and the way they relate to us. It is a template too for the way we relate to them. As the Word incarnate, Jesus relates to the Spirit and to the one he calls Father according to such a pattern. But through him this is also to become the pattern of our own relations with members of the trinity. The account of trinitarian relationships becomes a quite practical matter as the trinitarian character of Christ's own life and death extends into that of our own life and experience via the redemption we receive in him. This practical consideration of the meaning of the trinity for us continues into the next chapter.

For all its grandeur of scope – from God's own life to ours – my contribution to trinitarian theology here is still rather circumscribed. I do not try to uncover a whole raft of claims about the trinity in this fashion, by looking at New Testament accounts of Jesus; I provide no complete trinitarian theology on that basis. My primary interest is simply in the pattern of the relations among the persons, how they are ordered to one another – their *taxes*, to use the technical Greek term, or expressed more colloquially, the irreducibly different roles they play with respect to one another.

Indeed, my task of giving a trinitarian reading of Jesus' life and death is made much easier by presupposing, rather than arguing for, most of the basic claims of trinitarian theology. I assume, for example, that the persons of the trinity are distinct from one another not just in their actions with reference to the world but in and of themselves; that they are perfectly equal to one another in divinity, and that, for all their differences, they are perfectly one, utterly inseparable, for instance, in both their being and action. None of those claims is particularly controversial as I see it and offering support for them by taking a closer look at Jesus' life and death would probably make them only more controversial rather than less. Instead, I will be addressing an issue in trinitarian theology that remains contentious, particularly in discussions between East and West, and one that I believe can be helpfully clarified by this sort of treatment.

I do, however, think that all the points of trinitarian theology originated in conversation with an interpretation of Jesus' life and death of the sort I offer here. In discussing the pattern of trinitarian relations on biblical grounds I am following in the footsteps of these previous efforts, along a theological path of scriptural interpretation made easier, in certain significant respects, because of what I believe were their dogmatic achievements.

The New Testament does not of course contain in itself a very highly developed trinitarian theology; that only developed centuries later, at least in part because of all kinds of further pressures – theological, political, and so on. But the theologians engaged in these later efforts were all fully occupied with New Testament exegesis in particular. Their ideas about the trinity did not develop, then, simply by way of self-contained theological assumptions and infer-ences, in the effort, say, to reconcile the claim that Christ is divine with a prior commitment to monotheism. These theologians, moreover, did not concern themselves with the bare trinitarian formulas, quite few in number, which are the first places that modern theologians often look for biblical evidence in support of the trinity.[8] They con-cerned themselves instead with a whole raft of passages where rela-tions among Father, Son, and Spirit seemed to them to be the subject of either direct discussion or narration in some detail.[9]

Thus, the Word that becomes flesh in Jesus is taken to be clearly distinct from the Father and Spirit because in the gospel stories Jesus talks to the former and sends the latter. Jesus is not then the mere epiphany of the one he calls Father, a mere manifestation of him for certain purposes, but must represent a distinct divine principle in his own right in relation to the Father. Quite a number of passages

---

[8] Notably, Mt 28:19 calling for baptism in the name of Father, Son, and Spirit.
[9] See Wolfhart Pannenberg, *Systematic Theology*, trans. Geoffrey W. Bromiley, 3 vols. (Grand Rapids, Michigan: Eerdmans, 1991), vol. I, pp. 268–9.

suggest that Father, Son, and Spirit do not have interchangeable places in relationship to one another and for that reason are clearly distinct from one another. For example, the Son prays to the Father and the Father does not pray to the Son, the Son is sent by the Father and not the Father by the Son; the two therefore cannot be the same.

A whole host of other New Testament passages, however, suggest an equivalence of power and value among the three. For example, Father, Son, and Spirit are taken to be perfectly equal in power to one another in virtue of mutually reciprocal relationships that hold among them. Insofar as they are able to take on the same roles or functions with respect to one another, an equivalence of value among them is also established.

Their revealing one another is an example of such a mutually reciprocal relationship. In the life of the Son, on the one hand, the liberating character of the Spirit's work becomes apparent (see Luke 4:18–21); on the other hand, the Spirit is the one who makes the Son known (1 Cor 12:3). The same relationship of mutual revelation, as a synopsis of the narrated gospel, holds for Father and Son: "No one knows who the Son is except the Father, or who the Father is except the Son" (Luke 10:22). They also form mutual paths of access to one another:

> No one comes to the Father except through the Son, because we cannot know the Father, unless faith in the Son is active in us, since we cannot approach the Father in worship, unless we first adore the Son, while if we know the Son, the Father draws us ... By the preaching of the Father, the Father brings us to the Son.[10]

And they glorify one another. The Son glorifies or brings honor and renown to the Father by doing the glorious works of the Father for us but only because the Father has first glorified the Son by handing over to him their performance (John 17:1–4). Glorifying the one is

---

[10] Hilary of Poitiers, "On the Trinity," Book 11, section 33, p. 213. He is exegeting John 6:44, together with John 14:6.

therefore the equivalent of glorifying the other. To glorify the Son for what he accomplishes is to glorify the Father since the Son's own glory is from and of him; and the reverse, to glorify the Father for his goodness to us is to glorify the Son who carries it out.

Father, Son, and Spirit are inseparable equivalents of one another in virtue of the way they appear "in" one another, as these theologians like to say, following John 17:21. The love of the Father for us is manifest in what the Son does, in much the way a ray of light displays the character of its source. More generally, so as to hold of the very relationship between the first and second persons of the trinity:

> "He who looks upon the 'figure' of the only-Begotten, becomes keenly aware of the hypostasis of the Father." The analogy of a source of light and the light which it sheds is the relevant one: a person who apprehends the light shed apprehends at the same time its source, so that a single act of apprehension takes in the whole situation and the relations holding between its constituent elements.[11]

Father, Son, and Spirit seem to belong to one another and therefore to be nothing without one another. The Son is specifically the Son of this Father – his "only son, full of grace and truth" (John 1:14; see also Heb 1:5). And the Father is the Father of this particular Son – "my Father" (Luke 2:49; Mark 14:36; Mt 11:25) – and only thereby ours – "my Father and [therefore] your Father" (John 20:17). Who Jesus is as Son and who the Father is as Father are determined by their particular relationship with one another. This is no general relationship of sonship which includes both Christ and us, but a unique relationship between the two of them which we come to share in virtue of our connection with this one Son (1 Cor 1:9; Rom 8:29).[12] In much the same way, the Spirit is specifically the Spirit of this Father (see John 15:26; and 1 Cor 2:11–12) and as such the Spirit of

---

[11] John McIntyre, "The Holy Spirit in Greek Patristic Thought," *Scottish Journal of Theology* 7 (1954), p. 365, citing Basil's Epistle 38 on Hebrews 1:3.

[12] See Athanasius, "Four Discourses," Discourse 4, section 22, p. 441.

this particular Son (Gal 4:6; John 14:26); and only thereby ours (John 20:22: 1 John 3:24). It is in virtue of their relations with one another that they are what they are, in full mutuality of co-implication.

The whole story of the gospel is taken, moreover, to be their working a single action of salvation together, through equivalently divine capacities; they each act but always jointly by the very same powers for the very same end. Thus, the Father does nothing without the Son; the working and words of the Father appear in what Jesus himself does and says (John 6:45–6). "The Father teaches through the words of the Son, and though seen of none, speaks in the manifestation of the Son."[13] And the Son does only the will of his Father – not his own will in any contrast to it (John 5:19).

Yet the act of saving us remains each of theirs. In speaking the Father's words, for example, Jesus is not merely speaking the words of another as a mere prophet might, but speaks of himself his own words (John 14:10). "The Father works in the Son; but the Son also works the works of the Father."[14] The Son, in other words, is no mere conduit for the activity of the Father, but an active agent himself of the mission upon which the Father sends him, holding in himself the divine capabilities necessary for its achievement: "All things have been handed over to me by my Father" (Luke 10:22; Mt 11:27); "all that the Father has is mine" (John 17:10); and therefore the Son himself exercises the Father's powers of jurisdiction. The Son carries out what the Father performs, raising us, for example, from the dead, and he is able to do so himself because he has "life in himself" from the Father (John 5:26).

In sum, "there is from the Father one grace which is fulfilled through the Son in the Holy Spirit;"[15] each one works together as the very same one God.

---

[13] Hilary of Poitiers, "On the Trinity," Book 9, section 49, p. 172.

[14] *Ibid.*, Book 7, section 40, p. 135.

[15] Athanasius, *The Letters of Saint Athanasius concerning the Holy Spirit*, trans. C. R. B. Shapland (London: Epworth, 1951), Epistle 1, p. 94.

"The grace of our Lord Jesus Christ and the love of God and the fellowship of the Holy Spirit be with you all" (2 Cor 13:13) ... The Apostle does not mean that the things which are given are given ... separately by each person, but that what is given is given in the triad, and that all are from the one God.[16]

In their saving acts, Father, Son, and Spirit do not show up as replacements or stand-ins for one another, but each brings about the very presence and action of the others. Thus, in the actions of the Son one sees the Father; in the Son one has access to the Father. The Son does not replace the Father as his emissary. The Father works where the Son works. "God was in Christ reconciling the world to himself" (2 Cor 5:19). As Athanasius deduces from John 14:10 ("the Father who dwells in me does his works"), "what things the Son then wrought are the Father's works."[17] Rather than being a substitute for the Father, Christ is the power of the Father himself, Gregory of Nyssa concludes following 1 Cor 1:24.[18] Instead of standing between us and the Father as some sort of buffer zone, in Christ we gain access to the Father, enter into the very presence of the Father. "When we learn to know the Son, God the Father calls us; when we believe the Son, the Father receives us; for our recognition and knowledge of the Father is in the Son, who shows us in himself God the Father, who draws us, if we be devout, by his fatherly love into a mutual bond with his Son."[19] Even though Jesus seems to send the Spirit to take his place, in his apparent absence, "when we are enlightened by the Spirit, it is Christ who in him enlightens us ... We, receiving the Spirit of Wisdom, have the Son and are made wise in him ... When we are quickened by the Spirit, Christ himself is said to live in us ... So Paul declared that the works he worked by the

[16] *Ibid.,* p. 142.

[17] Athanasius, "Four Discourses," Discourse 3, chapter 13, section 6, p. 396.

[18] Gregory of Nyssa, "Against Eunomius," Book 12, chapter 3, p. 245; see also Book 6, chapter 3, p. 187.

[19] Hilary of Poitiers, "On the Trinity," Book 11, section 33, p. 213.

power of the Spirit were the works of Christ: 'For I will not dare to speak of any things save those which Christ wrought through me ... in the power of the Holy Spirit.'"[20]

The scriptural passages that suggest the irreducible distinctiveness of the persons need to be put together with those suggesting their inseparable unity, and these theologians therefore show a special interest in individual passages that seem to model how to do this. John 10:30 ("The Father and I are one") is one example. Augustine explains: "He did not say, I am the Father, or I and the Father *is* one [person]. But ... hear both 'one' ... and 'are' ... If 'one' ... then not different; if ... 'are' then both the Father and the Son."[21] John 14:10 is another. Hilary of Poitiers comments: "There cannot be one person only, for he speaks not of himself; and conversely, they cannot be separate and divided when the one [the Father] speaks through the voice of the other [the Son]."[22] The persons of the trinity are, in other words, distinct yet inseparable – a very basic claim of trinitarian theology.

But this putting together of the one set of passages (concerning non-interchangeable relations that distinguish them) with the other set (showing their equality and unity) also has rather more sophisticated theological consequences. The messages of both sorts of passage will be true if Father, Son, and Spirit are and do the very same thing through the very same divine power, but in different, non-interchangeable manners or fashions. For example, the Father appears in the actions of the Son; and the Son, in the Father's mission to and for us. These are reciprocal relations of co-inherence or co-appearance. But for non-interchangeable reasons. The former

[20] Athanasius, *Letters concerning the Holy Spirit*, Epistle 1, pp. 111–13. He is following here a whole host of mainly Pauline passages.
[21] Augustine, *Tractates on the Gospel of John 28–54*, trans. John W. Rettig (Washington, DC: Catholic University of America Press, 1993), Tractate 36, section 9, paragraph 3, p. 91 (John 8:15–18). The Latin reads, *ego et Pater unum sumus*: "I and the Father, we are one thing." See p. 91, fn. 29.
[22] Hilary of Poitiers, "On the Trinity," Book 7, section 40, p. 135.

holds because the Father is the Son's source or sender; the latter because the Son comes from him, is the one sent by him. In short, for the trinity generally: "The Father is in the Son, for the Son is from the Father; the Son is in the Father, because the Father is his sole origin."[23] As Gregory of Nyssa makes the point:

> "I am in the Father and the Father is in me," each of course being in the other in two different senses; the Son being in the Father as the beauty of the image is to be found in the form from which it has been outlined; and the Father in the Son, as that original beauty is to be found in the image of itself.[24]

By showing how the persons of the trinity are able to be one and equal while retaining their distinctiveness, remarks like these clarify how to reconcile both sets of passages.

I do not mean to downplay the difficulty and complexity of this kind of trinitarian reading of scripture. In recognition of that difficulty and complexity, I have gone, indeed, into some detail about what such a reading in support of the basics of a trinitarian theology looks like. Much more remains to be said; in fact, the development of trinitarian reflection through scriptural exegesis of this sort fills many volumes. The interpretation of any one passage in this trinitarian fashion is quite controversial, let alone a harmonized reading of them all across biblical books of different genres and historical contexts of formation. The New Testament clearly does not require interpretation like this; it results from reading it through the lens of a developing sense of the soteriological stakes of belief in Christ.

Those stakes I think have little to do directly with an opposition between monotheism and polytheism, although this is a common understanding of what fuels trinitarian speculation of the distinctive sort found in later Christian doctrinal formulations. It is not, in short, the divinity of Christ that presents a problem in and of itself,

---

[23] *Ibid.*, Book 3, section 4, pp. 62–3.
[24] Gregory of Nyssa, "Against Eunomius," Book 1, section 39, p. 94.

since any religious system at the time that one might label monotheistic (for example, Hellenistic Judaism or Neo-Platonism) already
included lesser divine principles (for instance, angels, divine ema-
nations, powers in heaven, or deified heroes) under the sway of a
supreme deity.[25] For reflection on Jesus to develop in the trinitarian
direction it does in Christianity two things have to happen. What is
achieved for us by him has to be of such moment that divine agency
throughout seems necessary to explain it. For example, Jesus
achieves for us some sort of deification or enjoyment of divine
properties like that of eternal life. A proof of divinity through
works is indeed the near constant refrain of theology in the early
church; the divine principles identified with both Jesus and the Spirit
have to be divine because they save. And the divinity of the agents at
issue must be of the highest sort; Jesus is no mere creature elevated to
a divine level, nor divine principle of a lesser sort. These other
possibilities are ruled out just in case there simply is nothing in
between God and creatures – no lesser divinities on the way to being
creatures, no creatures that are themselves something approaching
God. One has to be either one or the other, because creatures and
God are all that the world divides into.[26] Monotheism means, then,
that divinity is not a class term; divinity is not a kind of thing whose
defining characteristics might be displayed by many things to greater
or lesser degree. Given such an understanding of divinity, everything
responsible for the grace that only divine agency explains is just
God – the Father who sends Word and Spirit, along with the Word
and Spirit sent. They must all be of the same divine rank, since God is
a being without ranks, and the very same thing, if God is not a class
term. If the divine principles at work in God's saving action in Christ

[25] See Daniel Boyarin, *Border Lines: The Partition of Judaeo-Christianity* (Philadelphia:
University of Pennsylvania Press, 2004), especially chapter 5; Alan Segal, *Two Powers in
Heaven* (Leiden: Brill, 1977); and Larry Hurtado, *One God, One Lord: Early Christian
Devotion and Ancient Jewish Monotheism* (Edinburgh: T & T Clark, 1998).
[26] See, for example, Gregory of Nyssa, "Against Eunomius," Book 5, section 1, pp. 172–3.

are distinct from one another – as they clearly appear to be from the narration of that action – they are strictly one with and equal to one another.

The very life of God itself, consequently, must be directly mixed up with suffering, conflict, death, and disease in the saving action of Christ. The unusual claim, for the time, is that here the highest God has been made immediately accessible to us in the dire straits we find ourselves in. No buffer of intermediary semi-divine or more-than-human principles is necessary for God to be in contact with our suffering and sin. Jesus therefore mediates divinity and human-ity because he unites both and not because he is something in between. Divinity can be in direct contact with us without needing to fear its own contamination or loss of honor.

> If the sun ... is not defiled by touching the bodies upon the earth, nor is it put out by darkness, but on the contrary itself illuminates and cleanses them ... much less was the all-holy Word of God, maker and lord also of the sun, defiled by being made known in the body; on the contrary, being incorruptible, he quickened and cleansed the body also, which was in itself mortal.[27]

Divinity, in short, cannot be polluted.[28] There is no impetus, then, to say that trinitarian persons substitute for one another – doing the dirty work for one another. And no reason, for that matter, to think they could take the credit from one another; they are not rivals for divine honors, as we have seen, but glorify one another in mutually reciprocal ways. As strictly equal beings they are present with one another as the one God, perfectly united in their saving work.

[27] Athanasius, "On the Incarnation of the Word," trans. Archibald Robertson, in Philip Schaff and Henry Wace (eds.), *Nicene and Post-Nicene Fathers*, vol. IV, Second Series (Grand Rapids, Michigan: Eerdmans, 1957), section 17, p. 45.

[28] Cyril of Alexandria, *Commentary on the Gospel according to John*, trans. P. E. Pusey (Oxford: James Parker, 1874), Book 12, chapter 17, p. 657 (John 20:17).

Whether or not this is an accurate depiction of the theological pressures that fomented a trinitarian reading of scripture to begin with, I am in the different position of being able to assume the rudiments of an already developed trinitarian theology; I do not have to try to come up with it to begin with in conversation with these texts. For that reason, my own trinitarian narration of the gospel story need not present the same level of interpretive difficulty. Whatever one's other theological presuppositions, if one does not assume an already developed trinitarian theology, one is hard pressed to get one out of the New Testament. It is a long and hard theological road from scripture to the Christian ecumenical consensus of Chalcedon. If, however, one can assume certain Christological and trinitarian basics – that Jesus is the Word incarnate and that there are three persons in the one substance of the trinity who are perfectly equal and indivisible from one another – then it makes a great deal of theological sense to use the gospel stories to uncover more specifically what the relationships among them are like. If Jesus is the Word and the New Testament discusses his relationships with both the Spirit and the one he calls Father in recounting the character of his life and death, those relationships simply seem to be part of what is being narrated.

Whatever one's theological assumptions, moreover, this particular theological topic – the pattern of trinitarian relationships – is less fraught with interpretive difficulties in that information about these relationships can be drawn directly from the way they are narrated in the storyline and does have to be inferred from what Jesus says.[29] Whether one believes in the trinity or not, one can give a far simpler theological interpretation of the content of Jesus' farewell discourses

[29] The relationships among the trinitarian persons that are matters for direct statement without being part of the narrated action are ones, such as strict equality among the persons, that are not obvious when the trinity includes the human or takes human form. Or they are ones that are not obvious at first. They only become evident when the human is thoroughly made over in the resurrection of all flesh.

than a trinitarian one, especially when one attends to the immediate context of the narrated story of which they are a part.[30] When Jesus talks about his disciples being one with one another, and with the Father as he and the Father are one, that could very well simply mean, "I am carrying on with the mission set for me by the Father no matter how hard the road has become; and you should, too, as my disciples." The unity of the trinity is not, in any direct way at least, the obvious subject matter here if one considers the storyline. In the narrated action, to the contrary, when Jesus prays to the Father, in these farewell discourses and elsewhere, something about their relationship is clearly being suggested at the same time. It is the latter sort of narrated relationships upon which I concentrate.

How, then, are the relationships among the three persons of the trinity narrated in the gospel stories? Following a common theological summing up of those narrated relations, one can say the Father sends the Son on a mission, which involves his incarnation and earthly mission for our good, a mission that culminates with the Son's sending the Spirit to us upon his death, resurrection, and ascension back to the Father. The Son is from the Father, coming down or sent out to us into the world (e.g., John 3:13, 16–17, 34; 5:36; 6:29, 33, 38–9, 57; 7:28–9; 12:44–5, 49; 17:7–8; and so on), in sympathy with our plight (Heb 4:15; Phil 2:6–7), as the mediator of the Father's beneficent will to us (James 1:17), thereby reconciling us to the Father (2 Cor 5:18–19), offering the Father's own mercy and forgiveness (e.g., Mark 10:47–8; Luke 5:20–4; 7:47–8; Mt 9:2; 20:30), healing us of our infirmities and bringing us into conformity with the Father's own good intentions for human life. The Son is completely of the Father, receiving everything that is the Father's own (e.g., John 3:35; 17:9–10; Mt 11:27; Luke 10:22), granting access to the Father (Mt 11:27; Luke 10:22; John 1:18; 6:45–46; 14:6–7, 9), and making the very workings of the Father himself present in his own life and mission (e.g., John

---

[30] See, for example, *Calvin's Commentaries: The Gospel according to St. John*, trans. T. H. L. Parker, 2 vols. (Grand Rapids, Michigan: Eerdmans, 1993).

5:19–30; 6:37–9; 10:37–8; 12:49), his whole life amounts to doing the Father's will for us (e.g., John 5:30; 6:38, 57), with complete dedication to and prayerful trust in the Father's will despite all the struggles and hardships that commitment to it brings. This mission seems to involve the granting of the Spirit to us; the Spirit is one of the gifts that the Son is giving us from the Father (see Luke 11:11–13). And in granting it the life-giving mission of the Father continues through the Son's mediation (John 14: 26; 15:26). With that gift of the Spirit coming out to us, the Son returns to the Father (John 6:62; 7:33; 13:1, 3; 20:17; and so on), the mission upon which he was sent on its way to completion through his own Spirit.

The story then continues with a focus on what happens to us. Receiving that Spirit we become like Christ in his relations with the Father (see especially Eph 2:18; Rom 8:14–17; Gal 4:6–7). More particularly, the Spirit unites us to Christ in a way that gives us access to the Father and the Father's gifts (Eph 2:18). The Spirit connects us to Christ – by testifying to Christ (John 15:26; 16:13–4), being the one in whom we see and confess Christ (1 Cor 12:3), by making Christ present within us (1 John 3:24) and conforming us to Christ's own mind and pattern of living (1 Cor 2:10–16). Our connection with the Father is thereby established. Empowered by the Spirit, we are now able to pray to God as our Father (Gal 4:6–7; Rom 8:14–17), and participate in the Father's mission in imitation of Christ's own life (Rom 7:4–6; 2 Cor 5:17–18). Bound to Christ through his Spirit we gain the Father's favor and become recipients of the Father's gifts as Christ was; for example, we become with him the inheritors of eternal life (Rom 8:17; Gal 6:8).

The same general pattern of trinitarian relationships overarches the whole story, and pops up repeatedly within it (in that, for example, what happens in Christ's life recurs in ours through him). A common theological way of formulating the overarching pattern breaks it down into two movements. In a first movement Word and Spirit are sent out to us from the Father for our benefit, a sending out that is also a kind of descent in that it involves their entrance into a world of sin and death for our sake. The second movement is their accomplishing of that mission understood as both a return or offering back to the Father and an ascent out of a world of sin and death through transformation of it. In accomplishing the mission they make a return to the Father of what they have been asked to do, and in completing it they re-ascend to the position they had before being sent out. In so doing they both return and re-ascend with us. Our lives are turned back toward the Father in recommitment to him from out of the waywardness of our sin; and in being reunited with the Father we are elevated, from a world of misery and moral turpitude, to enjoy the gifts of divine life.

In short, the first movement is the undertaking by Word and Spirit of a mission for us from the Father; and the second movement is the accomplishment of that mission in its effect on us, a movement therefore by us to the Father that Word and Spirit enable and sustain. By beginning and ending with the Father, these two movements are joined in circular fashion. The Father initiates the movement, sends out Word and Spirit to accomplish it, and in accomplishing it they return, so as to bring us along with them.

The fulcrum or hinge between the two movements is formed by the gifts of Word and Spirit to us. The movement of outward and descending mission involves the bestowal on humanity – first on Jesus' own humanity and then on ours – of both the Word, as the shape or form of new life, and the Spirit, as the power to achieve it. A return to the Father – on the part of Word and Spirit, on the one hand, and humanity, on the other – is made insofar as something happens through their bestowal: humanity actually comes to take that shape by employing that power. Insofar as Jesus is the Word, the form of his life lays out or displays what the good for us is to involve; the character of that good is exhibited in the character of his life, death, and resurrection. The Spirit prepares, enables, and completes the giving of that good to humanity. The Son brings the Spirit to us as a power of new life; the Spirit conforms us to the shape or pattern of the Son. With the two of them, all the goods of the Father are ours, from the Father.

From my trinitarian narration of the story of Jesus Christ so far, it might seem that the descending movement, constituted by the initiative undertaken at the behest of the Father by Word and Spirit toward us, could itself be broken up into two discrete halves. The Father sends the Word to be incarnate and to undertake a mission of salvation as this incarnate one. And then the Word incarnate communicates the Spirit to his disciples after his death, at the point of his ascension to the Father. Using the common language of the trinitarian baptismal formula one could therefore conclude that the mission that the Son has from the Father, a prior relationship simply between the two of them, is the presupposition for the Spirit's being sent from the Son. This would be in keeping with the Western theological stress on the importance of the Son and on his relationship with the Father for the emergence of the Spirit; the Spirit is sent by both Father and Son together.

There are, in that case, two separable and sequential acts in the descending movement in which Son and Spirit are sent to us: the one moving from Father to Son, inclusive of the second person of the trinity's becoming incarnate and pursuing an earthly mission; the other, from Son to Spirit, focusing in particular on the death and ascension of Jesus, subsequent to which the Spirit is sent out by Christ, the Word incarnate, into the lives of his followers. In this way, the overall trinitarian movement Father>Son>Spirit would be made up of two different two-person acts, the one moving from Father to Son, and the other from Son to Spirit. The descending movement would then be trinitarian only in an overarching way, with the individual acts that constitute it exhibiting a binitarian character. This would be in potential contrast to the return movement in which the mission is accomplished in us, a movement that might more easily be considered thoroughly trinitarian in all respects: we do not have the Spirit apart from a relationship with the Word incarnate that gives the Spirit to us; and we also are not "sons" of the Father without the Spirit.

Closer attention to the scriptural narration, however, brings out the place of the Spirit in the first set of relations between

Father and Son in the descending movement.[31] The Spirit is already present and active in the Word's incarnation and performance of a mission from the Father prior to Christ's sending of the Spirit to his followers. The relationship between Father and Son becomes, therefore, more properly trinitarian: the Spirit enters within it right from the start and over its course. And this has the effect of complicating the way the Son is often thought, in the West at least, to send the Spirit. The Spirit is already active in Christ's life when the Spirit is sent to us from the Father by Christ; it is only because the Spirit is already related to him that the Son can send the Spirit to us. Relations between Son and Spirit are in this way more thoroughly canvassed (than they usually are in either East or West, although a lack of concern for this is typically viewed as an Eastern problem). Rather than a simple one-way relationship from Son to Spirit, in other words, the complex back-and-forth of their mutual interdependency is drawn out. And this more thorough treatment of relations between Son and Spirit then allows one to see the differences between the Son's sending of the Spirit and the Father's sending of the Spirit. The distinctively different roles of Father and Son in these trinitarian movements become more apparent (than they usually are on a Western view).

If one returns to the New Testament story with the role of the Spirit in the Son's own mission from the Father in mind, what stands out, first of all, is the Spirit's active role in the incarnation. The power to birth is associated with the Spirit not just in the new birth of Jesus' disciples, created or birthed anew in Christ's image by the Spirit's power (see, for example, Rom 8:14; Gal 4:6), but also in

---

[31] See, for example, Boris Bobrinskoy, *The Mystery of the Trinity*, trans. Anthony Gythiel (Crestwood, New York: St. Vladimir's Seminary Press, 1999); Edward Yarnold, "The Trinitarian Implications of Luke and Acts," *Heythrop Journal* 7/1 (1966), pp. 18–32; and Thomas Weinandy, *The Father's Spirit of Sonship* (Edinburgh: T & T Clark, 1995), chapter 3.

Jesus' own life: Jesus is born of or through the power of the Spirit.[32] "The child conceived in [Mary] is from the Holy Spirit" (Mt 1:20; see also Mt 1:18). Mary, in answer to her question about how she will conceive, is told: "The Holy Spirit will come upon you, and the power of the Most High will overshadow you; therefore the child to be born will be holy; he will be called Son of God" (Luke 1:35).

The Holy Spirit seems, then, to be preparing the way and enacting the Word's entrance into the world by way of the incarnation for the purpose of undertaking the Father's mission. The Word becomes incarnate in the person of Christ at the behest of the Father through the power of the Spirit. It is the Word that becomes flesh, but by means of the Holy Spirit, which makes that flesh to be that of the second person of the trinity, the true Son of God.

The Spirit would therefore establish Jesus' own Sonship in much the way that a number of mostly Pauline texts suggest the Spirit establishes ours (see, for example, Rom 1:3–4; 8:14; 2 Cor 3:18; see also John 3:5–6). Just as the Spirit makes us Christ's own so that we may be sons like him, the Spirit makes Jesus' own humanity that of the Son of God. In much the same fashion, in fact, the Spirit makes the bread and wine of the Eucharist into the body and blood of Christ that we eat and drink. There is an effective power here of the Spirit to join – the humanity of Jesus to the Word, us to Christ, and the bread and wine to the body and blood of Christ respectively – sufficient to give all of the former a new identity, the very identity of the latter.

By the power of the same Spirit, moreover, Jesus undertakes the mission of the Father over the course of his life and death. It is as one "filled with the power of the Spirit" (Luke 4:14) that Jesus ministers to the sick, the blind, and the captive (Luke 4:18; Mt 12:18, following

---

[32] For the parallel between our rebirth and Jesus' being born of the Spirit, see, for example, Augustine, *Tractates on the Gospel of John 55–111*, trans. John W. Rettig (Washington, DC: Catholic University of America Press, 1994), Tractate 108, section 1, paragraph 1, p. 279 (John 17:14–19): "Even according to the form of the servant [Jesus] was born of the Holy Spirit, of whom [his disciples] were reborn."

164

Is 61:1). "You know ... how God anointed Jesus of Nazareth with the Holy Spirit and with power; how he went about doing good and healing all who were oppressed by the devil" (Acts 10:38).

The Spirit itself seems to enter history along with the Word to empower Christ's public ministry. The Spirit is what gives Christ the ability to carry out the mission upon which he has been sent; he is therefore never without it. Everything Christ accomplishes for us is accomplished via the Spirit:

> Workings of miracles and gifts of healing come from the Holy Spirit. Demons are driven out by the Spirit of God [Mt 12:28]. The presence of the Spirit despoils the devil. Remission of sins is given through the gift of the Spirit [1 Cor 6:11] ... Resurrection from the dead is accomplished by the operation of the Spirit [see Rom 8:11; Phil 3:21].[33]

The Spirit leads (Mt 4:1) or drives (Mark 1:12) Jesus into the wilderness where his trust in the Father and the nature of his commitment to the mission is subjected to an early testing. Jesus enters and returns successfully from there full of the power of the Spirit (Luke 4:1, 14). In and through the power of the Holy Spirit, the close relation that he has with the Father is maintained under trial.

Indeed, the total orientation of Jesus' life and death toward the Father, constituting a kind of return to the Father for the power of the Spirit vested in him, is sustained through the Spirit. Thus, Jesus prays to the Father in the Spirit: Jesus "rejoiced in the power of the Spirit and said, 'I thank thee, Father, Lord of heaven and earth'" (Luke 10:21; see John 11:33, 41). He petitions the Father for us through his Spirit – to send that Spirit upon us (John 14:16–17). He does the Father's will completely – his very food is to do the will of the one who sent him and to accomplish his work (John 4:34) – as someone empowered by it.

---

[33] Basil, *On the Holy Spirit*, trans. David Anderson (Crestwood, New York: St. Vladimir's Seminary Press, 1997), chapter 19, section 49, p. 77; see also chapter 16, section 39, p. 65.

It is in the Spirit that Jesus speaks, acts, teaches, prays, heals and exorcises demons [e.g., Mt 12:18–21; 28]. It is also in the Spirit that He offers Himself as a sacrifice, consecrates himself [to the Father, John 17:19], and that this sacrifice is accepted by the Father [Heb 9:14]. The gift of his life by Jesus [in accordance with the Father's mission] is the gift of the Spirit Himself who is in him (John 19: 30–34).[34]

Because of this central role in the Son's execution of the Father's mission, the Holy Spirit could be said to be what unites Son and Father in bringing about and sustaining a conformity of wills between the one and the other; the Holy Spirit is the power by which their oneness of heart and action for us is manifested. In much the same fashion, the Spirit brings about our unity with Christ in establishing a conformity of life and purpose between ourselves and the Father.

In this respect Christ is the Son of the Father through the Spirit because the Spirit of his acts makes him one: he is the Son in that he acts like one, faithfully performing the mission upon which he has been sent. Not simply because his humanity has been united to the Word by the Spirit is he the Son, then, but because that unity with the Word brings with it the Spirit as an interior power for action in conformity with the Father's mission. In this sense "everyone *moved* by the Spirit is a son of God" (Rom 8:14; italics mine) – Jesus himself and we by way of him. Both aspects of the Spirit's working for us – to join us to Christ and thereby empower us for certain kinds of acts – are discussed by Cyril of Alexandria, following the imagery of John 15:1, this way:

it is his Holy Spirit which has united us with the savior Christ [and] connection with the vine produces … the dignity of Sonship … For just as the … vine ministers and distributes to the branches the enjoyment of its own natural … qualities, so the Only-Begotten Word of God imparts to the saints … an affinity to his own

[34] Bobrinskoy, *Mystery*, p. 88.

nature ... by giving them the Spirit ... and nourishes them in piety, and works in them the knowledge of all virtue and good works.[35]

The Spirit unites us to Christ and gives us thereby the power of the Spirit to live like Christ.

Jesus does not, then, merely act by way of the Spirit and under its direction; the Spirit is in him as his own power. If he is the Word, Jesus has the Spirit inseparable from it as his own. He has this power for his own in that he is divine, in short. But by way of that fact his humanity also has the same power; the Spirit thereby becomes the interior motor of a human life that enacts the Word's own mission from the Father.

At the baptism in the Jordan, which begins his public ministry, the Spirit of the Father comes down (Luke 3:22; Mark 1:10–1) and rests or remains upon Jesus' own humanity (John 1:32), to be the operative power of his own ministry. He is called by the Father his beloved son, and is the recipient of the gift of the Spirit apparently for that reason – as a favored or blessed son. Jesus, indeed, is full of the Spirit: God gives Jesus the Spirit without measure (John 3:34).

Because Jesus already has the Spirit for his own insofar as he is divine, it is his humanity that is at issue in his coming to have the Spirit at a particular point in his life – at the Jordan as a condition for his public ministry. Indeed, the Word that has the Spirit by rights here gives the Spirit to its own humanity at the behest of the Father, and thereby the event at the Jordan becomes properly trinitarian: the Word is active too – not just Father and Spirit – when Jesus receives the Spirit. Commenting on John 17:19 ("I sanctify myself"), Cyril of Alexandria makes the point: "And being holy by nature ... he is sanctified on our account in the Holy Spirit, not with another sanctifying him, but rather he himself working for himself the sanctification of his own flesh. For he

[35] Cyril of Alexandria, *Commentary on John*, Book 10, chapter 2, p. 363–4 (John 15:1).

CHRIST THE KEY

receives his own Spirit, and partakes of it, insofar as he was a man, but he gives it to himself, as God."[36]

Properly speaking, even the humanity of Jesus should have the Spirit for its own right from the start: if the Word has the Spirit, Jesus as a human being has access to that Spirit too, since he *is* the Word. The point would be that prior to his baptism and taking up of a public ministry, Jesus' having the power of the Spirit was not yet evident in his life; the start of his public ministry is when that fact begins to become evident. "After his baptism, the Holy Spirit was present in every action he performed."[37]

It is because the Spirit is so powerful a force in Jesus' own life that the Spirit can be given to the followers of Jesus through him (see Mt 3:11; Mark 1:8; Luke 3:16). The Spirit must dwell in Jesus' own humanity in order to dwell more widely in ours. As Irenaeus makes the point:

> For God promised that in the last times he would pour him [the Spirit] upon servants and handmaids that they might prophesy; wherefore he [the Spirit] did also descend upon the Son of God, made the Son of man, becoming accustomed to fellowship with him to dwell in the human race, to rest with human beings, and to dwell in the workmanship of God, working with the will of the Father in them and renewing them from their old habits into newness of Christ.[38]

The Spirit of God will rest on us (1 Pt 4:14) to transform our lives because the Spirit first rested on Christ to do the same.[39] The Spirit

---

[36] *Ibid.*, Book 11, chapter 10, p. 540 (John 17:19). For the same sort of interpretation of this passage, but without mention of the Spirit, see Augustine, *Tractates on John*, Tractate 108, section 5, paragraph 2, p. 282 (John 17:14–19).

[37] Basil, *On the Holy Spirit*, chapter 16, section 39, p. 65.

[38] Irenaeus, "Against Heresies," trans. Alexander Roberts and James Donaldson, in Alexander Roberts and James Donaldson (eds.), *Ante-Nicene Fathers*, vol. 1 (Grand Rapids, Michigan: Eerdmans, 1989), Book 3, chapter 17, sections 1–2, p. 444.

[39] Dumitru Staniloae, "The Procession of the Holy Spirit from the Father and his Relation to the Son, as the Basis of our Deification and Adoption," in Lukas Vischer (ed.),

168

rests on him, is contained within him, like a treasure in a treasury for further distribution; and for only that reason is he the treasurer, the keeper and dispenser, of that treasure to us.[40]

Both Son and Spirit are always in one another, indeed, in carrying out the mission of the Father; each manifests the other in the course of the mission, by working distinctively as Son or Spirit in and through what the other does. Thus, in Jesus, the incarnate Word, the Spirit becomes manifest on earth, working with power wherever Jesus works to heal and save. And as the power of Christ's working – the power that initiates, sustains, and accomplishes the Son's mission in Christ – the Spirit always makes its appearance in the form of the Son: the Son is the shape that such power takes.

Son and Spirit similarly appear together in us: the Spirit makes us Christ's – makes us belong to him (Rom 8:9) – and when we receive the Spirit we receive Christ to be the new shape of our lives. We are both the body of Christ and the temple in which the Spirit dwells (1 Cor 3:16); and the former because of the latter. The Spirit is what joins us together and animates the body of Christ as that comes to include us. We are the body of Christ only with his Spirit. And the proof of that Spirit is our coming to exhibit the shape of Christ's own life and death, for example, by dying and rising with him as participants in the Father's mission of love to the world. The Spirit is not genuine unless it is the Spirit of Christ (1 John 4:2–3).

Both become increasingly manifest together. The more evident the power of the Spirit in Jesus' life the more like a son he appears to be in successfully carrying out the Father's mission, and the more his own human life evidently takes on the shape that it is his mission from the Father to enact. Neither one is fully evident at first. The

Spirit of God, Spirit of Christ: Ecumenical Reflections on the Filioque Controversy, (London: SPCK, 1981), p. 179.

[40] I am following Gregory Palamas here as discussed by Staniloae, "Procession of the Holy Spirit", pp. 179–80, 182.

degree to which the power of the Spirit makes itself felt, not just for us but for Jesus' own humanity, grows over time.[41]

As the fact of Jesus' divinity becomes more apparent through the greater exercise of the power of the Spirit, his humanity thereby increasingly takes on the divine form of the Son. Along these lines, Athanasius interprets Luke 2:52 ("Jesus increased in wisdom, and in divine and human favor"): "As the Godhead was more and more revealed, by so much more did his grace as man increase before all men."[42] Athanasius does not simply mean that Jesus' human reputation increases – people have a higher opinion of him – as his divinity becomes clearer. An advance in his own human qualities – for example, in wisdom – happens as the power of God takes hold and reworks them into the divine form of the Son: "the manhood advanced in wisdom, transcending by degrees human nature and becoming deified, and becoming and appearing to all as the organ of wisdom for the operation and the shining forth of the Godhead."[43]

There is, then, some sort of historical progression in the successful display of the Spirit's power (though obviously not a continuous one, since in some sense the Spirit's effectiveness seems to decline over the course of Jesus' life as it leads to the cross). The Spirit is not transparently displayed at once in Jesus' life and work as the Word incarnate; it cannot be just to the extent that Jesus is engaged in a struggle with forces of sin and death throughout his ministry and most poignantly at his crucifixion. The Spirit's power and glory certainly cannot be fully evident in Jesus' own life from the first, because of the very mission on which the Word is sent. The Word does not appear during its incarnation on earth in the form of God but in the form of a servant – a servant whose very mission requires taking up the position of those burdened by sin and death.[44]

---

[41] See David Coffey, *Deus Trinitatis: The Doctrine of the Triune God* (Oxford University Press, 1999), pp. 42, 138, 148, 154–5.

[42] "Four Discourses," Discourse 3, chapter 28, sections 52–3, p. 422.

[43] *Ibid.*, section 53, p. 422.

[44] Gregory of Nyssa, "Against Eunomius," Book 10, section 4, p. 227.

It is only at the end of his life, with sin and death defeated through his own death and resurrection, that Jesus fully manifests the power of the Spirit.[45] His own humanity is only then glorified; it is only then that his humanity is genuinely full of the Spirit in the sense of being fully transparent to it. His humanity becomes at that juncture radiant, so to speak, with the Spirit as his prior transfiguration on Mount Tabor portended. The Spirit shines out of Christ's humanity and becomes both the light in which Christ's divine saving power is seen and a radiant power that his own humanity emits – transmits to us.[46] At this point of transparency to the Spirit, the efficacy for us of his own humanity also becomes evident. At only that point, in other words, is he able to send the Spirit to us through his flesh (John 7:39; Acts 2:33).

Because Christ's humanity is the pathway by which we receive the Spirit, his humanity must be fully transformed by the Spirit in order to give it, fully filled up with the Spirit in order for it to spill out and over to others. This filling up of his humanity with the Spirit seems to require the passage of time, being completed at the end of Jesus' life and not in the struggles leading up to it; Christ's humanity is full of the Spirit in a way that makes him a life-giving Spirit (1 Cor 15:45; 2 Cor 3:17), after his resurrection and not before. Not just in our lives, as is so evidently the case, but in Jesus' own human life, becoming full of the Spirit takes time. And for much the same reason: because of the struggle against our sinfulness. The untoward consequences of our sin for Jesus' own humanity, for example, need to be overcome through the power of the Spirit raising him from the dead (Rom 8:11; Phil 3:21).

What are the effects of these more complicated relations between Son and Spirit on the general pattern of trinitarian relations? The

[45] See James Dunn, "Jesus – Flesh and Spirit: An Exposition of Romans 1.3–4," *Journal of Theological Studies* 24/1 (1973), pp. 52–6. Flesh and Spirit overlap until the flesh is brought completely under the sway of the Spirit in Jesus' life first and then in ours.
[46] See Staniloae, "Procession of the Holy Spirit," pp. 180, 182.

basic effect is to make clear how the workings of Son and Spirit are not simply intertwined in their transformative effects on us, but in the very mission of redemption that they undertake from the Father. They are sent out at once together on that mission – right at its start and over its course, from the beginning of Jesus' life through to its end – and then beyond, as that mission spreads more widely into human history. The descending movement to us as that takes shape in the mission of Christ's own life is as much Father>Spirit>Son – the Father sends the Son on a mission by way of the Spirit who is the already active mediator of the Son's mission – as it is Father>Son>Spirit – the Father sends the Son to provide us with the Spirit. In just this intertwined way the transformative effects on us, understood as an ascending movement back to the Father, are as much ones in which the Spirit makes us sons oriented to the Father in prayer and service, following the pattern Spirit>Son>Father, as ones in which the Son gives us the Spirit, thereby sanctifying us, dedicating us to the Father's mission of love, following the pattern Son>Spirit>Father. Athanasius briefly summarizes the two inter-twined patterns in us this way: "When we partake of the Spirit we have the Son; and when we have the Son, we have the Spirit."[47]

In the latter case of what happens to us, the two patterns making up our ascent to the Father (Spirit>Son>Father and Son>Spirit>Father) are clearly collapsible. There is only one movement summarized either way: the Spirit that we receive from Christ binds us to him and enters within us to make our lives into a human image of the second person of the trinity in much the way Jesus' own Spirit-filled humanity was. But the previous two patterns that make up the descent now become collapsible too. They both summarize, from two different points of view, the fact that Son and Spirit are sent into the world in Christ for the sake of making a gift of both to us.

Son and Spirit work the mission of the Father together in mutually informative ways. The Spirit enters into human history to enable the

---

[47] Athanasius, *Letters concerning the Holy Spirit*, Epistle 4, p. 184.

Son's entrance and historical mission. And the Son is therefore never without the Spirit as the animating principle of his own life in service to the Father. The mission of the Son is to give us his own Spirit, which conforms us to himself. By way of the Spirit's own power, the Spirit is given to us through him.

There are clear irreversible relations and roles here maintaining the distinctiveness of the persons: the three are always working the same things together but they do not do so in the same ways. The Father commends the incarnation, the Spirit enacts it, the Son is the one who actually becomes incarnate – he is the only one to be identified with this human being, Jesus Christ. Son and Spirit are both sent by the Father but not in the same fashion; only the Son is incarnate, not the Spirit. The Spirit is the enabling and animating principle of the Son's taking on humanity in Christ, but the Spirit does not have that humanity for its own. The Son incarnate has a human body; the Spirit does not. We are said, accordingly, to be included in the humanity of the Son as members of his body and not in the humanity of the Spirit as members of its body. The Spirit simply unites us with, includes us within, that human body of the Son; in the Spirit we share directly in the Spirit of that body.

The Father sends the Son on a mission for us by way of the Spirit's power; the Son is therefore sent by the Father and not by the Spirit. The Spirit does not send the Son as the Father does because the Spirit is being sent by the Father too, along with him. The Son is for this reason Son of the Father and not of the Spirit. The Spirit is sent by the Father for the sake of the Son, to enable his mission and to complete it by uniting us to Christ and becoming in that way our own power for Sonship. The Son is also sent for the sake of the Spirit – but in his case in order to give the Spirit to us. *is this true of us?*

The Son is the shape of the Spirit's working, the form that the power of the Spirit takes, while the Spirit gives animated efficacy to that Sonship, provides the power in and by which that form of the Son is realized. The Spirit rests on the Son as his own possession; the Son does not rest on the Spirit. While the Spirit thereby gives the power of Sonship, the Son does not similarly provide the power to the Spirit that makes it Spirit. The Son gives the Spirit to *us*, but does not give *to* the Spirit in the way the Spirit gives to him, by empowering his acts as Son. If the Son gives anything to the Spirit it is, to the contrary, just the Spirit's shape; the power of the Spirit takes on in Christ the form of the Son's missionary action.

The Son sends the Spirit to us from the Father, but not as the Father does. The Spirit has already been sent out from the Father as a condition of the Son's own incarnation and mission; and therefore the Son cannot be sending the Spirit in the way the Father does. Unlike the Father, the Son can send the Spirit – specifically to us – only because he has already received the Spirit and felt the effects of its working within his own human life. Thus, the Son incarnate can send the Spirit only after he has been raised by Father and Spirit from the dead, the power of the Spirit having become fully manifest then in his own life.

This biblically augmented pattern of relationships can be generalized to hold of the relations among the trinitarian persons themselves, irrespective of their workings in the world, if one assumes that the trinity itself is at work in the world by way of the incarnation of the Word, and works as itself there.[48] We know something about the general way trinitarian persons relate to one another from the way the trinity works specifically for us because in those works we have access to the trinity itself and not to some sort of substitute interposed between us and the true God. The trinity at work for us is the genuine article and no counterfeit. Its very own movements are extending to us there.[49]

[48] See Karl Barth, *Church Dogmatics 2/1*, ed. G. W. Bromiley and T. F. Torrance (Edinburgh: T & T Clark, 1957), p. 260. The trinity is not only itself in relation to us, but also apart from us.

[49] I do not use a distinction between the "economic" and "immanent" trinity here; the complicated controversies surrounding those terms might obscure the rather simple points I am making. A distinction of that sort also easily misleads by suggesting the existence of two different trinities – exactly what I am trying to avoid. But, if one used

Thus, the Father's sending of the Spirit and Son for our sake says something about the relationship that the Father has with them. The Son is from the Father in himself and not simply in virtue of the mission for us. The Son comes out of him, is begotten of him as his eternal Son, and not just as the incarnate Son. The Son is of the Father, the Father's own issue and image, both eternally and in history: the Son perfectly exhibits what the Father is, not simply in what he does in the mission but in and of himself. He is everything that the Father is – except that he is not the Father. He manifests or lays out all that the Father is but does not become the Father. While being in himself everything that the Father is, he remains Son and not Father, because he is all this only by being of and from the Father.

The Spirit, not just in history but eternally, is the power – the loving inclination and impulse, one might say – behind the Father's begetting of the Son. The Spirit, indeed, is always from the Father for the sake of the relationship between Father and Son. Both in history and eternally, the Spirit itself comes forth from the Father to give rise to that relationship by enabling the Son's eternal begetting from the Father. The Spirit empowers the Son's perfect exhibition of the Father and thereby unifies them into a relationship of perfect conformity to one another. The Spirit perfectly conforms to the Father in being for the sake of that relationship between Father and Son; and perfectly conforms to the Son as the Son's own Spirit of Sonship.

those terms (as I do in the next chapter), one could say with Karl Rahner, for instance, that the economic trinity is the immanent trinity in its workings for us, meaning by that, that it is the same trinity constituted by the eternal relations of the persons to one another that acts as itself to redeem us in history via the incarnation. See Rahner, *The Trinity*, trans. Joseph Doncell (New York: Seabury, 1974), p. 35: "God relates to us in a threefold manner, and this threefold ... relation to us *is* not merely a copy, or an analogy of the inner trinity, but this trinity itself, albeit as freely and gratuitously communicated." And p. 39: "In Jesus and in his Spirit as we experience them through faith in salvation history ... the immanent trinity itself *is* already given ... The trinity itself is with us, it is not merely given to us because revelation offers us statements about it. Rather these statements are made to us because the reality of which they speak is bestowed upon *us*."

As in the historical mission of the trinity for us, the Spirit here too rests on the Son. With John of Damascus one can say, "we believe also that the Spirit proceeds from the Father to rest on the Son."[50] In so resting the Spirit becomes the very power by which the Son himself relates back to the Father. Gregory Palamas makes the point clearly: "The Word, the beloved Son of the Father, avails himself of the Spirit in his relationship with the Father ... [in that] he possesses the Spirit as the one who has come forth together with him from the Father and who abides in him (the Son)."[51]

Since it is the Spirit of and from the Father that animates the Son's own life, in laying out or exhibiting what he has from the Father, the Son by way of that Spirit mirrors back to the Father what the Father is for the Son, in a perfect return to the Father of what has been given to him. The perfect performance of the mission by the Son incarnate has as its correlate in eternity the perfect return to the Father of what the Father begets the Son to be. One might talk here indeed of an eternal emission of the Spirit from the Son that the incarnate Son's gift of the Spirit to us mirrors and that is reflected in the incarnate Son's own giving up of his Spirit on the cross back to the Father – "Father, into your hands I commend my Spirit" (Luke 23:46). The Spirit of the Father, as a Spirit of loving beneficence for the Son (see 1 John 3–4), is immediately sent back to the Father by the Son, displayed in the Son's own love for the Father – and not just for us.

By the Son's sending back of the Father's Spirit, the movement of the coming out of Son and Spirit is completed in the trinity just as the mission is on earth. In the Spirit, the whole of the trinitarian movement comes to term. The Spirit is a kind of "amen," a joyful

[50] John of Damascus, "Exposition of the Orthodox Faith," trans. S. D. F. Salmond, in Philip Schaff and Henry Wace (eds.), *Nicene and Post-Nicene Fathers*, vol. IX, Second Series (Peabody, Massachusetts, Hendrickson, 1994), Book 1, chapter 8, p. 9.
[51] Gregory Palamas, cited by Dumitru Staniloae, *Theology and the Church*, trans. Robert Barringer (Crestwood, New York: St. Vladimir's Seminary Press, 1980), p. 29,

sound, rounding off those loving relations between Father and Son that the Spirit itself bears up or sustains across their course.

In sum, Son and Spirit come forth together from the Father and return together in mutually involving ways that bind one to the other. There are not two separable comings out of Son and Spirit and then two separable returns of the one and the other, but in each case of coming out or return a single three-person movement in which they both come out or go back together in complex dependence upon what the other has from and gives back to the Father.[52] A number of biblically informed analogies help clarify the way this is the case.

Following Psalm 33:6 and biblical imagery of the second person of the trinity as the Word, one could say that the Word of God goes forth from the Father's mouth on the breath of the Spirit. That breath carries or sustains and empowers the Word. The breath is in the Word and goes out from it when spoken. So, for example, Gregory of Nyssa can say:

> we shall be brought to [an understanding] of the Spirit, by observing in our own nature certain hints and likenesses of its ineffable power. In our own case, indeed, "spirit" (i.e., breath [*pneuma*]) is a drawing in of the air ... In the moment we give expression to a word, our breath becomes an intelligible utterance which indicates what we have in mind.[53]

John of Damascus affirms much the same thing:

> The Word must also possess the Spirit. For in fact even our word is not destitute of the Spirit ... For there is an attraction and movement of the air which is drawn in and poured forth ... And it is this which

---

[52] See Bobrinskoy, *Mystery*, pp. 277, 278, 295, 302.

[53] Gregory of Nyssa, "An Address on Religious Instruction," trans. Cyril Richardson, in Edward Hardy (ed.), *Christology of the Later Fathers* (Philadelphia: Westminster, 1954), section 2, pp. 272–3.

in the movement of the utterance becomes the articulate word, revealing in itself the force of the word.[54]

One can also follow light imagery for God in the Bible and think of the second and third persons of the trinity coming out from the first like a ray and its radiance from a shining source of light. Again John of Damascus makes the point: "The generation of the Son from the Father and the procession of the Holy Spirit are simultaneous ... It is just the same as in the case of the sun from which come both the ray and its radiance [for the sun itself is the source of both the ray and the radiance]."[55] According to this imagery, they always accompany one another: the ray in its radiance; the radiance in the ray; the radiance both sustaining the ray, which becomes visible, for example, in it, and being given off by it in the form of the ray's own penumbral luminescence.

Biblical imagery of love between parent and offspring – specifically between father and son – can also prove illuminating. Rather than the Spirit being the love that emerges from the relationship between Father and Son (as it usually is for Augustine), the Spirit is the love that comes forth from the Father to beget the Son.[56] The Son is carried out of the Father by and in the Spirit of love; the Father begets the Son out of his own love for him, the Father's own Spirit of love proceeding out from the Father in the direction of the Son as the Son is being begotten. The love of the Son, reflecting back to the Father the Father's own love of him, is then carried along by the very

[54] John of Damascus, "Exposition of the Orthodox Faith," Book 1, chapter 7, pp. 5–6. See also Athanasius *De sententia Dionysii*, 23, cited by Thomas F. Torrance, *Divine Meaning: Studies in Patristic Hermeneutics* (Edinburgh: T & T Clark, 1995), pp. 267–8. This analogy of an exterior word stands in contrast to an Augustinian focus on an interior word.

[55] John of Damascus, "Exposition of the Orthodox Faith," Book 1, chapter 8, pp. 9, 11.

[56] For the Spirit as the love that emerges from Father and Son, see Augustine, "On the Trinity," trans. Arthur West Haddan and William Shedd, in Philip Schaff (ed.), *Nicene and Post-Nicene Fathers*, vol. III (Grand Rapids, Michigan: Eerdmans, 1956), Book 6, section 7, p. 100; and section 11, p. 103 (for example).

same Spirit of love. Dumitru Staniloae summarizes both movements of love this way: "Through the Holy Spirit the Son returns to the Father in order to love him through the Spirit, just as the Father causes the Spirit to proceed in order to love the Son through him, or because of his love for the Son."[57] One also finds the position clearly stated by Gregory Palamas: "The Spirit is like the mysterious love of the Father toward the Word mysteriously begotten; the Word and well-beloved Son of the Father makes use of this love himself towards the one who begot him."[58]

Putting the light and love imagery together in discussing the return of the Son to the Father and its dependence on the procession of the Spirit from the Father, Staniloae again writes: "The irradiation of the Spirit from the Son is nothing other than the response of the Son's love to the loving initiative of the Father who causes the Spirit to proceed. The love of the Father [that is, the Spirit] coming to rest in the Son shines forth upon the Father from the Son as the Son's love."[59] And he helpfully adds, since these relations among the persons of the trinity are also manifest in a way we can perhaps better understand in the effects they have on us: "in the same way ... the Spirit of the Father who is communicated to us returns to the Father in conjunction with our own loving filial affection for him."[60]

One can also use mind, will, and knowledge imagery (which is not specifically biblical but certainly has a long history from Augustine through Aquinas) to clarify how Word and Spirit go out and come back to the Father in interwoven, mutually dependent fashion. The Spirit and the Word come out from the Father together in the way the will to know and the word or thought known come out from the mind. Most simply stated, one's mind forms a thought through the desire or inclination to do so. The desire and the thought happen

---

[57] Staniloae, *Theology and the Church*, p. 30.

[58] Gregory Palamas, cited by Olivier Clement, *Byzance et le christianisme* (Paris, 1964), pp. 46–7, in Bobrinskoy, *Mystery*, p. 289.

[59] Staniloae, *Theology and the Church*, p. 31.   [60] *Ibid.*

together and are entangled with one another through relations of dependence on one another. The word, on the one hand, does not arise without the inclination. But, on the other, there is nothing to the inclination – the inclination comes to nothing – unless the word is formed. The desire rests in the word so formed, and is expressed in and through it.[61]

Although I have so far been stressing the way that the same general pattern of relationships among the persons of the trinity occurs both eternally and historically, the more exact nature and extent of the correspondence between relations among the persons of the trinity themselves and those relations as they enter upon a mission for our sake are complex issues. Even if the very same relations are simply being extended into the mission they undertake for us, when they incorporate the human in a situation of sin and death through the Word's incarnation, the relations that the members of the trinity have with one another come to reflect that fact. "Jesus of Nazareth … retains on earth those relationships to the Father and the Spirit which are his eternally, but he exercises them under the conditions of human life on earth."[62] The human world of sin and death into which the persons of the trinity enter should, in other words, make some difference to their relations with one another as a matter of course. Not everything, therefore, about the relations among the persons of the trinity in their mission for us also holds for their relations simply among themselves. What the differences are and how deeply they run are at issue, indeed, in controversies between East and West about the relationship between Son and Spirit. As the East often contends, might, for example, the Son's sending of the Spirit be merely a matter of the mission and nothing more?

---

[61] See, for example, Augustine, "On the Trinity," Book 9, chapter 12, section 18, p. 133. One can in this way read him against the grain of his own express statements in support of the idea that the Spirit proceeds from the Father and the Son.

[62] Leonard Hodgson, *The Doctrine of the Trinity* (New York: Charles Scribner's Sons, 1944), p. 68.

One such difference is the spreading out over time in the mission of movements that coincide in eternity. Not just the movements of Son and Spirit overlap in the relations among the persons themselves, but the movement of their coming forth and return also, as we have seen, coincide. Coming forth and return is a single trinitarian movement considered from vantage points that are only analytically distinct. For the Son to come forth from the Father is just for him to display all that the Father is for him, and in that very display the Father's own beneficence is returned by the Son to the Father.[63] In the mission that the Son and Spirit undertake for us, to the contrary, the return takes time. Empowered by the Spirit of the Father, Jesus as the Son of God incarnate, it is true, always does just what the Father wants him to do, and in that sense being the Son of that Father and making a proper return to him simply coincide. But, as we have seen, perfect return is delayed, hampered by the sin and death in human life that Son and Spirit face in the course of the mission.

Temporal movement is simply characteristic of the historical world into which Son and Spirit enter to do the Father's work; it is because the movements of the trinity take us along with them, in short, that they are laid out in time. Even in time, however, things happen at once; the main reason for a temporal lag here is that the mission involves struggle against the dire straits of sinful existence.

This is one of many differences made in trinitarian relations when they hit the human in a world of sin and death. Most center around the appearance of subservience and superiority in relations between Son and Father in the narrated gospel stories: Jesus talks about the Father as one greater than himself (John 14:28); he seems to do the Father's will with some reluctance since it involves his own suffering and death (Mt 26:39; Mark 14:35–6; Luke 22:42); he obeys the Father

---

[63] For this overlap between what the Father is for the Son and the Son for the Father, see Athanasius, "Four Discourses," Discourse 3, chapter 30, section 66, p. 430: "For by that good pleasure wherewith the Son is the object of the Father's pleasure, is the Father the object of the Son's ... pleasure ... and one is the good pleasure which is from Father in Son, so that ... the Son [is] in the Father and the Father in the Son."

in apparent subservience to the will of another (e.g., John 5:19); worships and prays to the Father for help, and so on.

The Spirit's influence on the Word in the passages we have highlighted earlier could also be taken as an indication of the subservience of the Son. Although this is not a particularly classical interpretation, Hans Urs von Balthasar is a contemporary theologian who makes much of it. According to him, Jesus submitted to the Holy Spirit who communicates the Father's will to him. The Spirit is in Jesus but in a way that is over him, driving him, for example, in a direction that no human would want to go – ultimately to his own death.[64] Jesus is totally occupied with the Spirit above him who is directing him in the ways of the Father.[65] Although his whole life is his mission and he freely consents to what the Father through the Spirit is telling him to do, he does not completely understand the will of the Father (Mark 13:32) and so must simply have faith and trust in it. Indeed, "the Spirit takes over the function of presenting the obedient Son with the Father's will in the form of a rule that is unconditional and in the case of the Son's suffering, even appears rigid and pitiless."[66]

Because the Son and Father are believed to be the equals of one another in and of themselves, the most common way in the history of Christian thought to explain the apparent subordination of the Son to the Father in the gospel narratives is with reference to Jesus' humanity. Jesus obeys and worships the Father insofar as he is a man. Obedience and worship are appropriate stances for a human being to take and reflect the disparity of status between a creature and God. Jesus is of course also the Word incarnate but divinity and humanity remain distinct in him, and therefore what is appropriately said of him in virtue of his humanity should not be confused

---

[64] Han Urs von Balthasar, *Theo-Drama*, vol. IV (The Action), trans. Graham Harrison (San Francisco: Ignatius Press, 1994), p. 364.

[65] Hans Urs von Balthasar, *Theo-Drama*, vol. III (Dramatis Personae), trans. Graham Harrison (San Francisco: Ignatius Press, 1992), p. 521.

[66] *Ibid.*, p. 188.

with what is said about him in virtue of his divinity.[67] The Word incarnate prays to the Father, but he does so insofar as he is a man and not insofar as he is God. Relations of subservience are in this way simply consequences of Jesus' humanity and indicate nothing about the fundamental character of the relationship between Father and Son.

One can also affirm, however, that there is something in the relations between Father and Son that corresponds to the suggestion *eternal* of inferiority in Jesus' relations with the Father; there must be, *obedience* since Jesus is the Word and behaving as himself in his relations with the Father. It is just that what corresponds to it is not properly characterized as a relationship of superiority and subordination. Corresponding to the apparently subservient relationship that comes about because the Son is sent on the Father's mission is the fact that the Son is of and from the Father, the fact that the Son arises out of the Father's own substance to be the perfect divine exhibition of him. This being of and from the Father, without the inclusion of the human within it, is a relationship of strict equality; the Son is no less divine, no inferior, because of it. Hilary of Poitiers, for example, makes the point this way, in explaining what about the relations between Father and Son both accounts for the subservience of the Son on the mission and implies no essential inequality of status between them:

> The giver is greater: but the receiver is not less, for to him it is given to be one with the giver ... The Father is therefore greater than the Son: for manifestly he is greater, who makes another to be all that he himself is, who imparts to the Son ... the image of his own unbegotten nature ... The Father therefore is greater, because he is Father: but the Son, because he is Son, is not less.[68]

---

[67] For a classic expression of this rule of "double account," see Athanasius, "Four Discourses," Discourse 3, chapter 16, section 29, p. 409.

[68] Hilary of Poitiers, "On the Trinity," Book 9, sections 54 and 56, pp. 174, 175. See also Book 11, section 12, p. 206; and Gregory Nazianzen, "Orations," trans. Charles Gordon Browne and James Edward Swallow, in Philip Schaff and Henry Wace (eds.),

Despite the difference that the humanity of Jesus makes here, the relationship between the Son and Father themselves therefore does not fall out of sync with the gospel narration of the way Jesus relates to the one he calls Father; a correspondence remains between them. Indeed, it is usual to interpret the latter relations in light of the equality between Father and Son, so as to highlight the equality of the two even there.[69] Passages such as "the Son can do nothing on his own" (John 5:19), "I do as the Father has commanded me" (John 14:31), "the Father has given me a commandment about what to say and what to speak" (John 12:49), "I speak just as the Father has told me" (John 12:50), and "I have not spoken on my own" (John 12:49), do not, in short, suggest the submission of Jesus' will to an external command. They indicate, instead, simply that the Son's work is the Father's work, that the Father's work is the very work that Jesus does. Jesus is not interpreted in these passages as downplaying his own role by humbly affirming his inferiority to the Father; he is interpreted instead as affirming his exceptional character among men – that what he is doing is by the Father's own charge. It is "as if the radiance should say 'All places the light has given me to enlighten and I do not enlighten from myself but as the light wills.'" The obedience of a subordinate is not being expressed here; it is as much as to say, "I am proper to the light and all things of the light are mine."[70]

Jesus is, indeed, obedient to the Father but in such a perfect way that what we ordinarily mean by obedience no longer holds. Unlike a subordinate, Jesus does not follow the orders of another; he is not taught from without what to do; he follows no external mandate. "What the Father knows, the Son does not learn by question and answer; what the Father wills, the Son does not will by command.

Nicene and Post-Nicene Fathers, vol. VII (Grand Rapids, Michigan: Eerdmans, 1983), Oration 29 (Fourth Theological Oration), chapter 7, p. 312.

[69] See Hilary of Poitiers, "On the Trinity," Book 11, section 12, pp. 206–7.

[70] Athanasius, "Four Discourses," Discourse 3, chapter 27, section 36, p. 414.

Since all that the Father has, is his, it is the property of his nature to will and know, exactly as the Father wills and knows."[71] *(of the Father)*
He does the work of the Father because he *is* the Word and therefore acts accordingly. His very humanity takes its shape from the second person of the trinity that he is, and that divine person naturally reflects or exhibits all that the Father is in perfect fashion. His whole life is therefore to do the will of the Father; he knows no other way. The will of the Father constitutes him rather than legislates to him from without.[72] Because it constitutes him, he knows what to do naturally or intuitively; he does what he does of his own accord, as his own idea, spontaneously. With what Word would the Father teach the Word incarnate? He already is that Word. The will of the Father, in other words, must be the teaching of his own heart even if a difficult one in that it portends his own suffering and death.

> His [Jesus'] will is indissolubly united to the Father. We must not think that what he calls a "commandment" is an imperious order delivered by word of mouth by which the Father gives orders to the Son, as he would to a subordinate, telling him what he should do. Instead, let us think in terms worthy of the Godhead, and realize that there is a transmission of will, like the reflection of an object in a mirror.[73]

In this way the Word incarnate's relations to the Father reflect those of the Word generally to the Father; they bring with them a perfect coincidence of intention. In creating the world, for example, the

---

[71] Hilary of Poitiers, "On the Trinity," Book 9, section 74, p. 181.

[72] In this way Jesus exhibits the ideal of human existence under God's "command" for Karl Barth: "It is not therefore added to his essence, to the man himself, as though it were originally and properly alien to him and he to it, and at some level of his being he were not determined by it ... He is himself in this determination" (Barth, *Church Dogmatics 3/2*, ed. G. W. Bromiley and T. F. Torrance (Edinburgh: T & T Clark, 1960), pp. 268–9). Matthew Boulton draws a distinction between constitutive and legislative commands in Barth's work; see his *God against Religion: Rethinking Christian Theology through Worship* (Grand Rapids, Michigan: Eerdmans, 2008), pp. 112–13, 186–92.

[73] Basil, *On the Holy Spirit*, chapter 5, section 20, p. 40.

Father says, "let us make man," "not that, as in the case of men, some under-worker might hear, and learning the will of him who spoke might go away and do it ... For the Word of God ... is the will of the Father. Hence it is that divine scripture says not that one heard and one answered ... [Others such as Abraham, Moses, and Zacharias, hear the command of God and have] the Mediator Word ... which makes known the will of the Father ... [But here] there is no questioning and answer, for the Father is in him and the Word in the Father."[74]

We have the tendency to interpret Jesus' relations with the one he calls Father in terms of subservient obedience because that is the relationship with the Father that is appropriate for us – whose wills are not in sync with the Father, and whose sinful inclinations have to be brought back into line with the Father against our engrained impulses. (Theologians who, unlike myself, believe obedience to be the means by which Jesus saves and the primary character of redeemed human existence also have theological reasons for such an interpretation.) The relationship between Jesus and the Father is not one of master and subordinate (or slave) but a relationship of perfect friendship or partnership in which the will of one naturally aligns with the other; here obedience follows from perfect fellowship (John 15:15). When our own humanity is one day fully re-worked into the image of the Son, this is what we will enjoy too: in heaven no command will sound but the voice of one's own heart.[75]

For all the differences, then, the general pattern of trinitarian relations repeats and is not altered. This indeed is one of the central contributions of the position argued for here. In most other accounts, the trinity falls out of sync with itself somewhere along

---

[74] Athanasius, "Four Discourses," Discourse 2, chapter 18, section 31, p. 365. See also Augustine, *Tractates on John 11–27*, trans. John W. Rettig (Washington, DC: Catholic University of America Press, 1988), Tractate 23, sections 8–9 (paragraph 1), pp. 220–2; section 11, paragraph 4, pp. 225–6; and section 15, paragraph 2, p. 230 (John 5:19–40).

[75] See Barth, *Ethics*, trans. Geoffrey Bromiley (Edinburgh: T & T Clark, 1981), pp. 500–3, 505.

the line and often quite fundamentally – what happens on earth is not reflected in heaven. Even von Balthasar, who wrongly, I believe, insists that the obedience of a subordinate must characterize the very relationship between Son and Father because Jesus exhibits that obedience, nevertheless espouses a "trinitarian inversion:" the Spirit leads the Son on earth but this reverses the relationship they otherwise have.[76]

Much more significantly, a failure to follow through on the correspondences between trinitarian relations generally and the gospel narration of them holds for both Eastern and Western theologies in the usual controversies between them over the place of the Spirit in those relations. The East, since Photius, the ninth Patriarch of Constantinople, typically maintains, on the one hand, that the Son's sending of the Spirit has no correlate in relations between the Son and Spirit themselves: the Father alone sends the Spirit.[77] The West, on the other hand, refuses to make much of anything of the Spirit's role in the sending of the Son. Each truncates the gospel story's significance for an understanding of the trinity, refusing to follow it all the way in formulating an account of relations among the trinitarian persons themselves.

Their reasons for doing so are often based on genuinely worrisome features of the other side's position.[78] For example, the East often simply refuses to recognize the significance of the Son's

[76] See, for example, *Theo-Drama*, vol. III, pp. 189–91; and vol. IV, 364–5.
[77] For a brief description of his position see Yves Congar, *I Believe in the Holy Spirit* (The Complete Three-Volume Work in One Volume), trans. David Smith (New York: Crossroad Herder, 1999), vol. III, pp. 57–60; Bobrinskoy, *Mystery*, pp. 286–7; and Walter Kasper, *The God of Jesus Christ*, trans. Matthew O'Connell (New York: Crossroad, 1984), p. 220.
[78] For helpful summaries and theological analyses of the controversies between East and West, see Lukas Vischer (ed.), *Spirit of God, Spirit of Christ*; Bobrinskoy, *Mystery*, pp. 279–303; Leonardo Boff, *Trinity and Society*, trans. Paul Burns (Maryknoll, New York: Orbis, 1988), pp. 200–5; Congar, *I Believe in the Holy Spirit*, vol. III, pp. 49–60, 174–214; and Kasper, *God of Jesus Christ*, pp. 219–22.

sending of the Spirit as a way of counteracting the Western threat to the distinctive place of the Father in the coming forth or procession of the Spirit. If the Spirit proceeds from both the Father and the Son – the so-called "filioque" of the Western modification of the Constantinopolitan Creed – then the Father loses his distinctive place in the trinity as the person from whom the others come. The unique role of being the originator and generator of the others is transferred to the Son so that Father and Son are confused.

The West usually replies that the non-communicable personal qualities of the Father are not being transferred to the Son but only the sort of powers that can be the Son's own. Or the claim is that the two work together "as one principle" so that the Father's property of originating others is not really taken over by the Son in and of himself.[79] The East convincingly retorts – to my mind – that the latter response either turns the coming forth of the Spirit into some sort of impersonal process, in which the operation of the trinity's essence is separated off from that of the persons in an unacceptable way, or makes the Son's role in the procession of the Spirit far less than what is implied by the conjunction "and" – the role of a mere hanger-on. The former response also suggests that the procession of the Spirit is a less than personal process, since it takes place in virtue of a non-person-specific divine nature shared by Father and Son. It illegitimately transforms into a general divine quality what is really a distinguishing characteristic of the Father. And this has the unfortunate consequence of implying that the Spirit is not an equal member of the trinity. If the power to generate another is not defining of the Father but part of the one divine nature shared among Father and Son, then the Spirit should share it too. If, as in the West, the Spirit is the only member of the trinity that does not

---

[79] For the former response see Henry Barclay Swete, *The Holy Spirit in the Ancient Church* (London: Macmillan, 1912), pp. 370–1; and Congar, *I Believe in the Holy Spirit*, vol. III, p. 87, 120. For the latter, see Congar, *I Believe in the Holy Spirit*, vol. III, pp. 98, 116; and Bobrinskoy, *Mystery*, p. 285.

give rise to another, then the Holy Spirit is not fully divine. And this is a major general worry in the East: the West slights the Holy Spirit. The Spirit is not an agent as the others are, figures in the movements of the trinity as a mere secondary expression of the more primary relationship between Father and Son, and becomes completely submerged in the Son's service.[80]

The West worries that Son and Spirit are not sufficiently distinguished from each other in saying simply that they both proceed from the Father. The Father is not split into two by these two originating movements and neither are their terms, Son and Spirit. The relationship that Son and Spirit have in virtue of their both coming forth from the Father does not itself therefore distinguish Son from Spirit, in the way, say, the relationship of begetting between Father and Son itself distinguishes Father from Son. The relationship between Son and Spirit is not, in short, a relation of opposition, a relationship like that between Father and Son in which the terms of the relation are opposed to one another. For the West following Augustine and Aquinas this is the primary way persons of the trinity are shown to be distinct.[81]

The East replies that proceeding is simply different from begetting: Son and Spirit come forth from the Father in different ways.[82] The specific Greek term in John 15:26 (*ekporeusis*) marks that difference: the procession of the Spirit is quite distinctive and not a procession in the general sense of the Latin term that holds for

---

[80] For an exaggerated but influential critique of the West of this sort, see Vladimir Lossky, *The Mystical Theology of the Eastern Church* (Crestwood, New York: St. Vladimir's Seminary Press, 1976), pp. 57–8.

[81] My talk of irreversible relationships and roles is a more general version of this sort of principle, but a more complicated one in that the relations that distinguish the persons are themselves trinitarian. That is, each relation that distinguishes or opposes one person to another always includes all three of them. For example, the Spirit comes out or proceeds from the Father as the power with which to beget the Son. The East, e.g., Photius, distinguishes persons by non-communicable properties rather than by relations of opposition. See Congar, *I Believe in the Holy Spirit*, vol. iii, p. 58.

[82] Congar, *I Believe in the Holy Spirit*, vol. iii, pp. 181, 202.

CHRIST THE KEY

both. The East declines, however, to say further in what the difference consists: "There is a difference between generation [of the Son] and procession [of the Spirit], but the nature of that difference we in no wise understand."[83] It remains a mere posit.

It is not indeed clear from the Eastern (Photinian) view what the relations, if any, are between Son and Spirit.[84] They can easily appear to be disjoined, coming forth on separate tracks from the Father, in ways that jeopardize the unity of the trinity. The Spirit's relations with the Father, for instance, seem to bypass the Son, and this might imply that our relations with the Father could too. If, to the contrary, we always approach the Father by way of the Son, a rather radical disjunction looms here between the relations of the persons of the trinity when they work for us and as they are in themselves.

Eastern theologians often propose the venerable old formula, "the Spirit proceeds from the Father *through* the Son" as an alternative to the West's "the Spirit proceeds from the Father and the Son" in order to meet such an objection – to show, that is, that Son and Spirit have a relation to one another. But this merely papers over the disagreement since it is not at all clear what "through" means here.[85] It could be interpreted in a strong sense to mean what the West most often means by "and:" the Son exercises the very power that the Father exercises in bringing forth the Spirit. Or, it might mean that the Father remains the sole originator, with the Son an inactive or passive participant, perhaps a mere conduit for a power not his own.

In general, the West is concerned about slighting the dignity of the Son. This is one reason why the West avoids considering the role of the Spirit in the Son's own sending. When the doctrine of the trinity was first being formulated, the place of the Spirit in the Son's own life was being used to suggest that the Son is nothing more than a Spirit-filled or Spirit-directed human, like any other prophet or anointed

[83] John of Damascus, "Exposition of the Orthodox Faith," Book 1, chapter 8, p. 9.
[84] Kasper, *God of Jesus Christ*, p. 218.
[85] See Congar, *I Believe in the Holy Spirit*, vol. III. pp. 185–8.

190

king of the Old Testament.[86] According to this argument, he is not the Son of God by being the Word who takes flesh but becomes the Son only when he receives the Spirit upon his baptism in the Jordan. The claim that the Spirit proceeds from both Father and Son excludes altogether this Son-making capacity of the Spirit in Christ's case, and ensures the fully divine status of the Son. If the Son has everything that the Father has and is in that way just as divine as the Father, the Son should also have the power to generate the Spirit. If the Father alone has this capacity, the West worries the Son is not the Father's equal. The fact that in the East the Father alone gives rise to both Spirit and Son might in fact suggest they are both subordinated before the majesty of the Father, that the Father is somehow uniquely and alone truly God.

The concerns on both sides are well taken, as I have been suggesting. The ways East and West address them are what is faulty. Neither side therefore effectively dodges the criticisms lodged by the other. Fuller attention, than either East or West typically gives, to what the biblical story implies about the basic pattern of trinitarian relations provides a better way to do justice to the legitimate concerns of both sides and thereby resolves the disagreements between them.

Following the import of the biblical story for the pattern of trinitarian relations, one can affirm with the East that the Father has the exclusive person-defining property of being the source of the other two. Both Son and Spirit come out of the Father in keeping with the way they are both sent out by him on a mission for us. The Father is the only unoriginated originator in the trinity; the Father gives rise to both Son and Spirit and they do not give rise to him. The Father is not the Father, it is true, without his Son and Spirit, just as Son and Spirit are not what they are without the Father; but it is nonetheless the case that Son and Spirit are from the Father and the

---

[86] See Bobrinskoy, "The Indwelling of the Holy Spirit in Christ," *St. Vladimir's Seminary Quarterly* 28 (1984), pp. 61–2.

Father is not from them. Despite the former reversible relations of being with one another, the latter relations of origin remain irreversible. Augustine makes the point this way for relations between Father and Son in particular: "He is not the Father if he does not have a Son; and he is not the Son if he does not have a Father. But still, the Son is God from the Father; and indeed, the Father is God, but not from the Son."[87]

The Father does receive back from Son and Spirit, but only the very same things he gave them. The Father, for example, gets back from the Son the very Spirit of love that the Father poured out on the Son in begetting him. Son and Spirit, to the contrary, receive from one another what they do not give as they emerge together from the Father. The Spirit receives its shape from the Son but not the power that the Spirit gives the Son; the Son receives its efficacy from the Spirit but not the form it bestows on the Spirit. The Father's reception is therefore of a different kind from the reception by which Son and Spirit emerge from him.

With the West one should say that the Son is actively involved when the Spirit proceeds from the Father; this is a simple consequence of the fact that, as we have seen, Son and Spirit come out from the Father together in a mutually conditioning fashion. But the Son is clearly not the source of the Spirit as the Father is, and therefore the simple conjunction "and" in the Western formula, "the Spirit proceeds from the Father and the Son," is inappropriate in suggesting a lack of distinction in this respect between the two. Contrary to the Western view, the Son is not the one the Spirit comes out of; the Father is the only source of the Spirit in that way. Although this is a crucial matter – without its shape the Spirit is nothing, mere dissipating air, so to speak – the Son is responsible simply for giving shape to the Spirit as it emerges from the Father.

---

[87] Augustine, *Tractates on John 28–54*, Tractate 29, section 5, paragraph 1, p. 17 (John 7:14–18); see also *Tractates on John 11–27*, Tractate 19, section 13, paragraph 2, p. 152 (John 5:19–30).

The Son can be said to cause the Spirit to proceed from the Father only in the sense that the Spirit emerges for the sake of empowering the Son to be the very explication or laying out of what the Father is. The Son does not produce the Spirit as the Father does but is the Spirit's reason for being. The Son, one might say, is the draw of the Spirit, the one to whom the Spirit is proceeding from the Father so as to animate. The Son cannot be the active or efficacious cause of the emergence of the Spirit as the Father is, if the Son receives his own animation and power to act as Son from the Spirit itself in this way.

The Son does breathe back out the Spirit, or (to change the metaphor) send back the Spirit of love to the Father, as the West stresses. But, contrary to the Western view, this is not the way the Spirit arises to begin with. The Spirit already exists in the Son; the Son has to have already received the Spirit as both emerge from the Father before the Son can send that Spirit, as, say, the Spirit of the Father's own love, back out again to the Father. The sending of the Spirit by the Son is a return movement, in clear analytic distinction at least from that out-going movement from the Father that includes both the proceeding of the Spirit and the begetting of the Son. The sending back of the Spirit by the Son does not, then, make the Spirit to be the Spirit; that happens when the Spirit emerges from the Father. Or, one might say, it is at most only part of what makes the Spirit the Spirit. The Spirit is the Spirit in virtue of the whole movement: emerging from the Father, into the Son, and then out again, to return.

The slighting of the Spirit that might come from including the Son in the process of its emergence – the Eastern worry – is here remedied by giving the Spirit, too, an irreplaceable role in the begetting of the Son. The Spirit is the love or power of the Father by which the Son is drawn out of the Father to be the perfect manifestation of all that the Father is. All that the Word lays out or explicates of the Father from him is given animated life by the Spirit. The mind's thoughts are conveyed by the word only as the breath remains in that word. The word, no matter how perfectly formed, has no life in it without the breath.

Just as we saw with the Son's distinctive role in the procession of the Spirit, the Spirit is not confused with the Father by being included in the process by which the Father gives rise to the Son. The Word does not come out of the Spirit as the Word does from the Father, but is carried away from the Father with the Spirit's support, like a word carried away by a breath of air from someone's mouth. The Spirit is not the source of the Son as the Father is, but is the Son's reason for being (in a way easily distinguishable from the way, as we said before, the Son is the Spirit's reason for being). The Son comes forth from the Father so that the Spirit – the beneficent or loving power of the Father – might be manifest in an appropriate, indeed perfect, way.

Indeed, neither Son nor Spirit is therefore slighted in comparison with the Father, as the West worries. They are both clearly the equal of the Father, because the Father never acts alone in giving rise to either of them. The Father does nothing of himself, even if he is in a unique way the source of the other two. The members of the trinity are equal to one another because they are always all actively involved in doing the very same things. They all play their indispensable roles in the complex movement by which Son and Spirit arise from the Father together.

Because the divine Word itself is now animated by the Spirit, the New Testament passages about Jesus' anointing with the Spirit need not imply, as the West fears, that Jesus is anything less than divine. It is not merely prophets who have the Spirit bestowed on them; the divine Word contains the Spirit too as a condition of its own existence. Those passages do not have to suggest that Jesus became the Son of God at a particular point in time. I explained above how they might be compatible with the idea that Jesus is the Son of God from the first, with the Spirit of the Father always for his own, in virtue of that very fact.

The worry about a disjunction or separation of Son and Spirit in the Eastern view is thoroughly dispelled here by the complex interrelations of Son and Spirit in both their emergence from and return to the Father. Because Son and Spirit arise from and go back to the Father together in a completely interwoven, interdependent fashion, there can be no question here of the Spirit's somehow bypassing the Son in relations with the Father; nor the reverse, of the Son's bypassing the Spirit.

Because Son and Spirit come out and return together there is also no question here of the West's focus on the Son being at odds with the East's highlighting of the Spirit. The very same complex movements of the trinity can be read with an emphasis either way; and thereby differences between East and West on that score are reconciled. Because they both come out and return together, either Son or Spirit can be viewed as the hinge of the whole movement, at the bend, so to speak, of the coming out and return. The Father begets the Son so that the Spirit can proceed from him and return: the Spirit is in that way the hinge. Or the Father causes the Spirit to come out of him so that he will have someone – the second person of the trinity – to love and be loved by: the Son is in that way the hinge. These are just two different ways of talking about the very same thing. More abstractly, the pattern of coming out and going back can be talked about as either F>sp>S>sp>F (with an emphasis on the Son), or F>s>SP>s>F (with an emphasis on the Spirit), because it is both at once.

By gathering as we have a general pattern of trinitarian relations from the New Testament stories, a pattern centered on the particulars of Christ's life but not limited to it, one can see the way the pattern recurs in all the trinity's workings for us beyond the events of New Testament narration: the Father is always and everywhere working to bring about what accords with the shape or form of the Son, efforts that are enabled, sustained, and completed in the power of the Spirit. As Athanasius remarks, "there is nothing that is not originated and actuated through the Word and in the Spirit."[88]

---

[88] Athanasius, *Letters concerning the Holy Spirit*, Epistle 1, p. 143.

For example, one can interpret the word and breath imagery of passages from Genesis and the Psalms in this way to suggest that God the Father creates the world according to the shape or form of the Word in the power of the Spirit.[89] The world is created according to Genesis through the word of God the Father: the Father speaks and the world comes into existence according to that word. And the form of that world seems to emerge through the power of a hovering spirit or sweeping wind (Gen 1:2). The creative Word of God the Father is in this way always accompanied by the animating breath of the Spirit that surrounds it: "By the word of the Lord the heavens were made, and all their host by the breath of his mouth" (Psalm 33:6); in making his will known in the world, "he sends out his word … and he makes his wind blow" (Psalm 147:18); "in wisdom" God makes everything and "when [God] send[s] forth [God's] spirit they are created" (Psalm 104:24, 30).

The creation of humans, too, as we saw in the first chapter, follows the same pattern of trinitarian relations, to make humans not just a reproduction or imitation of them but part of them. Human beings are created by the Father to be the image of the Son as that happens through the power of the Spirit taking up residence within them. This intention of the Father for us is fulfilled when the Spirit becomes more properly ours in a new way, in virtue of our humanity becoming the Son's own in Christ.

Armed with the general pattern of trinitarian relations one can also easily see the way the pattern recurs in our lives as we are joined to Christ's. (And here we are eventually carried out beyond scriptural narration into subsequently developing Christian experience of worship and service.) As the Word incarnate sends back the Spirit to the Father it is also sent out to us. This happens quite literally upon Jesus' death, but it also happens more generally, we have seen, as the work of Jesus' life is completed in the Spirit by perfectly manifesting that Spirit in and through his humanity;

---

[89] See Bobrinskoy, *Mystery*, pp. 26–31; see also Weinandy, *Father's Spirit of Sonship*, p. 26.

thereby what is achieved by his own humanity is extended in its efficacy to us.

The Spirit sent out to us makes it possible for us to enter into the trinitarian movements and follow along their own circuit of descent and ascent. The Spirit enables us first to ascend or return to the Father as Christ does with him. In this way the order of descent and ascent in the circuit is initially reversed for us, since we enter into it at the point of Christ's return to the Father. The Spirit joins us to Christ in his own movement of return borne by the Spirit. As Irenaeus makes the point: "this is the gradation and arrangement of those who are saved ... the advance through steps ... They ascend through the Spirit to the Son, and through the Son to the Father."[90] We are carried up to the Father by and with Christ's own movement to the Father when we have become one with him through the Spirit. Basil therefore says: "Through him we have our approach to the Father ... 'No one comes to the Father,' he [the apostle] says, 'except through me' [John 14:6]. Such is our way up to the Father through the Son."[91]

We then descend or return from the Father with the gifts of Son and Spirit. In virtue of our ascent to the Father, we receive from the Father what Jesus has, the abiding or resting of the Spirit in us, so as to be made sons in power like him, according to the usual trinitarian movement of descent, in which all the goods of the Father flow out of the Father in the form of the intertwined gifts of Son and Spirit. With that Spirit we have all the other gifts from the Father the Spirit brings – for example, eternal life and holiness – as these movements of ascent to the Father and descent from him occur repeatedly across the course of our lives (and deaths).

In sum, the Spirit inaugurates our ascent with Christ to the Father; and from the Father we then descend with the Father's gifts of Son and Spirit for our own.[92] As Basil remarks, "the way to divine

---

[90] Irenaeus, "Against Heresies," Book 5, chapter 36, section 2, p. 567.
[91] Basil, *On The Holy Spirit*, chapter 8, section 18, p. 37.
[92] Bobrinskoy, *Mystery*, pp. 153, 165.

knowledge ascends from one Spirit through the one Son to the one Father. Likewise, natural goodness, inherent holiness and royal dignity reach from the Father through the Only-Begotten to the Spirit."[93] "Sometimes [Christ] carries ... goods of grace from the Father to us; and other times he leads us to the Father through himself."[94]

What are we talking about more concretely here? What forms do such movements take in Christian lives? Our initial ascent to the Father with Christ requires us to be joined to Christ, to become Christ's own, through the power of the Spirit; and is therefore associated with baptism. The Spirit ministers to us at our baptisms in order to make us one with Christ, according to the Father's will.[95] United in baptism to Christ, before we fully manifest that unity in the sort of lives we lead, and simply for that reason moving along with him in his return to the Father, we ascend to the Father by being brought back as sinners before him, into his very presence just as we are with all our faults, to be found favorable in the Father's sight because of the company we keep. Justification (in a Protestant sense of that) is therefore a primary aspect of this ascending movement; it brings a sense of the Father's forgiveness and free favor into our lives. We can now approach the Father with boldness or confidence despite our sin because in and through Christ our relationship with the Father has become one of reconciliation, peace, and free access (see, for example, Eph 3:12; Heb 4:16; Rom 5:2). Our petitions will always be heard and answered. "If you who are evil, know how to give good gifts to your children, how much more will the heavenly Father give the Holy Spirit to those that ask him!" (Luke 11:13). For the same reason the ascending movement might be associated with prayers of petition and confession (which the Lord's Prayer mostly is). We pray with Christ in the Spirit for help in our weakness, for we do not know how to pray as we ought (Rom 8:26); we pray along with

---

[93] Basil, *On the Holy Spirit*, chapter 18, section 47, pp. 74–5.
[94] *Ibid.*, chapter 8, section 17, p. 34.   [95] Bobrinskoy, *Mystery*, p. 162.

Christ as he prays to the Father for us in the Spirit, so that we might come to be filled with the Spirit and its gifts (see John 14:16).

Our descent with the gifts of Son and Spirit from the Father can be identified with our receiving the power of the Spirit to be sanctified according to the form of Christ. The Spirit does not merely join us to Christ but, once we are so joined, enters within us as the power for new life according to the shape of Christ's own life as the Son incarnate. We are not just joined to Christ but are to be made over into him by the power of the Spirit we have from him. Attached to Christ by way of the Spirit's power to unite or bring together, we receive from Christ the Spirit as a quickening or animating power to live as he does.

Baptism is partly at issue here. We are not joined to Christ in virtue of our baptism without receiving thereby the Spirit for our own, as an available power upon which we might draw to reform our lives. One with Christ we have his Spirit, the same Spirit that animated and empowered his own life of service to the Father's mission. To the extent baptism involves our own acts of rededicating our lives to Christ through repentance for sin and conversion to new life, in being baptized, moreover, we make an actual beginning to draw upon that power. Our lives have already been transformed in an initial way through reception of the Spirit just to the extent we exhibit a faithful commitment of ourselves to Christ in being baptized.

Insofar as the gifts of Son and Spirit are actually transforming us in our descent from the Father, that descent is to be more closely associated with the Eucharist. The Eucharist is the place where the sanctifying power of those gifts is most strongly felt to enable and support a form of living in keeping with Christ's. Here the gifts of God in Christ are coming down to us for our sustenance, as energizing food for new lives. After baptizing us to be part of his own family or household as adopted children, God the Father in the Eucharist "discharges the functions of the provident householder in continually supplying to us the food to sustain and preserve us in that life into which he has begotten us by his Word."[96] Through our repeated engagement in Eucharistic practice, we manage to feed continually upon that life-giving Spirit coming to us through the gift of Christ's own humanity in the elements, so as to grow into and sustain under trial a Christ-like life. In the Eucharist the humanity of Christ gives to us the life-giving powers it has by way of the Spirit that rests upon it, enhancing and nourishing our lives as those powers enhanced and nourished his own humanity.

The Eucharistic service, moreover, repeats in miniature the whole movement of ascent and descent, going to the Father and receiving from him, through Christ in the power of the Spirit.[97] One with Christ through his Spirit we are lifted up with him – "lift up your hearts" – into the presence of the Father to receive gifts of new life from the Father – "the gifts of God for the people of God." We are offered ourselves as the bread and wine are offered to the Father so that all are made over into Christ's Spirit-filled humanity. The good things of the earth in forms that nourish our bodies – bread and wine – are first offered up in thanksgiving by us to the Father in Christ's own movement to him, and then received back from the Father as new Spirit-filled nourishment for new life in the form of Christ's own body and blood, through the power of the Spirit that makes those elements one with them. Irenaeus makes this point about offering to the Father in the Eucharist what one then gets back from him:

---

[96] John Calvin, *Institutes of the Christian Religion*, trans. Ford Lewis Battles, ed. John T. McNeill (Philadelphia: Westminster, 1960), vol. II, Book 4, chapter 17, p. 1360.

[97] See Bobrinskoy, *Mystery*, pp. 165, 167; and Cyprian Vagaggini, *Theological Dimensions of the Liturgy*, trans. Leonard Doyle and W. A. Jurgens (Collegeville, Minnesota: Liturgical Press, 1976), chapter 7. Thomas F. Torrance and Josef A. Jungmann also emphasize this but tend to associate ascent to the Father so exclusively with the humanity of Jesus that they overlook return as part of a divine trinitarian movement as well. See Torrance, *Theology in Reconciliation* (London: Geoffrey Chapman, 1975), chapter 4; and Jungmann, *The Place of Christ in Liturgical Prayer* (Collegeville, Minnesota: Liturgical Press, 1989).

It behooves us to make an oblation to God our maker ... offering first-fruits of his own created things ... with giving of thanks from his creation ... For God, who stands in need of nothing, takes our good works to himself ... that he may grant us a recompense of his own good things, as our Lord says: "Come, blessed of my Father, receive the kingdom prepared for you (Mt 25:34)."[98]

Using the imagery of Christ as both sacrifice for us, and the high priest who sanctifies that sacrifice, one can make the point about combined ascent and descent in the Eucharist another way. Offered up to the Father by Christ, and found acceptable in the Father's sight because of the already holy humanity of Christ with which we are joined, we are sanctified or made holy thereby in the power of the Spirit, as Christ's humanity already was so offered, accepted, and sanctified by the Father. In more detail, following a temporal sequence of consecrated elements and then sanctification of the faithful suggested by the Eucharistic service itself, one can say: Christ is the celebrant (Heb 3:31) who takes our gifts to the altar in heaven for the Father's blessing and approval; they come back to us as Christ's own body and blood, filled with every grace and blessing of the Spirit; and by blending that flesh with our own we become like Christ – Spirit-filled sons.[99] Jesus makes this same kind of Eucharistic offering of us in his own humanity as the incarnate one. In the incarnation itself he is offering our infirmities through himself to the Father, and they come back healed. "He receives them from us" – our hunger, weakness, and weariness – "and offers [them] to the Father, interceding for us, that in him they may be annulled."[100] "He takes our infirmities ... [and] sends up what is ours that it may be abolished, so the gifts which come from God, instead of our infirmities ... He too [does] receive, that man, united

---

[98] "Against Heresies," Book 4, chapter 18, sections 4–5, pp. 485–6.

[99] Vagaggini, *Theological Dimensions*, p. 227.

[100] Athanasius, "Four Discourses," Discourse 4, section 6, p. 435.

to him, may be able to partake of them."[101] With his own humanity glorified, Christ then makes an offering of us to the Father, in the same fashion with the same result: united to Christ, our human lives are well received by the Father so as to be exalted in the power of the Spirit in the way his was.

As a repeated act of worship the Eucharist continues the circle – from ascent to descent to re-ascent. In it we do not so much make an initial ascent to the Father for the first reception of gifts, coming down to us from him by way of Son and Spirit, as we go back to the Father with those gifts, and therefore the Eucharistic prayer is a prayer of thanksgiving for them. In part it is our own prayers of need, taken along with Christ as he prays to the Father for us and transformed thereby through the gift of the Spirit, that we now send back as Spirit-filled prayers of thanksgiving. Here is the worship of sinners being worked over, in and through the gift of the Spirit for our own, into the worship of praise for gifts received.

But more generally, one might say that in the Eucharistic celebration we are not merely taken along by Son and Spirit as they turn to or go to the Father, passive participants waiting to receive, but go on our own steam as well, as already Spirit-filled sons ourselves. Here we ascend to the Father in more the way Christ himself does, as those empowered by the Spirit within them to do so, as he was. In the Eucharist, "the presence of his Spirit in us means that Christ's prayer and worship of the Father are made to echo in us and issue out of our life to the Father as our own prayer and worship."[102] The Spirit of the risen and ascended Christ dwells within us to help us pray along with Christ the "Our Father."[103] We are always to pray in the Spirit (Eph 6:18) as Christ did (Luke 10:21). By being in us Christ and the Spirit themselves carry the prayers of ours that they make possible; they effectively unite our prayers with their own, to invoke the Father (see

[101] *Ibid.*, section 7, p. 435.
[102] Torrance, *Theology in Reconciliation*, p. 209.
[103] *Ibid.*, p. 183, discussing the views of Cyril of Alexandria.

Gal 4:6). In keeping with this idea of worship on the basis of gifts of Son and Spirit already received, one reads in the Pauline Epistles: "Let the word of Christ dwell in you abundantly ... teaching and admonishing one another by psalms, hymns and spiritual songs, singing sweetly to God in your hearts ... giving thanks to God the Father through him (Col 3:16–17); "Be filled with the Holy Spirit, speaking to one another in psalms, hymns, and spiritual songs, singing and making melody in your hearts to the Lord, giving thanks always for all things ... to God the Father" (Eph 5:18–20). And the Apostolic Constitutions of Hippolytus for the liturgy make a similar suggestion that could be summarized this way: "Father, we thank you, we beseech you, we glorify you through Jesus Christ, your incarnate Son, our high priest, head and mediator; and we do this in virtue of the Holy Spirit present in us, who gives us the power to do this."[104]

We already have the gift of the Spirit that puts us on the path of new life in Christ in virtue of our baptism, and therefore in the Eucharist we are re-ascending with those gifts, in a movement of prayer and worship made possible by them, to receive back even more from the Father. The gifts of Son and Spirit that are already ours are themselves strengthened in their influence upon us by the further gift from the Father of nourishment by the body and blood of Christ's own Spirit-filled humanity. In general, we bring to the Eucharist gifts we have already received in order to get them back transformed from the Father as a conduit of further gifts. From among the many gifts for which we are thankful to God, we bring the fruits of the earth received from God and get back the life-giving body and blood of Christ for our own as the source of further gifts through his Spirit such as holiness, healing, and eternal life. And so

---

[104] This is the summary of Hippolytus, *Apostolic Constitutions*, Book 8, by Vagaggini, *Theological Dimensions*, p. 220. See the full translation of Book 8 in R. C. D. Jasper and G. L. Cuming, *Prayers of the Eucharist: Early and Reformed* (New York: Pueblo, 1987), pp. 104–13.

on – the cycle continues in a never-ending liturgy. In this way – through repeated ascents – "every generous act of giving, with every perfect gift, is from above, coming down from the Father of lights" (Jas 1:17).

Ascent in general might be associated specifically with worship. We ascend to the Father by turning to him in confession of sin and petition for the gifts of Son and Spirit we therefore lack as sinners, in praise and thanksgiving for the reception of those gifts and all the rest of the gifts they bring with them, and in glorification of the one who is all three. Because it is a trinitarian movement along which we are carried, we worship in the ascent not just the Father but all three together, for example, in doxologies, such as "Glory to the Father, and to the Son, and to the Holy Spirit," that typically express the perfect mutuality, unity, and equality of all three. We pray not just to the Father but to every member of the trinity in ways that respect their distinctive roles:

> We may sometimes address ourselves to the Spirit or to the Son as well as to the Father ... But we shall not be confusedly addressing ourselves sometimes to one and sometimes to another without knowing when or why. We shall speak to the Spirit ... who moves and inspires us and unites us to the Son; we shall speak to the Son as to our redeemer who has taken us to share in his sonship, in union with whom we are united to his Father and may address him as our Father.[105]

One prays to the Spirit to come within one's life and give one the power to act in a Christ-like way as one does at the feast of Pentecost: "Come, creator Spirit, visit the souls of your own."[106] One prays to the Holy Spirit as Simeon the New Theologian does: "Come, true light! Come, eternal life! Come, hidden mystery! Come, nameless treasure! ... Come, O powerful one, who always makes, remakes, and

---

[105] Hodgson, *Doctrine of the Trinity*, pp. 179–80.

[106] Congar, *I Believe in the Holy Spirit*, vol. I, p. 108, citing the ninth-century hymn for Pentecost.

transforms everything by your unique power!"[107] One prays to Christ as one's mediator before the Father, as the one through whom all gifts from the Father are to flow and who already incorporates within himself all the gifts we are to receive in unity with him.

It is as workers of the Father's will in the world that we go out or descend from the Father empowered by the Spirit in Christ's own image. The Spirit that is to sanctify us, make us holy as Christ is, is a commissioning Spirit, empowering us to participate in Christ's own mission of loving service to the world. "As the Father has sent me, so I send you ... Receive the Holy Spirit" (John 20:21–2). Receiving from the Father the gifts of Spirit-filled Sonship in unity with Christ, we are to do as he did when sent out from the Father.

The Christian experience of service to God's mission for the world in this way assumes a properly trinitarian shape. "The formula of the Christian life is seeking, finding, and doing the Father's will in the Father's world with the companionship of the Son by the guidance and strength of the Holy Spirit."[108] More specifically, service takes the form of trinitarian descent: from the Father to become the image of the Son in the world by way of the power of the Spirit, or from the Father to live a Spirit-filled life with Christ in his mission for the world. Those are two ways of saying the same thing.

Son and Spirit are sent out to us in order to enable our return to the Father. But returned to the Father we are sent out with Son and Spirit again to do the Father's work of service to the world. The return brings with it another going out because in returning we are incorporated into the dynamic trinitarian outflow of God's own life for the world.

Descent could be understood as service to the world that follows the ascent of service to God. There would then be two sequential

[107] Cited by Congar, *I Believe in the Holy Spirit*, vol. II, p. 112. Of course there are many other gifts through the Spirit for which one might ask.
[108] Hodgson, *Doctrine of the Trinity*, p. 62.

205

movements here in different directions, distinguished by their respective goals or objects: a movement toward God in worship or toward the world in service to it. Worship itself models the relationship between the two. At the end of worship comes the benediction and we are then sent out like Christ into the world to do the Father's business in the power of the Spirit.

Just as they did in the life of the trinity itself, however, the two movements should properly coincide. Worship – explicitly God-directed action – is an essential dimension of the task we are given for the world's sake. And in serving the world we turn ourselves to God, in service to the God who loves it. The whole of our lives, inclusive of both worship of God and service to others, becomes in this way an offering to God, a form of God-directed service (see Rom 12:1). The two coincide for this reason in Christ's own human life. Christ is both worshipper and worker of the Father. Both his prayers and his life's work are offered by him to the Father; and they both come back from the Father to him, in the power of the Spirit transformed – completed, perfected in the end.

5 | Politics

When contemporary theologians want to form judgments about social and political matters they often turn immediately to the trinity for guidance. Rather than Christology, a theology of the trinity is enlisted to support particular kinds of human community – say, egalitarian, inclusive communities, in which differences are respected – or to counter modern individualism by greater regard for the way personal character is shaped in community. What the trinity is like is thought to establish how human societies should be organized; the trinity is taken to be the best indicator of the proper relationship between individual and community; and so on. Jürgen Moltmann, John Zizioulas, Miroslav Volf, Leonardo Boff, and Catherine LaCugna are all important names in this regard.[1]

Theological judgments here can seem very easy and clear-cut. For example, if the persons of the trinity are equal to one another, then human beings should be too. Figuring out the socio-political lessons of the trinity is a fraught task, however. This chapter systematically explores the complexities and perils of the attempt, and concludes it would be better to steer attention away from trinitarian relations when making judgments about the proper character of human ones

---

[1] See especially Jürgen Moltmann, *The Trinity and the Kingdom*, trans. Margaret Kohl (New York: HarperCollins, 1991); John Zizioulas, *Being as Communion* (Crestwood, New York: St. Vladimir's Seminary Press, 1993); Miroslav Volf, "'The Trinity is our Social Program:' The Doctrine of the Trinity and the Shape of Social Engagement," *Modern Theology* 14/3 (1998), pp. 403–23; Leonardo Boff, *Trinity and Society*, trans. Paul Burns (Maryknoll, New York: Orbis, 1988); and Catherine LaCugna, *God For Us* (New York: HarperCollins, 1991).

in Christian terms. Christology (specifically, a discussion of the character of Jesus' relationships with other people) is the better avenue for making such judgments: it is less misleading, far simpler, and much more direct.

This could seem an unexpected turn on my part. I spent most of the preceding chapter, after all, discussing the way the general pattern of relationships among persons of the trinity recurs in all God's dealings with the world and our dealings with God. But the applicability of relations among persons of the trinity to human relationships is not so simple or direct, for a number of rather obvious reasons, as I will show.

My first caveat about appeals to the trinity for socio-political purposes has to do with the inflated claims made for the trinity in contemporary political theology. Many contemporary theologians overestimate the progressive political potential of the trinity. Monotheism, it is alleged, supports monolithic identities and authoritarian forms of government in which power is held exclusively by a single leader or group. An internally diverse triune God, in which persons share equally with one another, avoids these dangers. Or so the story goes.[2]

Overlooked in this common contrast between the socio-political implications of monotheism and trinitarianism are the complexities of such theological claims (can monotheism and trinitarianism, for example, be this easily distinguished?), their fluidity of sense (might not monotheism or trinitarianism have multiple meanings?) and the possible variety of political purposes that each might serve. To limit myself to the last consideration for the moment: monotheism need not be all that bad in its political implications. Of course it can suggest rule by one: one God, one Lord – meaning one human lord. But monotheism can also suggest (particularly when understood to deny that divinity is a general category) that no one shares

---

[2] See Erik Peterson, *Der Monotheismus als Politisches Problem* (Leipzig: Jakob Hegner, 1935); Moltmann, *Trinity and the Kingdom*, pp. 192–202; Boff, *Trinity and Society*, pp. 20–4.

in divinity and therefore that no one can stand in as God's representative: no lord but God. Should representatives of God be permitted, nothing prevents their identification, moreover, with the whole of a people rather than its leadership. Both moves, away from centralized, divinely authorized rule, were probably typical of some ancient Israelites, if the anti-monarchy strains of the Hebrew Bible are any indication.[3]

Trinitarianism, furthermore, is not often – to say the least – historically associated with an egalitarian politics and respect for diversity within community. Trinitarian thinking arose in tandem with Christian support for an increasingly centralized Roman Empire, once Christianity became the state religion under Constantine. Indeed, the major theological arguments in favor of imperial rule were not at all obviously monotheistic but presumed a diversity of divine principles or powers. Thus, Eusebius argues in his "Oration in Praise of the Emperor Constantine" that the emperor has near absolute authority to govern the whole known human world as the agent and representative of the Word – a second divine principle among other divine principles – who rules the cosmos from on high at the supreme God's say so.[4]

Granted, Eusebius does not maintain what will later become orthodox trinitarian teaching. This is rule by one in a descending chain of delegated authorities, in which each such authority, starting with the Word, is subordinated to a preceding one. After the one God in the highest position, comes the one Word, who is in direct charge of the cosmos at the highest God's behest, and then comes Constantine as the sole supreme leader of the empire. But any effort to make a theology like this more orthodox, only exacerbates the

---

[3] See Jan Assman, *Politsche Theologie zwischen Ägypten und Israel* (Munich: Siemens, 1992), pp. 75–6. The problematic implication of the latter move is, however, a privileging of the whole nation over others, e.g., the Canaanites.

[4] Eusebius of Caesarea, "Oration in Praise of the Emperor Constantine," trans. E. Richardson, in Philip Schaff and Henry Wace (eds.), *Nicene and Post-Nicene Fathers*, vol. I (New York: Christian Literature Company, 1890).

problem. A fully divine Word, for example, could very well simply reinforce the authority of the emperor who rules as the Word does. In the more "orthodox" case the emperor would come to be identified, not with a subordinate principle executing the Father's will, but with a Word equal to the Father himself. Three absolute co-rulers, moreover, seem hardly better than one as a model for the responsible exercise of political power. And so on.

Behind this poor historical showing lies the ambiguous socio-political potential of trinitarian theology itself. Many aspects of classical trinitarianism seem at least politically awkward at first glance. Thus, contrary to respect for difference, divine persons are equal to one another because in some very strong sense they are the same. They are commonly said, for example, to be permanently different modes or manners of the same one concrete nature or substance.[5] For this reason, the Son is everything the Father is – just like the Father – except for the fact that the Son is not the Father.[6] The Son is not to be called "Father," because that term specifies a distinction of person, but all other predicates assigned to the Father in virtue of the Father's divinity – omniscience, omnipresence, holiness, righteousness, power – are rightly ascribed to the Son as well. The oneness or unity of the trinity – not just the equality of the persons – is often given the same sort of basis: identity of substance, concretely rather than generically understood.[7] Without some suggestion of tritheism, it is therefore difficult to argue that divine persons are different from one another in the way human persons properly are – able to go their separate ways, distinguished

---

[5] See G. L. Prestige, *God in Patristic Thought* (London: SPCK, 1952), pp. 102–3, 157–9, 168, 173, 213–15, 229–30, 234–5.

[6] Athanasius, "Four Discourses against the Arians," trans. John Henry Newman and Archibald Robertson, in Philip Schaff and Henry Wace (eds.), *Nicene and Post-Nicene Fathers*, vol. IV, Second Series (Grand Rapids, Michigan: Eerdmans, 1957), Discourse 3, chapter 23, section 4, p. 395.

[7] There are other ways, however, of making that point: for example, perichoresis, indivisibility, and the priority of the Father in the generation of the other two persons.

by their own particular projects and interests, never in exactly the same place at the same time, distinct individuals sharing a common humanity in a general sense, but not the same one humanity in the way the divine persons are the same one and indivisible divine being or substance, and so on. Taken as an indication of proper human sociability, here it seems humanity is subsumed by community with others. (Perhaps for this reason most advocates of a trinitarian social or political program err, to my mind, in the direction of a very strong communitarianism; this becomes the main point of looking to the trinity for social guidance.) The common theological view that divine persons are constituted by their relations, along with the idea of their indivisibility in being and act, is simply hard to square with a politics that would like to foster the agency of persons traditionally effaced in relations with dominant members of society – women, racial, or ethnic minorities, those over-identified with social roles in which their own needs and wants are given short shrift. Moreover, the various ways of ordering the divine persons, no matter how complex, still distinguish the persons by their unsubstitutable functions or places within such orders. The Holy Spirit, for example, customarily has to go third, as in the liturgically favored, biblically derived formula, "Father, Son, and Holy Spirit." Order among the divine persons is thereby ripe for justification of hierarchy. It easily supports claims of fixed social roles, and the idea that people are equal despite the disparity of their assignment to such roles. And so on.

The turn to the economic trinity – the trinity's working for us in the world as the New Testament recounts that – is no help on this score, although many socially and politically progressive trinitarian theologians seem to think it is. As I mentioned in the preceding chapter, New Testament accounts of Jesus' relations with the one he calls Father are much more subordinationalist in flavor than accounts of the so-called immanent trinity usually are: Jesus prays to the Father, subordinates his will to the Father, defers to the Father, seems ignorant on occasion of what only the Father knows, and so on.[8] This sort of hierarchical relation between Son and Father, a relationship of inferior to superior, very obviously suggests the propriety of human hierarchy.

Developing such a relationship between Son and Father in more detail according to the biblical economy might only deepen, moreover, its politically problematic potential. Pushing just a bit farther the general tenor of their relationship as interpreted by Hans Urs von Balthasar and Joseph Ratzinger, one could summarize the relationship between Son and Father this way: sent to his death by the Father, under relentless pressure from the Spirit, the Son exhibits in his human life the blind obedience of an inferior before the heartless command of an implacable superior, demanding from him nothing less than self-sacrifice and extreme acts of self-evacuation and self-renunciation.[9]

Finally, the inclusion of gendered imagery in classical characterizations of the relationships among the persons of the trinity themselves, and in the biblical account of their workings for the world has enormously problematic social and political ramifications. The pervasive Father–Son language of the New Testament in particular always holds the potential for rendering women second-class citizens of the church or effacing their contributions altogether. Granted, Father–Son language is always given a quite limited theological rationale in classical trinitarian theology.[10] The point is very much not to import gender into God. That is quite explicitly denied: "The divine is neither male nor female (for how could such a thing be contemplated in divinity ...?)," as Gregory of Nyssa says.[11] "Son and

---

[8] See, for example, John 14:28; Mark 10:18, 13:32; Luke 18:18 and Mt 19:16.

[9] See Hans Urs von Balthasar, *Theo-Drama*, vol. III (Dramatis Personae), trans. Graham Harrison (San Francisco: Ignatius Press, 1992), pp. 183–91; and Joseph Ratzinger, *Introduction to Christianity* (London: Burns & Oates, 1969), pp. 132–5.

[10] For an extended argument to this effect, see Kathryn Tanner, "Gender," in Mark Chapman, Sathianathan Clarke, Ian Douglas, and Martyn Percy (eds.), *Oxford Handbook of Anglican Studies* (Oxford University Press, forthcoming).

[11] Gregory of Nyssa, *Commentary on the Song of Songs*, trans. Casimir McCambley (Brookline, Massachusetts: Hellenic College Press, 1987), Seventh Homily, p. 145. See the

offspring bear no human sense."[12] The significance of the imagery is quite often limited simply to the idea that the one comes from the other and is of the very same substance with it – equal to it and not other than it. "He is called 'Son' because he is identified with the Father in essence; and … because he is of him."[13] The intent is to distinguish the second person from a creature that comes from God but is not equal to God. "Making" language therefore trumps "kinship" language when the Father's relations with the world are at issue: the Father does not act exactly like a Father in creating the world; the Father makes the world and does not beget it from his own substance.[14] The gendered imagery in classical trinitarianism is always considered in tandem, moreover, with other forms of biblical imagery of a quite impersonal sort – light and water imagery, for example.[15] Paired with these other images, the meaning of Father–Son language becomes quite abstract and relatively untethered from its specifically gendered associations. The point of Father–Son language becomes so general, indeed, that these impersonal images can be its functional equivalent for theological purposes. The Son comes

discussion of this text by Verna Harrison, "Male and Female in Cappadocian Theology," *Journal of Theological Studies* 41 (1990), p. 441. See also Gregory Nazianzen, "Fifth Theological Oration" (31.7), cited and discussed by Harrison, "Male and Female," pp. 456–7.

[12] Athanasius, "Defence of the Nicene Definition," trans. John Henry Newman, in Philip Schaff and Henry Wace (eds.), *Nicene and Post-Nicene Fathers*, vol. IV, Second Series (Grand Rapids, Michigan: Eerdmans, 1957) chapter 5, section 24, p. 166.

[13] Gregory Nazienzen, "Orations," trans. Charles G. Browne and James E. Swallow, in Philip Schaff and Henry Wace (eds.), *Nicene and Post-Nicene Fathers*, vol. VII, Second Series (Grand Rapids, Michigan: Eerdmans, 1983), Oration 30 (Fourth Theological Oration), chapter 20, p. 316. For more supporting evidence and analysis, see Tanner, "Gender."

[14] See, for example, Gregory of Nyssa, "Answer to Eunomius' Second Book," trans. M. Day, in Philip Schaff and Henry Wace (eds.), *Nicene and Post-Nicene Fathers*, vol. V, Second Series (Peabody, Massachusetts: Hendrickson, 1994), p. 252. For a fuller discussion of the point, see Tanner, "Gender."

[15] For a detailed account of different forms of biblical imagery and analysis of their comparative theological strengths and weaknesses, see Tanner, "Gender."

out of the Father, for example, like a ray from a source of light, so as to share its nature. No one set of biblical images, furthermore, is privileged; each has its particular theological strengths and weaknesses. Light imagery, for example, is usually considered far better than Father–Son imagery in conveying the inseparable, indivisible character of the two. Multiple images are therefore commonly employed together so that they might mutually modify one another's theological shortcomings.[16] But whatever the theological intent, the rhetorical punch of the language in practice is another thing altogether; and nothing erases the sorry history in which the importance of such language has been magnified out of all proportion, in defiance of these quite circumscribed understandings of its theological point.

One might grant too that in classical trinitarian thinking this is a Father who acts like a mother: he births or begets the Son. The terms that sum up the character of the activity in which the one person gives rise to the other are usually gendered male (probably, for one, because "father" is the dominant gendered term in the New Testament): this relationship of origination is like that between a father and son. But the more detailed descriptions of the activity seem very much in keeping with what only women can do – give birth. Notwithstanding the ancient biological theory in which the father is responsible for the substance of the child – the mother being a mere container for what the father contributes – of theological interest here is the way the Son emerges immediately out of the Father like a child birthed from its mother. The closeness of the relationship is at issue: the absence of any temporal or spatial distinction between originator and originated. Birth as the primary metaphor for developing whatever the Father is doing in relation

---

[16] See Gregory of Nyssa, "Against Eunomius," trans. William Moore and H. A. Wilson, in Philip Schaff and Henry Wace (eds.), *Nicene and Post-Nicene Fathers*, vol. v, Second Series (Peabody, Massachusetts: Hendrickson, 1994), Book 8, sections 4–5, pp. 204–6, especially p. 206; and "Answer to Eunomius' Second Book," p. 308. See Tanner, "Gender."

to the Son is therefore often quite strong in classical trinitarianism.[17] One might even say, following Psalm 120:3, as Hilary of Poitiers does, that the Son is begotten of the Father's womb.[18] And Mary, an actual woman, consequently becomes a prime analogy, especially since her birthing, like the Father's, is pure – without "intercourse and conception and time and travail"[19] – and requires no contribution from a sexual partner. She is the sole source of the entire humanity of Christ in much the way the first person of the trinity is the sole source of the second person's whole divinity: the Son only has a Father in the way the Son incarnate only had a mother.[20]

The potential here for a gender-bending use of gendered imagery – a Father with a womb – might very well present the best hope for avoiding the theological reinforcement of male privilege. Gendered imagery is "exceeded" in a "baffling of gender literalism," as Janet Soskice puts it.[21] "Roles are reversed, fused, inverted: no one is simply who they seem to be. More accurately, everyone is *more than* they seem to be ... the Father and the Spirit are more than one gender can convey."[22]

Nothing stops, however, talk of a Father with a womb from simply erasing the contribution of real women by usurping their place: a man can do everything now![23] The genders are not being bent here in a strictly reciprocal way. The Father is not simply more than any one

[17] See for example, Hilary of Poitiers, "On the Trinity," trans. E. W. Watson and L. Pullan, in Philip Schaff and Henry Wace (eds.), *Nicene and Post-Nicene Fathers*, vol. IX, Second Series (Peabody, Massachusetts: Hendrickson, 1994), Book 6, sections 9–11, pp. 99–101; section 35, p. 111; and Book 9, section 36, p. 167.

[18] *Ibid.*, Book 12, section 8, pp. 219–20.   [19] *Ibid.*, Book 6, section 9, p. 100.

[20] Gregory Nazienzen, "Orations," Oration 30 (Fourth Theological Oration), chapter 19, p. 308. See also Hilary, "On the Trinity," Book 12, section 50, p. 231.

[21] Janet Martin Soskice, "Trinity and Feminism," in Susan Frank Parsons (ed.), *Cambridge Companion to Feminist Theology* (Cambridge University Press, 2002), p. 146.

[22] Susan Ashbrook Harvey "Feminine Imagery for the Divine: the Holy Spirit, the Odes of Solomon, and Early Syrian Tradition," *St. Vladimir's Theological Quarterly* 37/2–3 (1993), p. 114.

[23] For an extended argument about the reinforcement of male privilege by these means, see Virginia Burrus, "*Begotten Not Made*" (Stanford University Press, 2000).

gender – male or female – can convey, but is already as Father everything that the other gender ordinarily betokens. The divine Father may act in the way a human mother does; and a human mother – Mary – may give birth in a close parallel to the way the divine Father does. But the genders are still clearly distinguished by ranking them across the division of human and divine. Women generally and Mary in particular may be privileged over men as the closest analogue on the human plane to divine generation, but they are nevertheless bested on a divine level by what only a Father is said to do. Quite commonly, moreover, the use of both paternal and maternal language merely reinforces gender stereotyping. The Father is also a mother because he is nurturing and compassionate and slow to anger, following, for example, Is 49:15 and 66:13.[24]

One might try to avoid gendered imagery altogether. But even when absolutely equal trinitarian persons of un-assigned gender are made the basis for socio-political conclusions, the essential related-ness of those persons easily leads to heterosexism. The importance of differences between male and female for the identity of human persons can simply be presumed and substituted within a trinitarian account of the essential relatedness of persons to suggest that the identity of a woman depends on her relationship to a male counterpart.[25]

Clearly, then, trinitarianism can be every bit as socially and politically dangerous as monotheism. Everything depends on how that trinitarianism (or monotheism) is understood and applied. Ignoring such complexities, by insisting upon the inherent privilege

[24] See Boff, *Trinity and Society*, p. 171.
[25] See Miroslav Volf, *Exclusion and Embrace* (Nashville, Tennessee: Abingdon, 1996), p. 187. Volf moves illegitimately here from a necessity of conceptual reference (from the fact that one term is defined with reference to another) to a necessary relation of fact (women must actually be related to men, e.g., married to them, in order to be themselves). The logical slippage involved becomes readily apparent when one considers other cases where terms are defined with reference to one another but where it would be absurd to infer a requirement of actual intertwined lives of intimacy: heterosexuality, for example, develops as a concept in relation to homosexuality, and so on.

of trinitarianism in this regard, leads one unfairly to rule out the progressive political potential of self-described monotheistic faiths, such as Judaism and Islam. It also promotes an unrealistically sharp distinction between monotheism and Christian trinitarianism. Trinitarianism is after all a form of monotheism, as Christians maintain; and monotheistic faiths, such as Judaism, have, at many periods of their history, allowed for the existence of subordinate divine principles and powers – for example, angelic messengers, personified names of God, and so on.[26] The idea that trinitarianism is inherently politically progressive comes to trade in this way on a highly restrictive sense of what trinitarianism can be. For example, trinitarian positions that are not associated with a progressive politics are presumed not to be really trinitarian or to have had their trinitarianism severely compromised.[27]

By ignoring trinitarianism's potential dangers and assigning them exclusively to monotheism, politically progressive trinitarian theologians are easily lulled, moreover, into a false sense of complacency. Coming up with a politically progressive trinitarianism is not impossible (or even inadvisable, given the non-trinitarian alternatives). But it is hard work; and the results have to be vigilantly guarded against the ineradicable possibility of their subsequent non-progressive use by others.

The only trinitarianism that is clearly more socially and politically progressive than (some forms of) monotheism is trinitarianism within a very specific range of interpretation and mode of application. Those lauding the political merits of trinitarianism over strict monotheism eventually make clear that this holds for trinitarianism only when *properly* understood and employed – in other words, for the sort of trinitarianism they are actively trying to construct. What these theologians are trying to do, indeed, is systematically modify as

---

[26] See, for example, Alan Segal, *Two Powers in Heaven* (Leiden: Brill, 1977).
[27] Moltmann in the *Trinity and the Kingdom* drifts in all three of these unfortunate directions; LaCugna in her *God For Us* in the last one.

many of the socially and politically problematic aspects of trinitarian theology as they can.

Thus, Moltmann and Volf argue that the persons of the trinity are not simply constituted by their relations without remainder.[28] Following Moltmann, politically progressive trinitarian theologians, such as Leonardo Boff, downplay the irreversible orders among the trinitarian persons in favor of the perfectly reciprocal perichoretic relations – relations of indwelling – among them: the Father is in the Son just as the Son is in the Father, and so on. It is these perichoretic relations that do the heavy lifting. The reversibility of these relations, rather than identity of substance, is what accounts for the equality of the persons. And they come to replace politically problematic alternatives, such as identity of substance, as the basis for the trinity's unity: "Their unity, rather than a unity of substance or origin (the Father), would be a unity of Persons, by reason of the reciprocal communion between them."[29] "Instead of speaking of the unity of God in terms of His one nature, [it is better] to speak of it in terms of the *communion of persons*."[30]

The theological merits of these politically progressive theologies hinge on how good the arguments are for such theological moves. One argument in their favor is simply the fact that such moves support a progressive social and political viewpoint; and I have no interest in denying that. But these social and political considerations hardly override the many theologically problematic features of the sort of trinitarianism typically advanced. Inexplicably to my mind, for example, no one has adequately addressed how the heavy load that perfectly reciprocal perichoresis carries in these theologies is compatible with their equally strong emphasis on the biblical economy, in which Jesus seems clearly to be acting in a non-mutual

---

[28] See, for example, Volf, "The Trinity is our Social Program," p. 410; and Moltmann, *Trinity and the Kingdom*, pp. 172–4.

[29] Boff, *Trinity and Society*, p. 84.

[30] Zizioulas, *Being as Communion*, p. 134 (italics in original).

relation of subordination to the Father. For example, the Son prays to the Father, but the Father does not pray to the Son; the Son does the will of the Father, but the Father does not do the will of the Son; and so on. In other words, not all the relations among the persons of the trinity in the biblical narration of them seem even close to being reciprocal ones, in which the persons can change places with one another, and little explanation is offered for this; that fact is for the most part just ignored.[31]

The very heavy emphasis on perfectly reciprocal relations among the members of the trinity and severe downplaying of any idea of their fixed positions in an order (for example, the persons are now often said to be all equally origins of one another, even if they are always properly named in the order Father, Son, and Holy Spirit)[32] seem, moreover, hard to reconcile with the usual ways of making clear that the persons are distinct from one another. The most common way in the history of theology is to talk about their being related to one another in some non-interchangeable way – the Father is related to the Son as the one begetting him but in doing so he is specifically the Father and not the Son – and to make a distinction on that basis between communicable or shareable pro-perties (what all the persons exhibit insofar as they are divine) and incommunicable ones (for example, the character of being Father is not part of what the Father gives the Son in begetting him).[33] Most socially and politically progressive theologies simply start from the assumption of distinct persons, taking this for granted as a feature of the biblical witness, and go on to talk about the unity of the trinity on that basis – as a function of how closely related the persons are to one another. But if the relationships they have with one another allow for no distinctions among them, it is hard to see how such a starting assumption helps. Their relations work to undercut the

---

[31] See Boff, *Trinity and Society*, pp. 138–9, where every biblically narrated relationship among the persons is said to involve their being in one another.
[32] *Ibid.*, pp. 145–7.   [33] See *ibid.*, pp. 88–9, for an explicit rejection of the latter.

distinctiveness of the persons that is simply assumed at the start and there is no remaining way to shore it up. Being in one another may simply presuppose that the persons are distinct from one another. They cannot be in one another, if they are not different from one another in some way or other to begin with.[34] But that fact does nothing to explain how or why they come to be different.

Other moves made by politically progressive trinitarian theologians suggest, to the contrary, that the persons of the trinity are *too* distinct from one another. Moltmann, for example, maintains that the persons of the trinity are not equivalent to their relations, in the way an Augustinian or Thomistic account of persons as subsistent relations would have it.[35] The existence of the persons needs to be distinguished from their relations, because, while the persons do not exist apart from the way they relate to one another, those relations presuppose, rather than bring about, the very existence of the persons. "It is true that the Father is defined by his fatherhood to the Son, but this does not constitute his existence; it presupposes it."[36]

Moltmann indeed asserts that it is simply impossible for persons to be their relations in any stronger sense.[37] But this is to give the trinitarian term "person" (a rather ill-defined placeholder for whatever there might be three of in the trinity) the modern sense of "human person" and then insist on taking it quite literally. It is impossible for human beings to enter into relationships unless they already exist; we have to exist before we relate. Or, to make the distinction between existence and manner of existence perhaps more properly (as Moltmann himself does in a later article), we can be said to exist because of certain relationships – in virtue, say, of being born

---

[34] See Miroslav Volf, *After our Likeness: The Church as the Image of the Trinity* (Grand Rapids, Michigan: Eerdmans, 1998), p. 209: "the distinctions between them are precisely the presupposition of that interiority, since persons who have dissolved into one another cannot exist in one another."

[35] Moltmann, *Trinity and the Kingdom*, pp. 172–4. See also Volf, "The Trinity is our Social Program," p. 410.

[36] Moltmann, *Trinity and the Kingdom*, p. 172.   [37] *Ibid.*

of a particular mother and father – whatever the characters we come to have by way of subsequent relations with others.[38] But why assume any of this must hold for divine persons?

Quite a bit more argument than Moltmann offers would be necessary to justify the use of a modern sense of "person" here with implications diverging so markedly from previous uses of personal language in trinitarian theology. Personal terms have long been employed to talk about the persons of the trinity – Father and Son are the prime examples. But that was to suggest the very constitution of such persons in and through their relations with one another:[39] there is no Father without this Son and no Son without this Father.[40] The point was to highlight their essential or constitutive relationality; personal language certainly was not used to distinguish the existence of a person of the trinity from the way it exists in relation to another.

When its terms are taken this literally, the argument clearly suggests tritheism. The persons of the trinity become very much like human persons. And therefore the trinity itself becomes a collection – tightly interwoven to be sure – of distinct persons on a very close – too close – analogy to a society of human persons.

No matter how close the similarities between human and divine persons, and between a human society and the unity of the trinity, differences always remain – God is not us – and this sets up the major problem for theologies that want to base conclusions about human relationships on the trinity. The chief complication is how to move from a discussion of God to human relationships, given those differences.[41] How exactly, in short, does a description of the trinity apply to us? Three more specific problems arise here.

---

[38] Moltmann, "Theological Proposals towards a Resolution of the *Filioque* Controversy," in Lukas Vischer (ed.), *Spirit of God, Spirit of Christ* (London: SPCK, 1981), pp. 164–73.

[39] Boff, *pace* Moltmann, properly points this out in support of the use of the modern sense of "person" to discuss the three. See his *Trinity and Society*, pp. 88–9, 115–16.

[40] For example, see Athanasius, "Four Discourses," Discourse 3, chapter 24, section 6, pp. 396–7.

[41] See Volf, *After Our Likeness*, pp. 191–200; and his "The Trinity is our Social Program," pp. 403–7.

First of all, the differences between God and us suggest we do not understand very well what we mean when using ordinary language to speak of the trinity. What the trinity is saying about human relations becomes unclear, because the meaning of the terms used to talk about the trinity is unclear. Divine persons are equal to one another but in what sense? The persons are in one another but what does "in" mean here? Divine persons are distinguished from one another by the character of their relations but who understands exactly what that character is? As Hilary of Poitiers says: "Begetting is the secret of the Father and the Son. If anyone is convinced of the weakness of his intelligence through failing to understand this mystery ... he will undoubtedly be even more downcast to learn that I am in the same state of ignorance."[42] What indeed does even the language of "person" suggest, if with Augustine we have to say that "the formula three persons was coined, not in order to give a complete explanation by means of it, but in order that we might not be obliged to remain silent"?[43] Because God is not very comprehensible to us, and certainly not fully so, discussion of the trinity, all by itself, seems of little help in better understanding human relationships. What we are puzzled about – the proper character of human society – is explicated with reference to what is surely only more obscure – the character of divine community.

Some theologians might respond that the problem here is too great a focus on the so-called immanent trinity. One can give a more definite sense to terms used of the trinity in light of the trinity's workings in the economy of salvation. One could explore, for example, what the unity of the trinity means in terms of the character of the fellowship enjoyed by Jesus and the one he calls Father.

[42] "On the Trinity," Book 2, section 9, p. 55. I am following here the more felicitous translation in Boff, *Trinity and Society*, p. 174.

[43] Augustine, "On the Trinity," trans. Arthur West Haddan and William Shedd, in Philip Schaff (ed.), *Nicene and Post-Nicene Fathers*, vol. III (Grand Rapids, Michigan: Eerdmans, 1956), p. 92. Again I am following the more felicitous translation in Boff, *Trinity and Society*, p. 143.

But unless one purports to know much more about relations among the trinitarian persons than is probably warranted, one is still left with very vague recommendations – typically about the social goods of equality, a diverse community, and mutual relationships of giving and receiving. All the hard, controversial work of figuring out exactly what any of that might mean – what sort or degree of cultural uniformity is required for community? how far can differences in a unified society go? – seems left up to the ingenuity of the theologian arguing on other grounds.

This is not necessarily a bad thing, to the extent it means that the trinity cannot give answers to political questions without socio-historical mediation – that is, without the need for study of the causes and consequences of present political circumstances using the best social, political, and economic theories available. But dangers remain. Should the theologian try, as commonly happens, to narrow down the senses of terms used of the trinity following what he or she thinks those terms mean (or should mean) when used of human persons and societies, the account of the trinity loses its critical edge on political questions and begins simply to reflect the theologian's prior political views. The trinity's concrete recommendation for politics in that case amount to little more than what the theologian already believes. Karen Kilby, citing a typical example, pointedly diagnoses the problem produced by this sort of procedure for specifying the meaning of trinitarian terms:

> First, a concept, perichoresis, is used to name what is not understood, to name whatever it is that makes the three Persons one. Secondly, the concept is filled out rather suggestively with notions borrowed from our own experience of relationships and relatedness. And, then, finally, it is presented as an exciting resource Christian theology has to offer the wider world in its reflections upon relationships and relatedness.[44]

[44] Karen Kilby, "Perichoresis and Projection," *Blackfriars* 81 (2000), p. 442.

The critical question, in short, remains unanswered: how is one to draw out the implications of the trinity for human society with any specificity, given how little one really understands about the trinity?

The second problem is that much of what is said about the trinity simply does not seem directly applicable to humans. The differences between God and humans stand in the way. Many of these differences that prevent a direct application have to do with the essential finitude of human beings. Human society could therefore take on the very character of the trinity in these respects in which they differ only if people were no longer human.

So, for example, it seems bound up with their essential finitude that human persons can only metaphorically speaking be in one another, if that means having overlapping subjectivities or agencies in the way the persons of the trinity do.[45] Because all the other members of the trinity are in that person, when one person of the trinity acts the others are necessarily acting too: "Each divine person acts as subject, and at the same time the other persons act as subjects in it."[46] Clearly this does not hold for human persons: I may enter empathetically into the one I love, but that does not mean I act when my beloved does.

> Another human self cannot be internal to my own self as subject for action ... Mutual love [is no] proof to the contrary ... Despite all the selflessness of love, it is not the beloved ... who is the subject of love within the loving self, but ... the loving self itself ... A self ... can embrace or "enter empathetically" into the other, but it is not a self that can indwell as a self that other. The indwelling of other persons is an exclusive prerogative of God.[47]

Divine persons, moreover, seem much more relational than human beings are. Even if one thinks (as I do not) that it is appropriate to make a real distinction between existence and character in

---

[45] See Volf, *After Our Likeness*, pp. 209, 211.
[46] *Ibid.*, p. 209. [47] *Ibid.*, pp. 210–11 (italics in original).

the case of trinitarian persons, human persons can still never be as closely tied to their relations with others as persons in the trinity are commonly thought to be.[48] Thus, it would be very unusual to suggest that trinitarian persons temporally precede the relations among themselves that make them what they are, in the way this happens in human relations. Human beings have no character to begin with as that is decisively shaped by what happens to them later. I therefore exist prior to those relationships with duplicitous significant others, for example, that end up making me a bitter, distrustful old person.

Character, moreover, in human beings is not as bound up with actual relations with others. I can be defined by certain relational capacities whether or not I ever actualize those capacities in my relationships with others. For example, my character might be constituted by the tendency to be suspicious before my relations with other people give me good grounds to be that way. For much the same reason, the character I come to have in virtue of my relations with others remains even when the original relations that gave rise to it end: I retain my character despite, for example, the deaths of the people and communities who have contributed most to it. The relational characteristics of trinitarian persons, to the contrary, are much more tightly a function of actual relationships. The Father, for example, is not defined as someone with the general capacity to beget someone, but as the Father who is and remains such only in begetting this Son.[49]

The character of a human person, moreover, takes different forms in the course of relations with different people. I always have the capacity to be more or other than I am right now. I have the capacity, for example, to be enormously engaging and incredibly funny; and the capacity to be hateful when made the brunt of ridicule. And

---

[48] See Thomas Weinandy, *Does God Suffer?* (University of Notre Dame Press, 2000), pp. 115, 119, 128, 134–5, 140, 207–8.

[49] See Giles Emery, "Essentialism or Personalism in the Treatise on God in Saint Thomas Aquinas?," *Thomist* 64 (2000), pp. 551–3.

therefore to know a human person in her relations with you is to know her only incompletely. Theologians generally do not want to say anything quite like that of the trinity. Trinitarian persons are fully themselves in their relations with one another and with us; trinitarian persons are not in themselves, for example, other than the persons they show themselves to be to us. And trinitarian persons do not become progressively more or other than themselves as their relations are extended, say, beyond themselves into the world. People at all times and places, therefore, relate to members of the trinity in their same fully realized characters.

Trinitarian persons are, moreover, always themselves in their relations with one another because they relate to one another immediately – without any externality or media that might disguise their true selves. Finitude prevents this from being the case in relations among human persons:

> Human beings relate to one another through mediating acts – words, hugs, kisses. While these actions bring about actual relations, the very fact that they are mediating acts means that human beings are never fully in communion with one another as they are in themselves. For example, if two people intensely love one another, their words and acts of love never fully express the whole of their love for the acts, being mediatory, do not fully embody or express the entirety of their love.[50]

Despite their intense relationality, trinitarian persons, moreover, remain irreducibly distinct from one another in ways that human beings cannot imitate. Father and Son remain in a certain sense absolutely different from one another in the trinity because, unlike the case of human fathers and sons, here the Father has never been a Son – the Father is always Father – and the Son never becomes a Father in turn – the Son is always Son.[51] The terms "father" and "son"

[50] Weinandy, *Does God Suffer?*, p. 207 fn. 62.
[51] See Athanasius, *The Letters of St. Athanasius concerning the Holy Spirit*, trans. C. R. B. Shapland (London: Epworth, 1951), Epistle 4, pp. 187–8.

in the trinity do not, in short, indicate general capacities, which a variety of individuals might exhibit, but are person-defining properties. In the human case, I am different from my mother in that I am my mother's daughter but I can also become like my mother by becoming the mother of a daughter myself; and therefore in being different from my mother I am not absolutely different from her. The human relations that distinguish people never simply define them and therefore one can lose the way one has been identified in virtue of those relations (one's identity as a daughter, say, once one's mother has been dead for thirty years) and take on others (the identity of a mother to one's own daughter) while remaining oneself. But persons of the trinity are too tied to their specific relationships – for example, to being Father and Son – to do this. They are too absolutely what they are – Son or Father – and too absolutely distinct from one another in their relationships for that to be possible.

Indeed, in the trinity relations of tremendous intensity never threaten the individuality of the persons in the way relations like that threaten to blur the identities of human beings. Unlike the case of trinitarian persons, the finitude of humans seems to require the policing of boundaries between themselves and others that breaks off relationships. I will never be my own person unless I can break away from the incredibly intense relationship I have with my mother. In the trinity, to the contrary, the persons are absolutely different from one another in the very intensity of the relationships they have with one another. It is because the relationship is so intense, so to speak, for both of them that the Father can only be a Father and the Son only a Son. Only in virtue of maintaining their relationship inviolate do they remain absolutely different from one another – the Father without any capacity whatever to be a Son because of it, and the Son nothing like what makes the Father Father in begetting him. They are themselves therefore only if the relationship maintains its intensity for both of them; and never more themselves by mitigating or somehow attenuating it.

Finally, human finitude also seems to entail that humans give of themselves so that others may gain in ways that often bring loss to themselves. In the case of trinitarian persons, to the contrary, their perfect equality is usually thought to involve giving without loss and receiving without increase. The first person of the trinity does not give all of itself to the second at any cost to itself; and the second does not receive from the first what is not already its own. Athanasius makes the point: the persons of the trinity "are not ... discharged into each other, filling the one the other, as in the case of empty vessels, so that the Son fills the emptiness of the Father and the Father that of the Son, [as if] each of them by himself is not complete and perfect."[52]

One could argue, as I have elsewhere, that loss in giving to others on the human plane is a function of a world in disarray and not a necessary consequence of simple finitude.[53] It is possible in principle for the world to be arranged in ways that make giving to others a benefit to oneself. But this simply brings us to the third problem.

Direct translation of the trinity into a social program is problematic because, unlike the peaceful and perfectly loving mutuality of the trinity, human society is full of suffering, conflict, and sin. Turned into a recommendation for social relations, the trinity seems unrealistic, hopelessly naïve, and, for that reason, perhaps even politically dangerous. To a world of violent, corrupt, and selfish people, the trinity seems to offer only the feeble plaint, "Why can't we all just get along?"[54]

In recognition of how difficult it is to translate the trinity directly into recommendations for a sinful world, theologians often propose that the trinity is only the "utopian goal"[55] or "eschatological

---

[52] Athanasius, "Four Discourses," Discourse 3, section 2, p. 394. See also, for example, Hilary of Poitiers, "On the Trinity," Book 3, section 13, p. 65; and Gregory of Nyssa, "Against Eunomius," Book 10, section 4, p. 226.

[53] See Kathryn Tanner, *Economy of Grace* (Minneapolis, Minnesota: Fortress, 2005), chapter 3.

[54] These are the famous words of Rodney King in response to the 1992 Los Angeles riots.

[55] Boff, *Trinity and Society*, p. 6.

destiny" of humans.[56] The trinity offers a social vision but one cannot expect it to provide a social program.[57] If the idea here is that human society, short of the eschaton, can be expected only to approximate the character of the trinity, that seems right. It is nevertheless a very odd eschatological goal or destiny that suggests we must leave behind what essentially makes us human if we are ever to get there.

The trinity as social vision also suggests the trinity helps direct the transformation of society in the meantime. Still to be answered, however, is once again the critical question of how the trinity is able to do so given the differences between God and us. How is the gap between sinful, finite human beings and the trinity to be bridged so that we can see its implications for the lives we actually live? For the same reason, the goal of trinitarian community that we are offered seems almost cruelly fanciful. A treasure is dangled before us with no clue as to how we might get to it from the desperate straits of social relations marked by violent conflict, loss, and suffering.

One strategy for bridging the gap is to supplement the move down from the trinity, when envisioning human society, with a move up, from below.[58] In other words, from what one knows about human life, one can figure out the manner and extent to which human relations are able to imitate trinitarian ones. The trinity tells us what human relations should be like ideally. The understanding of humans as creatures and sinners tells us what sort of approximation of the ideal we are in fact capable of. "By describing God, in whose image human beings are created and redeemed, the doctrine of the Trinity names the reality which human communities *ought* to image. By describing human beings as distinct from God, the doctrines of creation and of sin inform the way in which human communities *can* image the Triune God, now in history and then in eternity."[59]

---

[56] Volf, "The Trinity is our Social Program," p. 405.   [57] *Ibid.*, p. 406.

[58] See Volf, *After Our Likeness*, p. 200; and "The Trinity is our Social Program," pp. 405–6.

[59] Volf, "Trinity is our Social Program," p. 407 (italics in original).

For example, knowing what we do about human beings, we can assume the closest approximation to the perichoretic relations among trinitarian *persons* is the mutual conditioning of *characteristics* among human beings.[60] Human beings are the unsubstitutable agents of their own acts; they cannot, as mentioned before, have overlapping subjectivities. But they can have mutually conditioning characters. My character is formed as I am influenced by others, just as the character of others is formed in and through relations with me. "In this mutual giving and receiving, we give to others not only something, but also a piece of ourselves, something of that which we have made of ourselves in communion with others; and from others we take not only something, but also a piece of them."[61]

As this example suggests, the danger of such a strategy is that the trinity fails to do any work; it does not tell one anything one did not already know. We do not need the trinity to tell us that human beings condition one another by way of their relationships. We do not even need the trinity to tell us that persons are catholic in their conditioning by others.[62] There is nothing especially trinitarian about the idea that individuals are a microcosm of the whole world's influences. That is a commonplace affirmation in philosophy and recourse to the trinity adds nothing of substance to it.

Presumably the trinity might add something substantive were one to ask about the *sort* of relations with others that properly condition personal identity. If the trinity is any indication those relations should be loving ones in which the other is concerned for one's own good. The focus, to the contrary here, simply on whether and to what extent human identity is relational deflects attention from this more substantive and less formal question.[63] The point becomes simply an attack on individualism, for example: "Being a person is fundamentally different from being an individual or a 'personality,' for a person cannot be imagined in himself but only within his

---

[60] Volf, *After Our Likeness*, pp. 211–12.   [61] *Ibid.*, p. 211.
[62] *Ibid.*, p. 212.   [63] See, for example, Zizioulas, *Being as Communion*, pp. 105–7.

relationships."[64] The kind of relationships these should be is never raised as a focal issue. If they are destructive or detrimental to oneself or others, should one not distance oneself from the relations that make one what one is?

This oddly formal focus is also a problem for the other major strategy of bridging the gap between divine and human, and has a broader cause, to be discussed later. This other major strategy looks to the economic trinity for help in bridging the gap.[65] One does not have to bring an account of the trinity together with what one knows about the limits of human life to figure out how human relationships could come to approximate trinitarian ones. The economic trinity – how the trinity acts in saving us – instead makes that clear, because what one finds in the economic trinity itself is the trinity brought closer to what humans are capable of.

For example, in the economy the trinity appears as a dialogical fellowship of love and mutual service between Jesus and the one he calls Father, the kind of relationship that human beings could imitate because it is one in keeping with their finitude – in contrast, say, to perfectly mutual indwelling or perichoresis. In the economy the persons of the trinity seem more like separately constituted human persons acting harmoniously together in a jointly agreed upon common project. It might appear that they simply agree to act together in concert because of the love they share for one another and for us. In relations among the persons of the trinity themselves, to the contrary, something more than dialogical fellowship takes place. The will of the Son (for example) naturally corresponds to the will of the Father because in a significant sense they have only one will. Instead of a fellowship of wills, one finds an identity of will. It is only when the Son is sent on a mission into the world by the Father that the Son seems to have a will of his own leaning, in theory at least, in some other direction – for example, the will to maintain his own human life by avoiding crucifixion. The Son incarnate's own will therefore seems to be brought into conformity with the will of the Father, in something closer to the way the will of one human being might be brought into harmony with another. The unity that follows from having the very same will – a unity based on unity of nature or substance – is not anything that human beings can imitate. But a perfect harmony of wills like this, by way of perfect fellowship in a common project, is.

The same goes for sin. By entering a world of sin and death for us, the economic trinity itself provides the clue to how trinitarian relations should be lived out in a world of that kind, thereby obviating the need for theological speculation. For example, those trinitarian relations take the broken and sorrowful form of a Father losing his own Son by way of a death undergone for the sake of others. Following the way of the trinity in the economy means following the way of the cross, in short. Miroslav Volf eloquently makes the point:

> Jesus demanded not so much that we imitate the divine dance of love's freedom and trust, but the divine labor of love's suffering and risk. The love that dances is the internal love of the Trinity; the love that suffers is that same love turned toward a world suffused with enmity. The first is the perfect love of the world to come; the second is that same love engaged in the transformation of the deeply flawed world that is.[66]

Because this strategy seeks to close the gap by thinking of trinitarian relations as more like the human ones of our experience, a similar problem to the one that beset the previous strategy arises, however. The closer trinitarian relations in the economy seem to human ones, the less the trinity seems to offer advice about how to move beyond what we already expect from life given human limits and failings. The trinity simply confirms what we already know and solidifies our chastened hopes under the circumstances. We all have

---

[66] "The Trinity is our Social Program," p. 413.

some sense of what dialogical relations of loving fellowship are like; and that is all we should expect of our lives on trinitarian grounds. We all know about the way death severs relationships and about how obedience to a good cause often comes at the price of sacrifice in troubled times; and the trinity offers nothing more.

Pushing imaginatively beyond those experiences to something better – something more than a unity of mere will and love, something more than sacrifice – would seem to require the trinity to be something more for us too. Without being more, the trinity's potential for critical, informative commentary is simply deflated. But to the extent the trinity does hold out something more – for example, a perichoretic unity and not one of mere will and love – the usual problem of bridging the gap between human and divine simply reappears unaddressed. The alternative to bridging the gap is simply to tell us that in these respects the trinity is not a human hope – for this world at least.[67]

This strategy of closing the gap also tends, rather curiously, to be insufficiently economic. Our salvation is at the center of the economy, after all. But the focus in this strategy on how the trinitarian persons relate to one another in the economy tends to displace interest in what the trinity in entering our world in Christ is trying to do for us. As Moltmann never tires of emphasizing, one should concentrate on the difference that the economy (for example, the incarnation) makes for God. In Moltmann's case this is closely tied to soteriological concerns: what is happening in and among the trinitarian persons themselves opens up a place for the world of suffering and sin to enter the divine life and so be overcome. But such a strong focus on relations among the persons of the trinity themselves in the economy easily fuels the temptation to see those relations as the very meaning of salvation for us in an altogether abstract

---

[67] The previous quotation from Volf ("The Trinity is our Social Program," p. 413) seems to suggest this when read in light of what he says on p. 405. There are only some respects in which the trinity can be a model for human community.

way. In other words, the idea that human relations should take on their character becomes an end in itself, apart from any more concrete consideration of what those relations among divine persons are actually doing for us in the economy – for example, bringing about the end of death, sin, and suffering in human lives.

My own strategy for closing the gap also looks to what the trinity is doing for us – what is happening in the life of Christ, in short – to answer the question of how the trinity applies to human life. Human beings are not left to their own devices in figuring out what the trinity means for human relations. Instead, the trinity itself enters our world in Christ to show us how human relations are to be reformed in its image.

The trinity does not do so, however, in the way the previous strategy suggested – by showing us a form of itself that we can hope to approach and thereby providing us with an external model to which we might more easily conform.[68] The trinity in the economy does not close the gap by making trinitarian relations something like human ones, but by actually incorporating the human into its very own life through the incarnation. We are therefore not called to imitate the trinity by way of the incarnation but brought to participate in it. A significant difference exists between the two:

> To view the Trinity as an external model that human relationships should reflect ... has no biblical basis (significantly, the New Testament does not use the idea of the image of God in this way), and [it] is only artificially combined with the ... idea [that we come to know, and participate in, the relations among Father, Son, and Spirit in and through what Christ does].[69]

---

[68] For criticism of the modeling idea, see Paul Fiddes, *Participating in God* (Louisville, Kentucky: Westminster John Knox, 2000); Richard Bauckham, "Jürgen Moltmann's *The Trinity and the Kingdom of God* and the Question of Pluralism," in Kevin Vanhoozer (ed.), *The Trinity in a Pluralistic Age* (Grand Rapids, Michigan: Eerdmans, 1997), pp. 160–2; and Alistair McFadyen, "The Trinity and Human Individuality," *Theology* 95 (1992), pp. 12–14.

[69] Bauckham, "Moltmann's *Trinity and the Kingdom*," p. 160.

Rather than make itself over in a human image of community we can imitate in order to close the gap, the trinity in the economy (as we saw in Chapter 4) makes over human life in the trinity's image by way of our entrance into its own life through Christ. By joining us to those relations Christ gives us the very relations of Father, Son, and Spirit to be the new form of our own. The second person of the trinity takes the humanity united to it into its own relations with Father and Spirit; and we are to enjoy those same relations through him by the power of the Spirit. In Christ we are therefore shown what the trinity looks like when it includes the human, and what humanity looks like when it is taken up within the trinity's own relationships. If these relationships among Father, Son, and Spirit in which humanity now participates have implications for human ones, they are being worked out in and through Jesus' own human life as it takes a trinitarian shape.

The gap between divine and human is not closed here by making the two similar to one another, but by joining the two very different things – humanity and divinity, which remain very different things – into one in Christ via the incarnation. Trinitarian relations need not be like human relations in order for humans to be taken up into them. The fact that God is nothing like humans does not stop the human from being joined to the Word in Christ or us from being joined with Christ in the Spirit, so as to be children of the Father by grace, sharing in Jesus' own relations with Father and Spirit.

Because the gap is not closed in the way the usual appeal to the economic trinity closes it, one avoids the problematic trade-off mentioned earlier: the more trinitarian relations seem similar to human ones (and therefore relations that human beings could imitate) the less the trinity tells one anything one did not already know about them. Gone too is the basis for hope in the idea that trinitarian relations are sufficiently close to human ones to be imitated by us. Now hope is fueled by how *different* the trinitarian relations, in which we are to be incorporated, are from anything with which we are familiar under the constraints of finitude and sin. The difference between the trinity and us now holds out hope for a radical improvement of the human condition. The trinity is not brought down to our level as a model for us to imitate; our hope is that we might be raised up to its level.

Finitude is no longer a problem here either. Finitude does not make trinitarian relations inaccessible to us since human relations come to image trinitarian ones as they are swept up into them and not as they become like them in and of themselves. Human relations need not somehow become more than human themselves in order, thereby, to approximate the trinity. Human relations, which remain fully human, image the trinity only as they are joined up with its own life – by participating in it in the strong sense specified in the first chapter. Humans do not attain the heights of trinitarian relations by reproducing them in and of themselves, by mimicking them, in other words, but by being taken up into them as the very creatures they are. They come to share a divine form of existence, not their own by nature, by becoming attached to it.

The usual strategy of looking to the economy – the trinity at work in the world – seems stuck on the idea that the trinity appears to us in the economy as a model for our imitation because it fails to follow the economic workings of the trinity all the way down to their impact on us. In other words, that strategy stops with relations among trinitarian persons in the economy – for example, the Son incarnate doing the will of the Father – and makes them a model for human ones rather than following through on what the economy of the trinity itself is suggesting about human relations. Jesus' life, in short, exhibits not just the sort of relations that humans, in the image of the Son, are to have with Father and Spirit – relations of worshipful dedication to the Father's mission, empowered by the Spirit – but, in his relations with other people, Jesus also shows how those relations with Father and Spirit are to work themselves out in community with other people. If one wants to know how a trinitarian life impacts one's relations with other people, this second part of the story is very obviously the place to look: Jesus' relations with other people constitute the sort of human relations that the economy of the trinity itself specifies. Jesus' way of life toward other people as we share in it *is* the trinitarian form of human social life.

It is not at all clear, however, that Jesus' relations with other people are trinitarian by following the trinitarian pattern of his relations with Father and Spirit. The human being Jesus relates to Father and Spirit in much the way the second person of the trinity does. Because Jesus *is* the second person of the trinity, he retains as a human being the same sort of relations with Father and Spirit that he has as the second person of the trinity. This is a very direct translation of trinitarian relations into a human form. But none of that is true for Jesus' relations with other people; they are simply not the direct translation of trinitarian relations into a human form in the same way.

Indeed, if one takes into account the whole story of the economy – both parts of it – and avoids isolated attention to what is narrated about the relationships among the trinitarian persons, it is not at all apparent that the one side establishes the pattern for the other: Jesus' relations with Father and Spirit do not appear in any obvious way to be the model for his relations with other human beings in the story. Rather than establish the pattern for human relationships, Jesus' relations with Father and Spirit are – quite obviously – the sort of relations that it is appropriate for humans to have with Father and Spirit. These are the kind of relations with Father and Spirit we are supposed to have by virtue of being united with Christ through the power of the Spirit so as to share in his life. We are to worship the Father following the precedent of Jesus' own prayers, carry out the will of the Father as human beings filled up with and empowered by the Holy Spirit as Jesus was, which means working for the well-being of others as Jesus did, and so on. But why think we will relate to other humans in the process in anything like the way we are to relate here to Father and Spirit?

One can make the same rather obvious point in light of the way we are incorporated within the trinitarian life by being joined to Christ.

When humans are incorporated into the trinity through Christ, different people are not spread across the trinity to take on its pattern; instead, we all enter at the same point, we all become identified with the same trinitarian person, members of the one Son, sons by the grace of the Holy Spirit; and move as a whole, as one body, with the second person of the trinity in its movements within the dynamic life of the trinity. The trinity does not therefore in any obvious way establish the internal structure of human community, the unity of the trinity being what makes human society one, the diversity of the persons establishing its internal complexity. Instead, the one divine Son and the one divine Spirit are what make human society one; we are one, as the Pauline texts suggest, because we all have the same Spirit and because we are all members of the one Son. And the diversity of this human community is internal, so to speak, to that one Spirit and one Son; the diversity is a diversity of gifts of that Spirit and of that one Son's bodily members. Rather than establishing the pattern of unity and diversity in human community, the trinity establishes more what that one united but diverse body of Spirit-filled sons by grace does, how it moves; the whole body of Christians moves together in the way any single human being, united to Christ's own life, follows a trinitarian dynamic.

There are of course New Testament passages that suggest the unity between Son and Father is what unity in human community is to be like: Jesus asks his Father "that they may be one, as we are one" (John 17: 11, 22); "I ask ... that they may all be one. As you, Father, are in me and I am in you, may they also be in us" (John 17: 20–1; also 22–3). Rather than reading these passages as some brief for understanding the unity of human persons on an analogy with unity among persons of the trinity, one can, however, take them to be indicating simply the centrality of Christ, and of his relations with the Father, for our relations with the Father. Christ's unity with the Father is what ensures our unity with the Father, in that our relationship with the Father comes by way of him. Because the Son and Father are one, when we take our identity as a community from life in Christ, we will be one with the Father in something like the way he is, through him. The point of "as" in these passages is not to highlight the similarity between our unity with the Father and Jesus' unity with him but the difference: the community between Jesus and the Father cannot be imitated by us, it is exceptional, because based on what Jesus alone enjoys as the Word incarnate – a unity of nature with the Father.[70] We, to the contrary, are one with the Father only through grace by way of Christ. Thus, Athanasius argues:

> If ... it were possible for us to become as the Son in the Father, the words [in those verses of John 17] ought to run ... as the Son is in the Father ... But by saying "in us" [there is] pointed out the distance and difference; that he indeed is alone in the Father alone, as only Word and Wisdom; but we in the Son, and through him in the Father.[71]

In short, "the Son is in the Father in one way [by nature]; and we become in him in another [by grace]."[72]

There is a community-forming aspect to our relations with the Father by way of Christ, but again these passages can be taken simply to highlight the importance of Christ's own relations with the Father for it. *Through* the Son we will one day unite together (be completely of one mind and heart) to do the will of the Father – be one with the Father is his mission for the world – as Jesus was. Christ is one with the Father, perfectly doing the Father's will, and therefore by being united with Christ we shall all be one by being one with the Father as Jesus was, united in doing the Father's will in the way Jesus did. Christ is what unifies us in our relations with the Father, as both a gift to us and as an example for us. Summarizing the import of John

---

[70] See Athanasius, "Four Discourses," Discourse 3, chapter 25, sections 19–25, pp. 404–7; and Augustine, *Tractates on the Gospel of John 55–111*, trans. John Rettig, Fathers of the Church Series (Washington, DC: Catholic University of America Press, 1994), Tractate 110, especially pp. 289–90.

[71] Athanasius, "Four Discourses," Discourse 3, chapter 25, section 21, p. 405.

[72] *Ibid.*, section 24, p. 407.

17:23, Athanasius discusses the centrality of what Christ does to unify us in relation to the Father this way: "Father, as you have given to me to bear [this body], grant to them your Spirit, that they too may be one and may be perfected in me."[73] And he affirms the centrality of Christ as example to the same end: "As he, being the Word, is in his own Father, so ... we too, taking an exemplar and looking at him, might become one towards each other in concord and oneness of spirit."[74]

The way Jesus exhibits in a human form the relations among Father, Son, and Spirit, has an effect, of course, on his relations with other people: Jesus relates to other people in highly unusual ways, which have everything to do with his relations to Father and Spirit. The way the persons of the trinity relate to one another over the course of Jesus' life, relations among the divine persons in which we are to share by being united with Christ in the Spirit, bring with them changed relations among human beings. The Son is sent by the Father into the world, and empowered by the Spirit, to carry out a mission that brings him into a relationship with us. A life empowered by the Spirit in service to the mission of the Father for the world means that Jesus is with and for us, and that we, in turn, are to be with and for one another, in the way that mission specifies.

The character of that mission, as Jesus' own way of life makes clear, is to inaugurate a life-brimming, Spirit-filled community of human beings akin to Jesus in their relations with God. The mission means bringing in the kingdom or new community that accords with Jesus' own healing, reconciling, and life-giving relations with others. This way of being is what the trinitarian relations as they show themselves in the economy – Jesus' praying to the Father and serving the will of the Father in the power of the Spirit – amount to in human relational terms. Jesus' relations with Father and Spirit make his whole life one of worshipful, praise-filled, faithful service to the Father's mission of bringing in the kingdom; that is to be the

---

[73] *Ibid.*, section 23, p. 406   [74] *Ibid.*, section 19, p. 405.

character of our lives too, both in and out of church, as we come to share Jesus' life. We are to participate in the Father's mission for the world, mediating the life-giving Spirit of Christ through union with him. Glorified, worked over into Christ's image, so as to take on his shape in relations with other human beings, we are to form the citizens or members of a new kingdom or community with Christ as both the director and forerunner of the sort of new lives we are to lead together.

The question then becomes what the kingdom has to do with the trinity that works to bring it about. To what extent is the kingdom, in other words, not just the consequence of a trinitarian life like Jesus' in relation to Father and Spirit, bound up, part and parcel of it for that reason, but also reflective of the trinity's own character? A lot depends here on exactly what one thinks the kingdom is like. I would venture that the kingdom is like the trinity in that both are supremely life-affirming of all their members, organized to bring about the utmost flourishing of all. Both are paradigmatic instances of what I have called elsewhere a community of mutual fulfillment in which the good of one becomes the good for all.[75] The trinity is coming to us to give us the sort of life-giving relations of mutual flourishing that the trinity itself enjoys.

There is an analogy then with the trinity, but not a very specific one. What one gets out of the trinity here for an understanding of the kingdom one might also find by treating any number of other theological topics – the incarnation, for example. The incarnation too – but in a significantly different manner from what one finds in the trinity – sets up a kinship, in this case between humanity and divinity, a community of now mutual fulfillment in that the human is to benefit from what the divine already enjoys. In some ways, indeed, the incarnation is a better analogy for the sort of human community or kingdom to be set up. When every human being becomes one in Christ this overrides in a significant sense forms of

[75] See Kathryn Tanner, *Economy of Grace*, pp. 75, 79, 82, 84, 101, 142.

already established kinship that would otherwise keep people apart; this is an unnatural community one might say in much the way humanity and divinity in Christ are an unnatural community, made up of what is naturally disparate and dissimilar. More like the relationship between humanity and divinity in Christ than the trinity, this is a community of previously diverse persons brought together only by something different from all of them that they share – Christ.

Whatever the case, the analogy here is no more with the trinity than with the incarnation. And that means the analogy is not specifically with the trinity at all. The crucial principles that bring out the connection between the trinity and the kingdom – for example, the principle that relations among the members should promote the flourishing of all – are more general than anything the trinity itself – or the incarnation, for that matter – exhibits. The same general principles of community can be found in the trinity, the incarnation, and the kingdom.

There is more than an analogy, then, between the kingdom and these principles, in that the kingdom is simply a case of them. The various cases of the principles – the trinity, the incarnation, and the kingdom – form, however, only analogues with one another, because these very general principles take different, quite particular shapes depending on the very different things at issue. For example, in the trinity the members benefit from all *being* the same thing in different modes or manners; in the kingdom, the members all benefit from *sharing* or participating in the same thing – the very glory of God.

Now that we see that the kingdom to come is the sort of human community the economic trinity itself specifies, it becomes very difficult to sustain the merely formal and abstract preoccupations of much trinitarian political theology. One can no longer stop with attacks on individualism or on monolithic social identities and fail to consider the character of society more concretely. Even non-individualistic, internally diverse communities must be subject to further critical scrutiny with reference to the goals to which they are dedicated. Are those communities dedicated to anything like what Jesus was dedicated to in his relations with other people? Are they dedicated to policies ensuring the comprehensive well-being of all their members, especially the disempowered, following Jesus' own concern for the physical and spiritual well-being of the poor and suffering?

Replacing the idea of modeling human relations on the trinity with the idea of sharing in the life of the trinity as it works for the world also makes a small but significant contribution to resolving problems of gendered language. It prevents one from making too much of gender differences by lining them up with different persons of the trinity, and thereby reinforcing them. All persons, of whatever gender, are to be associated with the very same person of the trinity – the second one, the Son – for the same reason and in the same way – by virtue of what the Spirit of Christ does for them.

Such a shift in perspective certainly is a major help in addressing the other problems mentioned earlier. For example, difficulties in understanding the immanent trinity present no problem because the trinity provides direction for our social relations by other means – by showing us how Jesus relates to other human beings. We do not need to comprehend the trinity any better, to fathom it more fully, in order to draw inferences about human community from it; we can look instead to the character of Jesus' human relationships to understand its implications for human life more directly.

The present strategy of looking to the economy avoids, moreover, both the temptation among politically progressive theologians to downplay Jesus' subordination to the Father, and the temptation among less progressive ones to play it up. There is no impetus to do either because one does not expect Jesus' relations with Father and Spirit to be offering a model for human relations. Jesus' relations with Father and Spirit are what our relations to the triune God are to be like – relations of worship and service to the trinity's mission for the world – relations that subordinate humans to God in a perfectly appropriate way. One can therefore do justice to the economy in suitably nuanced fashion, taking into account the specifics of the scripturally narrated relationship at issue. What scripture is trying to tell us here, for example, is not the kind of relationship that human beings are to have with one another, but the sort of relationship that holds specifically between Jesus, the Word incarnate, and the Father. We will one day share in that relationship through unity with Christ but only in ways that are in keeping with our being merely human and not divine by nature as Christ was.

One no longer has a reason, in short, to expect all relationships in the gospel narratives to take exactly the same form whatever their subject matter. One can instead attend to the specific differences of these relationships as the New Testament recounts them. The same general pattern of trinitarian relations may recur (as we saw in the last chapter) but this always happens in differentiated ways that reflect the inclusion of the human within those trinitarian relations and the difference between Christ and us. Human relations do not share in the relations among the persons of the trinity in an undifferentiated fashion – as if the trinity were simply a group of friends expanding their social circle to include new members.[76] As we saw in the last chapter, humans do not have exactly the same relationship with members of the trinity as the persons of the trinity do – let alone the same kind of relationship with one another.

In this differentiated view of the way the trinity enters our world, Jesus himself does not have exactly the same relationship with Father and Spirit in the economy as the Word considered apart from the incarnation does. The same pattern may recur but the specifics can be quite different. In contrast (for instance) to the perfect equality of the trinitarian persons in and of themselves, Jesus, the Word incarnate, seems subordinate to the Father in that he obeys the Father at least apparently against his own best interests, and so on, as we have talked about before. Unlike what should be the case within the trinity, relations of dependence between the Word incarnate and

[76] Bauckham, "Moltmann's *Trinity and the Kingdom*," pp. 160–1.

the other members of the trinity are not fully mutual, once again because of the real difference his humanity makes to those relations. For example, the way the Word incarnate depends on Father and Spirit for the continued life of his own flesh after death is not matched by any dependence of their lives on his, as befits the fact that the Word incarnate is not simply the Word but a human being as well. Because Jesus is a finite human being and not merely the Word who enjoys perichoretic relations with the other members of the trinity, the perfectly indivisible way in which Son and Father are found in and with one another seems to give way in the economy, as suggested earlier, to become something more like a dialogical fellowship among separable people of concerted will.

One can give a similarly differentiated account, moreover, of the way Jesus relates to others, divine or human, depending on whether one considers Jesus in his humanity or his divinity. Thus, Jesus relates to other human beings as their savior in virtue of the power he has as the Word of God; and he relates to them as their fellow sufferer in sharing with them a humanity that needs to be elevated and healed from the effects upon it of a conflict-ridden, death-dealing world. In a similar fashion, Jesus' relations to the Father and Spirit insofar as he is divine do not perfectly match the relations he has with them insofar as he is human. For example, while it reflects the fact that as divine Son he is all that he is of and from the Father, Jesus' relations to the Father take the specific form of worship only insofar as he is a man.

Human beings share in trinitarian relations as mere human beings with all the differences that finitude and sin appropriately make to those relations. When humans image the trinity they do not conform exactly to the relations between the Son incarnate and the Father. For example, Jesus' whole life from the very beginning is lived in perfect correspondence to the Father's will for the kingdom, while our lives come only secondarily into an imperfect correspondence with it because of our finitude and sin. Because we are only human, we share, moreover, in those relations by way of Christ and not in his place, as if we were his equivalent. And that means when we relate to other human beings in the trinitarian fashion of Jesus' own life, we do not do so in exactly the way he does. Because he is divine, Jesus has a superior position in relating to other people – he saves them, for example – and we do not.

Finally – because of the differentiated way in which human relations are formed in the image of the trinity – one need not fear that basing political recommendations on the trinity will produce either an unrealistic politics or an uncritically complacent one. The different fashions in which the same pattern of the trinity appears means that a trinitarian politics can be realistic. One no longer need expect or demand a simple reproduction everywhere of the relations that members of the trinity have with one another – where they are clearly inappropriate, where they simply seem inapplicable. Political recommendations based on the trinity gain realism as they follow the highly differentiated ways the trinity works within the world; trinitarian political recommendations become appropriately gauged thereby to the actual character of humans.

Yet, uncritical complacency is also overcome. The workings of the trinity in the world that seem to be of a character we can easily imitate are for the sake of, are the means to, something more: life-giving relations of perfectly mutual flourishing that the divine persons themselves enjoy. Complacency is overcome by a sense that there are heights of relationship above our own, ones that our relations with one another in themselves can only strive to approximate without ever matching – at the highest, relations among perfectly equal trinitarian persons swirling in and out of one another with such a completely realized fullness of mutual communication that any need for loss or gain is thereby excluded. Without taking on the character of such perfection in and of themselves, human relations might hope to gain that height by being united with the trinity and thereby incorporated within its own life, as the trinity itself makes that possible by its coming graciously into the world to us in Christ.

6 | Death and sacrifice

Serious attention to the incarnation enables one to revise traditional descriptions and explanations of the saving significance of the cross so as to do justice to the criticisms that feminist and womanist theologians rightfully lodge against classical atonement theories.[1] This is among the more controversial claims to be found in my *Jesus, Humanity and the Trinity*.[2] I expand upon the argument now, and show how it provides a nuanced and subtle reworking of classical images for the cross – the primary test case for my purposes here being images of sacrifice.

Reflecting to some extent theological differences about the nature of sin and salvation as well as the complexity of the event itself on a Christian understanding of it (for example, this event involves both God and humanity in Jesus' person, and both Jesus' sinless humanity and the acts of sinners against him), descriptions of what is happening on the cross are notoriously diverse among the followers of Jesus, beginning at least with the New Testament. The cross is the final expression of God's wrathful condemnation of sin, the place where sin, and the suffering and death it entails, are borne by Christ and put

---

[1] For summary statements of feminist and womanist worries, see Elisabeth Schüssler Fiorenza, "The Execution of Jesus and the Theology of the Cross," in *Jesus: Miriam's Child, Sophia's Prophet* (New York: Continuum, 1994), pp. 97–128; and Delores Williams, "Black Women's Surrogate Experience and the Christian Notion of Redemption," in Paula M. Cooey, William R. Eakin, and Jay B. McDaniel (eds.), *After Patriarchy: Feminist Transformations of World Religions* (Maryknoll, New York: Orbis, 1991), pp. 1–13.

[2] Kathryn Tanner, *Jesus, Humanity and the Trinity* (Minneapolis, Minnesota: Fortress, 2001).

to death, destroyed. The cross is the ultimate expression of God's loving choice to be with sinners, in all the sufferings of a spiritual and physical sort that burden human life in its sinful condition. The cross is the final act of divine humiliation, or the intra-trinitarian act whereby the second person of the trinity is abandoned by the first, in a divine self-emptying that makes room for a world of pain, sin, and death within the very life of God. It is the cultic sacrifice to end all sacrifices. It is the agonizing birth of the new creation to be revealed in the resurrection of the dead and in the new life of those dedicated as Christ was to God's cause. On the cross we find the final form of perfect obedience to God's will, or a man laying down his life for his friends. We see our own sin: the culminating rejection of Christ's mission of love as that takes shape in the execution of a religious and political subversive at the hands of imperial power.

These various descriptions of what is going on when Jesus is crucified have distilled over the centuries into distinct models of the atonement, each developing more thoroughly particular aspects of them and usually offering in the process some explanation for the saving significance of the cross. Thus, the moral example or moral influence model of the cross (stemming from Abelard) stresses the way Jesus' dying for us is the perfect manifestation in human form of God's self-sacrificial, condescending love, a helpful example for our imitation or morally powerful influence, spurring us to a similar love. According to the *Christus Victor* model, God is engaged on the cross in a decisive battle with the forces of sin and death, overcoming the devil for our sake. Restoring the beauty and order of the world lost by our dishonoring of God, Jesus, on Anselm's vicarious satisfaction model, offers up to death his own sinless life in honor of God, thereby rendering the satisfaction that humans owe to God but in a divine way that their dishonoring of God demands and merely human lives cannot provide. On the penal substitution model, typical of the Reformation but found as early as Athanasius, Jesus on the cross, through his perfect obedience and/or by suffering the punishment due violators of the law, fulfills the law's terms and exempts human sinners from penalties otherwise owed. On the happy exchange model associated with Luther, Christ takes on our sins and puts them to death on the cross while we put on Christ's righteousness through our faith and in that way find acceptance before God.

The disconcerting differences of opinion, and even outright conflict, among these models encourage efforts to construct typologies of their essential differences and establish criteria for their evaluation. The models differ, for example, on who is responsible for the crucifixion – the devil, human beings, God, or Jesus as the one consenting to his death and going willingly to it. They differ on who or what is changed via the cross: God (God's wrath changed to mercy); human beings (our hate for God changed to love, our fear before God's wrath changed to trust); or the whole situation (through the cross a new sort of relationship is set up between God and human beings). The models differ on the one effecting change: God brings it about or we do by following the way of obedience that Jesus models for us on the cross. Christ effects the change primarily through the powers of his humanity (for example, insofar as he is obedient), or through his divinity (in case God is battling the devil on the cross for rights of jurisdiction over us). The models differ on whether the cross is an interruption of God's relations with us or part of a continuous effort – for example, to win us back from the devil, or to express love for us in a way that will finally get through to us. And so on.

Criteria for evaluation have become somewhat standard by this point in the history of theological argument over the atonement and I understand feminist and womanist criteria to be very much in line with them. One consideration, certainly, is the unappealing or one-sided character of God that many of the models imply. God in the moral example or influence model might seem a sentimental patsy, without righteous anger or horrified concern for the destructive and wayward effects of sin on human life. On the vicarious satisfaction model, God appears more concerned about slights to God's own dignity than the sufferings of a death-filled world. Here and in the penal substitution model, God seems restricted in the expression of love by a rigid law or penal code of God's own construction. In many cases, one suspects God derives pleasure or satisfaction from death and suffering. Feminist worries about the cross as a model for abuse are perfectly continuous with the last concern, which hardly seems especially objectionable or outlandish in its basic form.

The outdated character of the mechanism of atonement in many of the models is a question too. Contributing factors here include, for example, the loss of the honor code among superiors and subordinates and penitential frame that gave Anselm's theory its cogency; and the modern sense (certainly since the Enlightenment) that an injustice would be done if another were punished or had to be obedient to the law in one's place. The womanist concern that classical atonement theories trade on ideas that would condone the surrogate status of black women – their having to do the dirty work for whites – and play down the now so obvious injustices of that surrogacy, seem an unproblematic example of the latter well-justified worry.

Another major question is the degree to which these various models leave other aspects of the gospel story, the other major dimensions of Jesus' life according to Christian understanding, unexplored or unimportant. The moral influence and vicarious satisfaction models, for example, slight the importance of the resurrection. The incarnation easily drops out of view on the penal substitution model: someone has to die or be obedient since those are the terms of the law but presumably the merely human quality of Jesus' acts is sufficient to meet the terms of any original contract or covenant that God sets up with us. The public ministry of Jesus is not obviously important on any of the models and this point in particular feminist and womanist theologians make forcefully.

Feminist and womanist theologians remind us that the death of Jesus must be brought into connection with his public ministry in a way that does not slight the saving importance in its own right of that ministry. The two are connected appropriately, feminist and womanist theologians tell us, if Jesus' ministry gave rise to the opposition that brought about his death, or if the message of the cross is to stay the course in dedication to the mission of God despite the costs in suffering and death to oneself that are likely in a world marked by sin. These connections between Jesus' death and his ministry turn one's attention away from any exclusive focus on Jesus' death and toward the character of the mission – for example, to the healing nature of Jesus' interactions with others, his acceptance of sinners among his close associates, and practices of inclusive table fellowship. Obedience to the mission, as that is pointedly displayed on the cross, is all well and good but the more important point is what the mission is to which Jesus' life is dedicated. It is true that obedience unto death is a proof of supreme dedication, but death, in and of itself, is an impediment to the mission and not in any obvious way its positive culmination. If the mission of God continues, it is despite Jesus' death and not thanks to it. Rejection and death stand in the way of the mission and must be overcome in a resurrected life that moves through and beyond death. To the extent the cross is simply the culmination of the sinful world's rejection of Jesus' mission, it presumably would have been better – a sign of the kingdom's having already come – if the suffering and crucifixion of Jesus had never happened. The new covenant or community of God that Jesus struggles to bring into existence would ideally not include them.

Feminist and womanist theologians in this way prevent human sin, along with all the religious and political aspects of the sinful situation that led Jesus to his death, from being eclipsed, as they tend to be, in models of the atonement in which God brought Jesus to his death or such a death was necessary to satisfy divine requirements. Identified as the consequence of human rejection and sin, the horror of the cross stands out in an unmitigated way: the death and suffering of an innocent victim, in and of themselves, are in no respect good; there is nothing saving about them as such. Once again, this reminder that theologians must remain cognizant of the sinful horrors of the cross, of the fact that this is a brutal, bloody death suited to a world of sin, is fully compatible with quite traditional and longstanding criteria for evaluating atonement theories (especially within Reformation circles).

Of course a feminist and womanist focus on Jesus' ministry can itself become one-sided, and therefore susceptible of critique according to some of the same general criteria. Despite the obviously climactic character of Jesus' passion in the gospel narratives of his life and the focus on it in Pauline writings especially, the cross can fall out of consideration altogether except as something simply negative. The usual recourse of feminist and womanist theologians is to dismiss the idea that there is anything saving going on in the crucifixion. Discussion of religious and political opposition to Sophia's prophets, among whom Jesus is numbered, can take the place of any further need for theological investigation into how Jesus saves us despite such opposition – how he saves in and through the extreme opposition that his mission faced and in contradiction to it.

A model of atonement based on the incarnation, I suggest, would supplement feminist and womanist theologies on this score, thereby deflecting criticism of them while resurrecting, so to speak, a nearly forgotten form of classical atonement theory. Following Thomas Torrance, one can say: "Union with God in and through Jesus Christ who is one and the same being with God belongs to the inner heart of the atonement."[3] Incarnation becomes the primary mechanism of atonement. Such a mechanism replaces altogether vicarious satisfaction and penal substitution, with their obvious problems from both feminist and non-feminist points of view; and provides a different underpinning than usual for the *Christus Victor* and happy exchange models.

---

[3] Thomas F. Torrance, *The Trinitarian Faith* (Edinburgh: T & T Clark, 1988), p. 159.

The happy exchange model is easily combined, as it is in Luther and Calvin, with a penal substitution view of the mechanism of atonement: sin needs to be put to death for justice to be done and Jesus does so on the cross by bearing our sins, putting them on. The primary mechanism of atonement on the happy exchange model would in that case be the legal one of the penal substitution model: the requirements of the law are met on the cross.

Christus Victor is not a model at all in that it fails, per se, to address the question of the mechanism of the atonement. Christ is battling the forces of evil and sin on the cross but how is the battle won? Gustaf Aulén, who is primarily responsible for the modern currency of this classical idea, associates the *Christus Victor* model with a ransom theory: God buys back or redeems humans from imprisonment or enslavement to sin and death by way of the cross. He also associates it with the bait-and-hook account of what happens on the cross that one finds, for example, in Gregory of Nyssa.[4] If one excises the fishing analogy, which has important non-legal connotations, the latter idea is that the devil takes Jesus to his death, as if he were a sinner whom death can rightfully claim; the devil thereby oversteps his bounds and loses rights to us. But the historical currency of these accounts of the atonement is just as restricted as the penitential and feudal conceptions that underlie Anselm's.

Aulén is aware that the *Christus Victor* model has some connection with the incarnation. But he understands the incarnation as merely a necessary prerequisite for the fight to be engaged: God has to enter into the sphere of sin and death, by becoming human, in order to fight sin and death. If the fight culminates on the cross, there is a continuity to the struggle across Jesus' life and death. The struggle begins with the incarnation where the fight is engaged, reaches a climax of intensity on the cross, and then moves through it to the victory of resurrection.

---

[4] Gustav Aulén, *Christus Victor: An Historical Study of Three Main Types of the Idea of Atonement*, trans. A. G. Hebert (London: SPCK, 1965), especially pp. 63–71.

Aulén does not see, however, that the incarnation is the very means by which the fight is waged and won. This claim is fundamental nonetheless to the early church theologians to whom he appeals. All of them view the incarnation, understood as the Word's assumption of humanity – the Word's uniting of humanity to itself in such a way as to make humanity its own – as the key to the salvation of humanity. It is in virtue of the incarnation that humanity is saved – first the humanity of Christ himself and then through him that of every other human being, one with him. Humanity is purified, healed, and elevated – saved from sin and its effects (anxiety, fear, conflict, and death) – as a consequence of the very incarnation through which the life-giving powers of God's own nature are brought to bear on humanity in the predicament of sin. Humanity is taken to the Word in the incarnation in order to receive from the Word what saves it.

The connection of incarnation with the happy exchange model becomes in this way easy to see so that the happy exchange model's association with penal substitution is broken. The happy exchange of the atonement is just a case of the saving communication of idioms that the incarnation brings about. As a result of the incarnation, the characteristics of human life become the (alien) properties of the Word, and thereby the properties of the Word (its holiness, its life-enhancing powers) become the (alien) properties of humanity in a way that saves humanity from sin and death.

The saving effects of the incarnation on this classical model are felt throughout Christ's life but no more so than on the cross, where those life-giving powers of the divine nature of Christ are so much needed – remedying the loss of the humanity of Christ's own powers of life as they ebb away in full physical and spiritual torment. The application of these ideas about the saving efficacy of incarnation to what is happening on the cross as to every other aspect of Jesus' life is quite clear in these same early church figures. Thus, Gregory Nazianzen maintains that the Word, in becoming incarnate, "bear[s] all me and mine in himself, that in himself he may exhaust the bad, as fire does wax, or as the sun does the mists of the earth; and that I may partake of his nature by the blending."[5] He avers again: "So he is called man ... that by himself he may sanctify humanity and be as it were a leaven to the whole lump; and by uniting to himself that which was condemned may release it from condemnation, becoming for all men all things that we are except sin – body, soul, mind, and all through which death reaches."[6] Gregory of Nyssa makes much the same point: "Although Christ took our filth upon himself, nevertheless he is not himself defiled by the pollution, but in his own self he cleanses the filth, for it says, the light shone in the darkness, but the darkness did not overpower it."[7] And he makes the point again in a way that quite explicitly applies to the cross: "Although he was made sin and a curse because of us, and took our weaknesses upon himself, yet he did not leave the sin and the curse and the weakness enveloping him unhealed ... Whatever is weak in our nature and subject to death was united with his deity and became what the deity is."[8] The incarnation indeed is the underlying mechanism of the bait-and-hook fishing analogy found in Gregory of Nyssa:

> In order to secure that the ransom in our behalf might easily be accepted by him who required it, the deity was hidden under the veil of our nature, that so, as with the ravenous fish, the hook of the deity might be gulped down along with the bait of the flesh, and thus, life being introduced into the house of death, and the light shining in darkness, that which is diametrically opposed to light and life might

[5] "Orations," trans. Charles Gordon Brown and James Edward Swallow, in Philip Schaff and Henry Wace (eds.), Nicene and Post-Nicene Fathers, vol. VII, Second Series (Grand Rapids, Michigan: Eerdmans, 1983), Oration 30 (Fourth Theological Oration), section 6, p. 311.

[6] Ibid., section 21, p. 317.

[7] Gregory of Nyssa, Adv Apol. 26, in Werner Jaeger (ed.) Gregorii Nysseni Opera (Leiden, 1960–), vol. III, Part 1, p. 171, cited by Torrance, Trinitarian Faith, p. 162.

[8] Gregory of Nyssa, Ep. adv. Apol., cited by Torrance, Trinitarian Faith, p. 162, fn. 56.

vanish; for it is not in the nature of darkness to remain when light is present, or of death to exist when life is active.[9]

Perhaps most explicitly Cyril of Alexandria says:

> There was no other way for the flesh to become life-giving, even though by its own nature it is subject to the necessity of corruption, except that it became the very flesh of the Word who gives life to all things ... There is nothing astonishing here, for if it is true that fire has converse with materials that in their nature are not hot, and yet renders them hot since it so abundantly introduces to them the inherent energy of its own power, then surely in an even greater degree the Word who is God can introduce the life-giving power and energy of his own nature into his very own flesh.[10]

Understood with reference to the incarnation, atonement returns to its English lexical roots: at-one-ment – a sense of the atonement that now can no longer be limited to the cross. Humanity is at one with the divine in Jesus. This is true on the cross as much as everywhere else in Jesus' life and that is what is saving about it.

Keeping this in mind, it becomes readily apparent how an incarnational account of the cross severely undercuts legal or contractual interpretations of the saving mechanism of the cross, typical of the vicarious satisfaction and penal substitution models. If God saves by assuming the very life of suffering and death to which Jesus is subjected, God's saving response to the events of the cross is not sufficiently external to them to make sense of a forensic analogy. God's saving act does not follow Jesus' obedience the way a reward follows the doing of good works. Nor does God's saving act follow Jesus' self-sacrificial death in the way release from debtors' prison follows the payment of a debt. In sum, God's saving action

[9] "The Great Catechism", trans. William Moore and Henry Austin Wilson, in Philip Schaff and Henry Wace (eds.), *Nicene and Post-Nicene Fathers*, vol. v, Second Series (Peabody, Massachusetts: Hendrickson, 1994), chapter 24, p. 494.

[10] *On the Unity of Christ*, trans. John McGuckin (Crestwood, New York: St. Vladimir's Seminary Press, 1995), pp. 132–3.

can no longer be viewed, in the temporally subsequent sense required by a forensic analogy, as any kind of legally mandated response – to what Jesus does on the cross, to his obedience, self-sacrifice, or suffering unto death. Saying any of that makes God's action to save come too late, too far after the fact. Instead, God is taking saving action from the very first in that here these human acts and passions are the Word's own.

To discuss God's saving action in legal or contractual terms is also to misunderstand the causal connection between what happens on the cross and God's action to save. What happens on the cross does not evoke what God does to save, in any strong sense. Those saving acts flow to the humanity of Christ in virtue of an already present community with that humanity – the strongest possible community in which what is the Word's becomes humanity's own – a community that holds prior to the meeting of any conditions and which in its intimacy obviates the need to meet them.

It is true that what happens on the cross is a precondition for salvation in some sense – just not in the way forensic models presume. If the powers of the Word are to reach humanity suffering under the forces of sin and death, the Word must assume, become one with, a life of that sort, as Jesus goes in suffering and abjection to the cross. The idea that Jesus must be obedient unto death, humiliated on the cross, in order to be exalted, means only that – not that Jesus is exalted, resurrected, as a reward. It simply means (as Athanasius makes clear in his interpretation of Philippians 2) that the Word must take on humanity as we know it in all its horrors if the powers of the Word are to be translated to that humanity in a saving way.[11] If anything more about Jesus' humiliation as a precondition of God's saving action is suggested, it is that Jesus had to be

---

[11] Athanasius, "Four Discourses against the Arians," trans. John Henry Newman and Archibald Robertson, in Philip Schaff and Henry Wace (eds.), *Nicene and Post-Nicene Fathers*, vol. IV, Second Series (Grand Rapids, Michigan: Eerdmans, 1957), Discourse 1, chapter 11, section 44, p. 332.

humiliated on the cross for the sake of salvation the way one has to be sick to go to the doctor, not the way one has to swallow one's pride and make amends in order to be forgiven, let back into another's good graces.

More subtly perhaps, the incarnational model of the atonement undercuts the sense of vicariousness in the satisfaction and penal models. In the claim that Jesus dies for us, the primary meaning of "for us" is benefit rather than legal substitution; Jesus dies to benefit us so that we will no longer have to live as we do in a sin-afflicted, death-ridden world. Jesus, as the Word incarnate, does act on our behalf: he steps into our place to act as our advocate and thereby does for us what we cannot do for ourselves. But in Jesus the Word makes our cause its own and does for us what we cannot do in virtue of the kinship established between the Word and humanity via the incarnation, because of the bond of the Word with humanity that the incarnation brings about. It is this incarnational identification of the Word with humanity rather than Jesus' simple standing in our place before the law that makes Jesus our substitute in the prosecution of our cause. Jesus does not represent us, stand in for us, primarily by taking on the position of guilty, death-deserving persons before the law. That, once again, is not what "died for us" has to mean here.

If the incarnation is often so evidently in the early church the basic model of salvation that extends to the cross, why does the incarnation drop out of modern accounts of the atonement, even among theologians such as Aulén with a special interest in the early church? One possibility is that Greek philosophical assumptions lie behind the account of how the incarnation saves and contemporary people no longer find those assumptions plausible. (For example, the incarnation trades on a Platonic reification of universal terms such as "humanity.") The incarnation would fall victim, then to the Hellenization thesis which Protestant liberalism, following Adolf Harnack, popularized. Even if true, however, the implausibility of its philosophical assumptions hardly explains why the incarnation is not at least included among the many models of atonement that contemporary mores and cultural assumptions render problematic. Such a charge, moreover, is unlikely to be true. As the earlier quotations clearly indicate, the saving efficacy of incarnation is not commonly explained by any technical philosophical means, but through the use of examples that are rather "homey" and commonsensical even to modern ears. We are told to think of the way darkness is overcome by light, or the way wood catches fire when set next to a flame. There is nothing particularly objectionable here, compared to modern worries, for example, about the injustice of putting innocent people to death, or especially time bound in its incomprehensibility to contemporary people, in the way the feudal code of honor underlying the vicarious satisfaction model now seems to be.

A much more plausible explanation for absence of attention to it is that incarnation is being understood – misunderstood – in ways that make it hard to see its connection with the cross. One such misunderstanding is to see the incarnation in a narrow temporally indexed way – that is, as simply referring to Jesus' birth – and therefore separated from the cross by the whole intervening span of Jesus' life. The incarnation, however, refers primarily to the fact that the Word has assumed or united the humanity of Jesus to itself. That assumption of humanity by the Word is of course responsible for the fact that the man Jesus exists at all; it is therefore a way of talking about Jesus' birth. But it also underlies and makes sense of what happens over the whole course of Jesus' existence, from his birth to his death and beyond: his whole human life and death are that of the Word incarnate. On an understanding of incarnation as the underlying precondition for the whole of Jesus' life and death, it makes perfect sense, as one finds in some quotations I cited, to associate the verses of the Gospel of John that introduce the birth of Jesus – the light shines in the darkness (John 1), and so on – with the death of Christ. There too, indeed especially on the cross, one finds the light coming into the darkness.

To see the connection with the cross one must also not think of the humanity that the Word assumes as anything other than humanity adversely affected by the consequences of sin and in that sense fallen. One must not identify that humanity, for example, with the pure, pre-lapsarian humanity favored in medieval accounts of the incarnation. If the humanity assumed by the Word were itself in such great shape, it would have no need of becoming any different by being one with the Word. Since the humanity of the man, Jesus, who is without sin, nevertheless represents humanity in need of salvation, such an account of incarnation has every reason to stress the awful human conditions that the Word assumes in becoming incarnate. The humanity of the Word is humanity suffering from fear and distress, persecution by others, anxiety before death, betrayal and isolation, separation from God – all the qualities of death-infused, sin-corrupted life that require remedy. The cross then exemplifies in paradigmatic fashion the very character of human life that the Word becomes incarnate to reverse by making its own. Far from turning attention away from the cross, this account of incarnation understands all the struggles of Jesus' life as the Word made flesh in light of it.

Finally, one must not understand the saving effects of the incarnation to be immediate. If that were so, humanity would be saved right at the start of Jesus' life, and the cross would have no significance. For example, Jesus' own humanity would enjoy resurrected life from his birth, without having to move through death to gain it. If the incarnation saved humanity immediately, incarnation would become an alternative to atonement on the cross and not an explanation for what is saving about it: humanity would be saved by the incarnation rather than by anything happening on the cross. One must say, instead, that humanity suffering under the weight of sin is reworked in a process of salvation over time, from Jesus' birth up to and through his death. The incarnation remains a constant but its effects are not. Salvation, what the incarnation brings about, takes time, in short; salvation is a form of temporal, historical process, involving struggle with the forces of sin and death, and the sort of changes that typify any human life, sinful or not.

To understand this, one must see the humanity that the Word assumes as an historical humanity, one that alters and grows. "The child grew and became strong … Jesus increased in wisdom and in years" (Luke 2:40, 52). And one must see it as a humanity needing to be changed because of the forces of sin and death afflicting it. There is consequently in Jesus' life a passover, a genuine way or passage, from corruption to incorruption, from a life suffering from sin to one free from its effects.[12] Each moment of Jesus' life as it happens is being brought into connection with the life-giving powers of the Word, and the reworking of each of them takes time. Jesus is not saved from death, therefore, until he dies and not saved from the terrible consequences of his rejection in a sinful world until he suffers them, at which time those aspects of Jesus' human life are taken up by the Word and subject to a process of reworking through the powers of the Word.

The way this incarnational model of the atonement addresses feminist and womanist worries is I hope evident by now. Here is a God who works unswervingly for our good, who puts no value on death and suffering, and no ultimate value on self-sacrifice for the good, a God of gift-giving abundance struggling against the forces of sin and death in the greatest possible solidarity with us – that of incarnation. Contrary to a great deal of feminist and womanist theology, there is something saving about the cross here, but there is nothing saving about suffering, death, or victimhood, in and of itself. All those cruel and bloody features of the cross that feminists and womanists worry atonement theories positively evaluate are here identified in no uncertain terms with the world from which one needs to be saved. The mechanism of atonement does not mitigate the horrors of the cross, but highlights them: they are what gives

---

[12] John Meyendorff, "Christ's Humanity: The Paschal Mystery," *St. Vladimir's Theological Quarterly* 31 (1987), pp. 15–31.

salvation by way of incarnation its urgency. Nothing stands in the way, moreover, of a quite realistic appraisal of the religious and political reasons for Jesus' execution, since they make all the more evident the sinful, conflictual, and death-dealing world that the incarnation of the Word works to heal.

Nor need feminists and womanists worry unduly in this case about the tendency of atonement models to foster one-sided and narrow prescriptions for human action by elevating certain features of the cross to salvific status. Nothing of the human character of Christ's going to the cross – for example, Jesus' steadfast dedication to the cause of God at such great cost to himself – is a condition in any strong sense of its being saving. Or, one might say everything about Jesus' life that involves intimacy with the human condition for the sake of saving it is a condition of salvation in a weak sense. Jesus is obedient to the mission of God and that is a good thing but this obedience is itself the *result* of the same fact of incarnation that accounts for the saving character of the cross: Jesus perfectly follows the mission from the Father upon which the Word has been sent because he *is* the Word. Obedience cannot, moreover, be a matter for isolated preoccupation, in the effort to live as Christ does. An incarnational model of atonement insists upon the relationship between the cross and the rest of Jesus' life, since the mechanism of salvation on the cross is at work throughout the whole of Jesus' life. And the effects of this salvific mechanism – its point – are, indeed, much clearer away from the cross than on it – for example, in Jesus' healing ministry to the sick and the outcast, the advent of the new community of God, and Jesus' resurrected life.

Along the way, we have been discussing several cases where images commonly used of the atonement are seriously reinterpreted and critically revised on the basis of an incarnational model – for example, language of obedience, contractual images, and the idea of Jesus as a "stand in" for us. But I turn now in a more concerted way to images of sacrifice, since that imagery is often what feminists and womanists are most worried about – because of its possible lauding of self-sacrifice. The model of incarnation throws a whole new light on such imagery especially when the historical complexity of that imagery's associations is better recognized.

Sacrificial imagery in the New Testament is quite complex, reflecting in great part the varied character of both Old Testament descriptions of sacrifice in ancient Israel and contemporary Temple practice (along with the fact that the governing political context for New Testament writings is a Greco-Roman one, in which sacrifice also plays an important role). If Christians assume there is something saving about Jesus' death, this association with cultic sacrifice is perhaps quite natural: the blood (of animals) is key to establishing and maintaining cultic relations with God, God's presence in the Temple. Christ's death therefore comes to be discussed in terms of communion sacrifice: "This is my blood of the new covenant" (Mark 14:24; see also 1 Cor 10:16; 11:25), a reference perhaps to the sacrifices that Moses performed to seal the covenant (Ex 24). Christ is the lamb of God, the paschal lamb, slain as a sign of the favor of God that would bring Israel's redemption from Egypt and its establishment as a new people under divine direction and protection (see 1 Cor 5:7; Eph 5:2; 1 Peter 2:9; 3:18). Problems in or interruptions to a close relationship with God (moral fault or cultic impurity) are rectified through the blood of cultic sacrifice (see Heb 9:22). Christ's death on the cross is therefore discussed perhaps most frequently in terms of expiatory sacrificial rites (for example, in Rom 3:24–5; Heb 2:17; 1 John 2:2; 4:10, and Rv 1:5) – those rites that wipe away sins or cultic impurities for the individual or whole community. Since none of these sacrifices involves the sacrifice of a human being, it perhaps makes sense that there are other New Testament references to the Abraham and Isaac story – Abraham's bringing his own son to be sacrificed; Isaac's willingness to be sacrificed (Rom 8:32). There are also suggestions of non-cultic sacrifice of a moral sort. Jesus is like those martyrs for the people under persecution (see 4 Macc) who lay their own lives of self-sacrificial service before God as a pointed reminder of and appeal to God's steadfast love of God's people.

References to the Fourth Servant Song of Isaiah 53 in descriptions of the Last Supper seem to have the same import.

With this understanding of the historical complexities of New Testament references to sacrifice in mind, one can see how many of the standard atonement models distort the understanding of sacrifice that originally grounds its use for describing the cross. Legal or contractual interpretations are cases in point. While the animal sacrificed in an expiatory rite may be standing in for the one for whom the sacrifice is offered (the man offering it lays his hands on its head in some act of identification perhaps), there is no legal connotation of the sacrificial act as a satisfaction or payment of a penalty.[13] The rite is not propitiatory: its point is not to change God's wrath to mercy, but to wipe away fault or impurity in ways that a God already desirous of communion with us institutes.[14] Benefits do not come back to the offerer because the conditions of something like a contract have been fulfilled but because the rite trades on God's unbroken faithfulness to a decision to be with those engaged in Temple service. Propitiation is not the reason why the rite wipes away sin; no real explanation is offered. God simply wants to reinstate God's people to full communion with God and this is what God tells God's people to do in such cases.

It is sometimes maintained that ideas of propitiation or placation according to a kind of legal contract are a Greco-Roman influence: Greek content is being introduced into New Testament references to Israelite practices.[15] But even in so-called propitiatory ritual acts in a Greek or Roman context – sacrificial rites designed to gain the favor of the gods for the city – the relationship is not specifically contractual. The idea is to maintain good relations, social communion, via

[13] Robert J. Daley, *The Origins of the Christian Doctrine of Sacrifice* (Philadelphia: Fortress, 1978), pp. 34–5.
[14] See Frances M. Young, *The Use of Sacrificial Ideas in Greek Christian Writers from the New Testament to John Chrysostom* (Philadelphia Patristic Foundation, 1979).
[15] See Young, *Use of Sacrificial Ideas*; and Stanislas Lyonnet, *Sin, Redemption and Sacrifice* (Rome: Biblical Institute Press, 1970).

gifts; social relations generally, whether among human beings or between human beings and gods, are simply constituted by gifts, back and forth. Votive rites – pledges of future offerings upon receipt of a blessing ("I will do this for you, oh gods, if you do this for me") – only obligate the offerers and not the gods. An offering is obligated in case the gods act for one's benefit but the gods remain free to give or not as they see fit.

A fuller sense of the historical complexities of sacrifice disrupts too any atonement theory that focuses on the death of Christ to the exclusion of attention to the social and political circumstances that surround it. Sacrifice is all about the establishment of communion and exclusion in social terms, and about how community is to be organized.[16] Sacrifice is a kind of social mimicking and reconstitution of biological bonds. The way a sacrificial animal is taken apart and those parts redistributed – who gets what part – mirror social arrangements; social connections are indeed symbolically constituted through such rites. There is undoubtedly then political import to the way Jesus' death is a sacrifice. The character of that sacrifice might very well be tied to the practices of community formation advocated by Christians, according to Jesus' own model in his ministry. The political import of Christian refusal to participate in the sacrifices of the Roman state is commonly recognized, but the socio-political ramifications of sacrifice need to be brought more centrally into the discussion of what it might mean to say that Jesus' death is itself sacrificial. What forms of exclusion, community, and social organization are implied by it?

Modern atonement theories have the tendency, moreover, to read modern ideas of sacrifice into the New Testament references to

---

[16] See Marcel Detienne, "Culinary Practices and the Spirit of Sacrifice," in Marcel Detienne and J.-P. Vernant (eds.), *The Cuisine of Sacrifice among the Greeks* (University of Chicago Press, 1989), pp. 1–20; Nancy Jay, *Throughout Your Generations Forever* (University of Chicago Press, 1992); and Stanley Stowers, "Greeks Who Sacrifice and Those Who Do Not," in L. Michael White and O. Larry Yarbrough (eds.), *The Social World of the First Christians* (Minneapolis, Minnesota: Fortress Press, 1995), pp. 293–333.

sacrifice (or to make sense of all of the references in light of the last, moral sort mentioned above).[17] Sacrifice for us is a primarily non-cultic act involving self-renunciation for others. It is a sorrowful act in which what is sacrificed is not offered to anyone but is considered simply a necessary cost to oneself of doing what is right. Self-sacrifice in this way becomes a sign of degree of dedication, a mark of disinterested effort for another's good. The cultic sacrifices of Israel (and Greece) are arguably quite the opposite: they are all rites that either celebrate or end in joyous communion – between human beings and God and among the human beings so blessed. The important point of the sacrifice is not the fact that one has given up something, since the people offering the sacrifice are often the ones who go on to eat it. Sacrifices that take the form of a holocaust – in which the animal or grain is completely lost to the worshipper by being burned – seem to suggest, not so much the renunciation of what is one's own as a return to God of what is already God's, the return to God of prior gifts on God's part to us (of at least the first fruits of those gifts) as an appropriate act of thanksgiving. Expiatory holocausts – in which the burning of the entire animal seems a way of wiping out sin or ritual impurity that interrupts communion with God – should therefore be understood to reinstate meal fellowship. The joy of God's presence is their presupposition and end.

Atonement theories that make the death of Christ saving have the tendency to overemphasize the importance of death to sacrificial rites.[18] Certainly, the cross is associated with sacrifice because Jesus dies there for our sins, but that does not mean death is the center of the rites with which the cross is being associated. Calling Jesus' death a sacrifice might indeed be a way of drawing attention to something taking place on the cross other than death. Particularly when

[17] See Daley, *Origins*, pp. 2–4.
[18] See J.-P. Vernant, "A General Theory of Sacrifice and the Slaying of the Victim in the Greek Thusia," in *Mortals and Immortals* (Princeton University Press, 1991), pp. 290–301; and Sarah Pierce, "Death, Revelry and Thysia," *Classical Antiquity* 12/2 (1993), pp. 219–61.

sacrifices are viewed as establishing and maintaining community between God and human beings by their eating together, killing the animal has the same sort of significance it would have in any meal: the animal needs to be killed in order to be eaten. Even when the animal is not eaten (but burned), this seems a way of indicating that the food is reserved for God – no one else can eat it. "The holocaust and the vegetable offering ... which are wholly burned by fire [are like] a feast set for a superior in which the host does not share."[19] Expiatory rites – which seem to focus on the animal's death as a way of erasing fault or impurity – are an exception only when one fails to see them in light of the communion and thanksgiving meals that they reinstate and sustain. Understanding expiatory rites in this broader communion-rite frame, one might see the expiatory character of Jesus' "sacrifice" on the cross in a similar way – with reference to the images of communion sacrifice that occur before his death (again in Mark 14:24) and after – when Jesus eats with his disciples before his ascension and at a prophesied eschatological banquet (Mark 14:25). The point of Jesus' death being its provision of a meal is indeed a primary feature of Reformation interpretations of the Eucharist; it is central, for example, to John Calvin's argument that the Eucharist is a meal and not a sacrifice, a meal subsequent to the sacrifice on the cross that makes it possible. Even without the connection to communion sacrifice, it is possible to argue that what expiates in these rites is not the death of the animal per se, but the blood poured out at death. Blood purifies and reconnects across separation because of its life-giving powers – "the life is in the blood" (Lev 17:11).

While being mindful of the historical complexities of sacrificial imagery is important in these ways to the assessment of Christian atonement models, it is not sufficient. One must be mindful too of the way the cross is not a sacrifice. The political execution of a

[19] John Dunhill, "Communicative Bodies and Economies of Grace: The Role of Sacrifice in the Christian Understanding of the Body," *Journal of Religion* 83 (2003), p. 86.

previously beaten subversive on a polluted site outside the city gates is not anything close to the sacrifice of an animal without blemish in the Temple at the hands of a priest. Sacrificial language is obviously being applied to something that is not a cultic sacrifice in order to throw some novel interpretive light on the cross. But this means that the differences from ordinary sacrifice should also be salient – much more salient than they are to modern people for whom cultic sacrifice is not a daily occurrence, for whom the cross is the only reference to cultic sacrifice they know. When such differences are clear, something novel is being said about the understanding of sacrifice appropriate here. Viewing the cross as a sacrificial act from the perspective of the incarnation is one (admittedly somewhat anachronistic) way of developing such differences and thereby seeing what is odd about the meaning of sacrifice when applied to the cross.

Understood as an act of redemption that follows from God's decision to be incarnate – understood indeed as a continuation of God's decision to make humanity its own in Christ – God's action on the cross to save takes center stage. The sacrifice of the cross is then viewed accordingly – as a rite performed by God and not human beings. God is sacrificing there for us and our salvation. If the work is done by God, the object of that work is human existence in its plight of sin and death. The sacrifice is not directed here to God but from God to human beings. Humans are not offering anything to God; God is giving to us.

If the man who dies on the cross is not just a man but God as well, then in a sense God is both the one sacrificing and the one sacrificed. The whole act is God's. An expiatory rite where human beings kill something that they might otherwise use for their own sustenance is turned into a situation where God gives everything necessary, where God contributes all the elements, where God gives completely to us. God's being the substitute for human property in an expiatory rite in this way undercuts any element of human self-renunciation in a rite of that sort: since God is the victim, we do not have to sacrifice anything ourselves, anything whose use might otherwise have contributed to our well-being.

But none of this takes away from the fact that the one sacrificed – killed – is the human being, Jesus. The suffering, dying human being, Jesus, is the one sacrificed. The rite is directed as we have said to the human, performed for the human in its circumstances of suffering and death. Any expiatory rite is focused on the human predicament – on the problem of sin or cultic impurity – and this feature is only accentuated by saying that God, rather than human beings, performs this rite of expiation for our sake.

The humanity of Jesus suffering under the burdens of sin and death is the sacrifice but one must also remember that to sacrifice, literally, is to make sacred or holy – that is the sort of transformation that occurs through the rite, that is the point of the rite now directed to humans in all the ugliness and brutality of their sinful situation. To sacrifice is, in other words, to sanctify. Looking ahead to his arrest, Jesus says in his farewell discourses, "for their sakes I sanctify myself, so that they may be sanctified" (John 17:19). Despite the fact that it takes place on the cross, this sanctification is not being identified with death but with life. Life is being brought to Jesus on the cross, as his resurrection makes clear. To be sacrificed, so as to be sanctified, is now not to die but to live, in a perfected and purified form.

Death is significant here because death is what is being sanctified or transformed in the passage from death to life, and not because death is what does the sanctifying. God does not work sanctification by bringing Jesus to the cross, by killing him – human beings do that. In keeping with the focus on the life in the blood of the sacrificial animal, the "how" of this sacrifice is the life-giving power of the Word rather than the power of death. The life-giving properties of the Word are what sanctify Jesus' humanity – healing his wounds, raising him from the dead, bringing him back to community with his disciples.

Here death does not bring about the transfer of the sacrificial object to God, the transfer of this human being into God's possession, into the realm of the divine. Death itself (along with sin, rejection, and conflict) is instead what is being transferred to God by way of the already given fact of God's assumption of mortal flesh. Dying, suffering humanity is God's own because this humanity is that of the Word incarnate. Here God purchases us, in the sense of acquiring us as his own people, through the life-giving blood of Christ in the way God always acquires a people – through a covenantal communion with them (1 Peter 2:9; Titus 2:14; Acts 20:28). Now this covenant of shared life amounts to incarnation, the assumption of the humanity of Christ, however dire its straits, as God's own.

Sacrifices in general are performed in order that humans may cleave to God, form a union with God.[20] This sacrifice of incarnation is no different: it gives us access to God (as the Epistle to the Hebrews says). But here, in virtue of the incarnation, God cleaves to us before the expiatory sacrifice associated with the cross; on the cross, expiatory sacrifice thereby loses its appearance of being a condition for communion with God. For example, God's forgiveness of us on the cross is offered before any confession on our part of sin or impurity, which is crucial to expiatory rites. From the cross, without waiting for their repentance, Jesus asks the Father to forgive his tormentors and executioners – just as Stephen does while being stoned (Acts 7:60). The expiatory rite associated with the cross is not then preparatory to communion sacrifice; a communion sacrifice has already taken place in Jesus' person, in and through the incarnation.

Here is a sacrifice indeed without any sort of preparatory rite of purification. The humanity of Christ on the cross enters into the holy of holies just as it is: defiled by sin's effects, and blemished and impure through contact with death and the curse of the cross. No purification of the human is required in order for it to be in contact

[20] See Augustine, *City of God*, trans. Henry Bettenson (New York: Penguin Books, 1977), Book 10, chapters 3–6, pp. 375–80.

with the holy. Nor, for that matter, need the holy itself be purified of our sin and impurity, as in expiation rites on the Day of Atonement. The cross makes clear that the holy simply cannot be contaminated by contact with sin or impurity. There is, accordingly, every reason to bring the sinful, the death-ridden, and the impure, as they are, into direct contact with the holy: such contact is the very means of their sanctification, as the incarnation makes clear.

It is through direct contact of the human with the divine by way of the incarnation that sacrifice is overturned: Jesus is the sacrifice that ends sacrifice (Heb 10). Sacrifice ordinarily brings about communion with the divine in a way that respects and enforces distance. Sacrificial systems differ, indeed, in the degree to which they stress that distance. But Israelite sacrifice (like Greek and unlike Vedic sacrifice) perhaps "consecrates the unattainable distance that henceforth separates them" even as it "seeks to join the mortal with the immortal."[21] For example, the more expiatory rites come to the fore, as they arguably do after the Exile, the more fault and alienation are foregrounded in rituals that nonetheless bind humans to God. Like the Pythagorean critics of Greek sacrifice, Christian descriptions of the cross as a sacrifice would therefore be proposing a kind of closeness of contact or proximity with God that undercuts the very presuppositions of sacrifice for both Greeks and Jews – distance.

This has its social consequences. Through an alimentary code – a code that concerns eating – sacrifice is concerned with the careful delimitation and allocation of the place of human beings: human beings are neither the animals they sacrifice, nor the gods they worship.[22] Talking of the crucifixion as the sacrifice of a God/man, blurs the difference between sacrifice (to which the animal victim is thought to consent) and murder, between animal victims and human sacrificers, between human sacrificers and God – the very

---

[21] Vernant, "General Theory," p. 297.
[22] I am paraphrasing Vernant, "General Theory," p. 297.

divisions that found human civilization according to the presuppositions of sacrificial rites. The human divisions that sacrifice enacts by way of entrance and exit to the holy, by way of restrictions and inclusions to meal fellowship, by way of the parceling out of animal parts, are threatened with effacement as well. Since Jesus shares our sufferings, weakness, and trials and yet is the very blood spattered upon the inner sanctuary of God's presence, every Christian, like the high priest on the Day of Atonement, now has access to the holy of holies through him (Heb 4:15–16; 10:19–20).

Let me try to bring all this together in conclusion. Humans are not to offer sacrifices to God. God to the contrary makes gifts to us for use on our behalf (for which we are admittedly to be grateful in "sacrifices" of praise and thanksgiving). The whole of Jesus' life – before, as after his death – is such a life-giving sacrifice given by God for us to feed on, for our nourishment.

Putting those gifts to use for the good of themselves and others, human beings become living sacrifices (Rom 12:1). Not sacrifices sanctified in death, but in the lives they live, for life. Humans no longer offer gifts to God to be consumed in fiery holocausts – since God needs nothing but wants to give all, since God does not destroy what God uses for God's own purposes. Instead humans make a proper sacrifice in life-enhancing use, for the good of human life, of what God gives them in sacrifice – the life-enhancing powers of the Word. The direction of these living human sacrifices becomes in this way the same as God's: toward the satisfaction of human needs, the reversal of the effects of sin on human life. Service to the neighbor becomes the reality designated by "sacrifices to God." Here we see a connection with the sacrifices of martyrs, but a connection that now downplays their deaths in that it calls attention to lives dedicated wholly and unswervingly to God's mission of life, as Jesus' was. As one martyred for refusing to sacrifice said:

> We have been taught that [God] has no need of streams of blood and libations and incense. We praise him to the utmost of our power by

the exercise of prayer and thanksgiving for all things wherewith we have been supplied. We have been taught that the only honor that is worthy of him is not to consume by fire what he has brought into being for our sustenance but to use it for ourselves and those who need, and with gratitude to him to offer thanks by solemn hymns for our creation.[23]

---

[23] Justin Martyr, "The First Apology," trans. Alexander Roberts and James Donaldson, in Alexander Roberts and James Donaldson (eds.), *Ante-Nicene Fathers*, vol. I (Grand Rapids, Michigan: Eerdmans, 1989), chapter 13, p. 166; translation slightly altered following Everett Ferguson, "Spiritual Sacrifice," *Aufstieg und Niedergang der Römischen Welt* II 23/2 (1980), p. 1172.

7 | The working of the Spirit

This final chapter explores the split or bifurcated understanding of how the Spirit works that is typical of modern Christian thought and practice. On the one side of this split (perhaps the dominant side in modern times), the Spirit is thought to work immediately – both instantaneously and directly, without any obvious mediating forms – in exceptional events, rather than in the ordinary run of human affairs, upon the interior depths of individual persons, apart from the operation of their own faculties, in ways that ensure moral probity and infallible certainty of religious insight. On the other side of the split, the Spirit is thought to work gradually, and without final resolution, in and through the usual fully human and fully fallible, often messy and conflict-ridden public processes of give and take in ordinary life. On this second view, the Spirit does not begin to work where ordinary sorts of human operation come to an end. To the contrary, the Spirit works through the whole of those ordinary human operations, in and over their gradual and apparently meandering course, to surprising, indeed unpredictable, effect. The one side stresses, then, immediacy, interiority, privacy, singularity, and the bypassing of the fallibility and sinful corruption of the human in both the Spirit's operations and effects; the other side, historical process, mediation, publicity, surprise within the course of the commonplace, and the ability of the Spirit to make do with the fallibility, corruption, and confusions of human life for its own purposes.

This second way of understanding how the Spirit works holds great potential, I suggest, for the contemporary science-and-religion dialogue.[1] It resonates with both the method and conclusions of contemporary scientific investigation into the complexity of natural processes. It is therefore an appropriately modern understanding of the Spirit.

But it also a fully traditional one. It is the way one would expect the Spirit to work if one formed one's ideas about that from the way God works in Christ. Christ is the key, in other words, to the working of the Spirit.

While presaged by earlier controversies (which also concern, as I suggest in a moment, questions of religious authority), this bifurcated understanding of how the Spirit works is peculiar to modern times. It erupts in the sixteenth and seventeenth centuries – in Britain in particular – around the disputed question of "enthusiasm." Radical sects in Britain, associated with the zeal of Puritan extremism, millenarianism, and new prophecy – Fifth Monarchy Men, Levellers, Diggers, Quakers, and Ranters, to name just a few – claimed direct divine inspiration and special revelations in their opposition to established church and social orders, culminating in the upheaval of the English Civil War in the mid seventeenth century. But this sort of controversy over the way the Spirit works has a wider geographical range and reflects very general religious trends typical of the period.[2]

In the first place, this split in views of the Spirit has everything to do with a number of other splits or bifurcations that are characteristic of modern religious thought and life generally. Many of these, like the one here, involve a split between interior and exterior, personal and public. Faith, for example, divides in modern times into the faith by which one believes and the faith one believes in, faith as either personal trust or assent to the propositions making up

---

[1] The two views eventually converge, we will see, in response to criticism of one another. But they retain a fundamental difference of opinion about how the Spirit works.

[2] See Michael Heyd, "The Reaction to Enthusiasm in the Seventeenth Century: Towards an Integrative Approach," *Journal of Modern History* 53/2 (1981), p. 264 (for the controversy's specifically modern character), and pp. 275–6 (for its international range).

a public confession of faith, a bifurcation underlying the opposition between Protestant pietists and Protestant scholastics since the seventeenth century. Like what happens at both poles that carve up in modern times an earlier more integrated view of faith, especially the first view of the working of the Spirit narrows down an earlier account, splinters off certain aspects of a previously widely shared view of the Spirit and gives them undue emphasis. Of course the Spirit can work without mediation, and in a completely antagonistic relation to the operations of our usual faculties, but now this occasional course becomes the Spirit's typical one. The second view of the Spirit, on my reading of it, is not so much the opposite extreme, an equally one-sided, narrow view, as the attempt to bring back the fuller picture in an updated way.

Perhaps more obviously proving my point here about its modern character, the split in views of the Spirit also has everything to do with the bifurcation between faith and reason that breaks out in modern times. Christian factions do not simply line up here on one side or the other of the split – irrational faith versus faithless reason – as equally one-sided devolutions from a previous more harmonious integration of religious and rational forms of assent and commitment. The question for Christian controversy primarily concerns whether the split between the two is to be affirmed or not. When reason challenges the faith, should the claims of reason be repulsed as an inappropriate incursion on faith's rightful domain, or should efforts be made to reconcile the two on a new basis?

In the case of the Spirit, the challenge from rational reflection seems to be based on the recognition of the fully human character of religious processes, a recognition hard to square with the usual claims to religious authority – claims to be speaking, for example, a divine word or truth. Those who speak in God's name, who predicate their own authority on God's, are merely human beings, with their own narrow interests, erroneous views, partial perspectives, and moral failings. Appeals to the Spirit that think of it as an unmediated divine influence on human life, bypassing human faculties and human historical processes, repulse this challenge by fundamentally accepting the terms of it. Such appeals accept that fully human historical processes and religious ways of sanctioning claims are incompatible with one another. Appeals to the Spirit – unlike appeal to a more apparently humanly mediated scripture or church tradition – can simply erase the influence of those historical processes and with them any challenge to religious authority. God simply spoke to me directly, overthrowing in an instant everything that I would otherwise have believed, and therefore the unquestionable authority of what I now believe is assured. W. C. Braithwaite captures nicely the religious dynamic here on the part of so-called enthusiasts such as the early Quakers, in which a refusal to acknowledge human processes provided confidence in religious claims. "They believed that inspiration gave infallibility, a belief that men have often held with respect to the writers of scripture, and they had to learn, with the help of some painful lessons, what we are learning today about the writers of scripture, that the inspired servant of God remains a man, liable to much of human error and weakness."[3]

Unquestionable authority, which this understanding of the immediate working of the Spirit shored up, could then be extended to other more compromised, because more obviously humanly mediated, sources of religious authority. Especially in more mainstream Protestant circles it becomes common to argue that the traditional authority of church teaching and practice stems from the authority of scripture, and that the authority of scripture depends, in turn, upon the fact that the authors of it were inspired by the Spirit in the aforementioned way. Out of the blue, singled out without rhyme or reason, apart from anything they were in and of themselves, the biblical writers were taken up by the Spirit as its passive

[3] W. C. Braithwaite, *The Beginnings of Quakerism* (1923), p. 109, cited by Geoffrey Nuttall, *The Holy Spirit in Puritan Faith and Experience* (University of Chicago Press, 1992), p. 54.

mouthpieces. In a way that contravened the whole character of their human circumstances, when they appeared to speak themselves, the Spirit was speaking in their place.

The second view of the working of the Spirit – the public, messy view – contests the initial opposition between religious sources of authority and fully human processes, and offers a picture of the Spirit's working that reconciles the two. In so doing, one can argue, it counters modern trends in the understanding of the way God operates while accepting, to a greater extent than the other view of the Spirit does, a modern realism about human nature.

Rather than taking the place of human reason (for example), divine inspiration works through its exercise. As one of the Cambridge Platonists puts the point, "reason is always the means of apprehension, and 'that is not revealed, which is not made intelligible.'"[4] Yet no illusions are held about inspiration's instrument: "for fallible to fail, is no more than for frail to be broken; and for mortal to die."[5] Every human being and all human beings together, without exception, are fallible, prone to corruption from partial interests and narrow-mindedness, and therefore in need of correction, their taken-for-granted views properly subject to change over the course of time, and properly laid open to challenge from competing views. God need not, however, work independently of these facts of the matter, from outside them, but in them. Thus the always judicious Richard Baxter writes:

> Doth the Spirit work on a man as on a beast or a stone? and cause you to speak as a clock that striketh it knoweth not what; or play on man's soul, as upon an instrument of music that hath neither knowledge of the melody, nor any pleasure in it? No, the Spirit of God supposeth

---

[4] Benjamin Whichcote, *Whichcote's Aphorisms* (London, 1753), p. 1168, cited by H. R. McAdoo, *The Spirit of Anglicanism* (London: Adam and Charles Black, 1965), p. 89.

[5] Benjamin Whichcote, *Select Sermons* (1698), cited by McAdoo, *Spirit of Anglicanism*, p. 89.

nature, and worketh on man as man; by exciting your own under-standing and will to do their parts.[6]

And the early Puritan Richard Sibbes confirms: "The Spirit of God moveth according to our principles, it openeth our understandings to see that it is best to trust in God; it moveth so sweetly, as if it were an inbred principle, and all with our own spirits."[7] Bucking Enlightenment trends in the understanding of divine agency, God's working is not identified here with exceptional, occasional interventions that interrupt the ordinary operations of natural processes. One deceives oneself, the Cambridge Platonist Henry More suggests, "to suspect the special presence of God in anything vehement or unusual."[8] One is wrong, according to Thomas Hobbes, if one thinks "faith and sanctity are not to be had by study and reason, but by supernatural inspiration ... Faith and sanctity are not miracles, but brought to pass by education, discipline, correction, and other natural ways."[9] God is as much at work in the ordinary run of things as in unusual happenings, because the usual run of things is not being understood from the first in naturalistic terms, as if what happened there took place on its own, apart from God's agency. Benjamin Whichcote, another Cambridge Platonist, makes the point: "They are not to be blamed as neglecting or undervaluing the idea of grace ... who remind men that they should use reason and the principles of creation, and those who 'take offence to hear reason spoken of' are mistaken, for these things have a more than human foundation."[10]

---

[6] Richard Baxter, *Practical Works*, ed. W. Orme (1830), vol. IV, p. 226, cited by Nuttall, *Holy Spirit*, p. 169.

[7] Richard Sibbes, *Works*, ed. A. B. Grosart (1862), vol. I, p. 197, cited by Nuttall, *Holy Spirit*, p. 36.

[8] Henry More, *Enthusiasmus Triumphatus* (London, 1712), pp. 11–12, cited by Truman Guy Steffan, "The Social Argument Against Enthusiasm (1650–1660)," *Studies in English*, University of Texas Publication No. 4126 (1941), p. 52.

[9] Thomas Hobbes, *Leviathan* (London, 1651), p. 172, cited by Steffan, "Social Argument," p. 58.

[10] Benjamin Whichcote, *Several Discourses* (London, 1701), no. 23, cited by McAdoo, *Spirit of Anglicanism*, p. 87.

If human life is what it is (for all the corrupting influence of sin) because of God's working and not in independent self-sufficiency from God, there is no reason to think that God is working more the less we are. And that means we cannot rule out a divine sanction for beliefs we come up with on "our own" – for example, on the basis of the ordinary operations of our reason in conversation with others who disagree with us. The very fact that we come up with them in that way does not exclude their having divine sanction; God might very well be behind them for all that. So, for example, if God's laws for human life are given indirectly through human processes of judgment over time, it might very well be that the "voice of men [and women] is ... the sentence of God himself," as Richard Hooker suggests.[11]

God is likely to be behind the beliefs we hold, however, only in their very status as temporary, changing, site-specific, fallible truths. If God usually works with, rather than overriding, the ordinary character of human life, we have every reason to think that God sanctions thereby the limited, fallible, correctable truths typical of it. It is as changing and defeasible truths, then, that human claims would gain divine sanction. Rather than split off divine sanction from the mutable with human origins, we can admit that what God wants for human life can be altered, corrected, and improved over time to suit changing circumstances. For example, as Richard Hooker argues, it is the subject matter and not the source of a law that establishes whether it holds in the same form for all time; a law made for mutable people is itself properly alterable whether God or mere human decision is behind it.[12]

Divine sanction consequently does not bring with it an insistence on indefeasible certainty or uncontestable veracity. Something about the human is changed through the working of the Spirit, but it is not

---

[11] Richard Hooker, *Of the Laws of Ecclesiastical Polity* (1593), 2 vols. (New York: Dutton, 1969), vol. I, Book 1, section 8, paragraph 3, p. 176.

[12] See Hooker, *Laws*, Book 1, section 15, paragraph 3, pp. 221–2.

the fully finite character of our acts. Surely divine influence here is for the purpose of remedying the sinfulness of human operations. But removal of sin simply means the elevation, strengthening, purification, and improvement of those operations and not the discarding of their finite human character. When human processes become Spirit-filled, they are not made more than human themselves. Instead, something about their human character changes. From the chaotic formlessness of many uncoordinated voices or the shapeless convergence of multiple causal trajectories comes a new direction for human processes. Something definite emerges from our acts in history, as we work together and against one another, something that is not fully imaginable, controllable, or foreseeable by us – certainly not predictable from any one of our personal perspectives as individuals. Different too is the shape of human processes, their new communal organization and orientation. One with Christ through his Spirit we are bound together to be a community with a trinitarian form of life in service to others.

Reviewing the argument between the first and second ways of understanding the Spirit in light of the modern problematic just discussed might clarify the issues a bit further. Most generally, the recognition that human processes mediate God's working opens up to question claims to divine validation and in that way threatens to overturn the whole apple cart in which unquestioned assurance and a divine sanction for what one believes typically go together. Both critics and defenders of the faith who maintain the unmediated working of the Spirit accept the idea that the primary point of claiming a divine validation for religious assertions is to support their unquestionable authority. Understanding the same challenge more narrowly, one can say the existence of any inferential process at all behind a claim of divine validation opens it to question, by allowing one to ask: "But how can you be sure? Perhaps it is only a mere human being speaking, from a limited and interested point of view, and not God?" Appeals to the direct, immediate working of the Spirit on individual persons are from this point of view an attempt to regain an unquestionable self-evidence for the divine sanction of religious beliefs, using the resources available for this purpose in the empirical philosophies and scientific methods of the day. This is not mere hearsay; I am not forced to put my trust in the word of others (the writers of scripture or church teachers) about what God has done, a trust that might conceivably be misplaced. Nor am I left to draw the conclusion of divine direction of my life from indirect evidence (say, from the holiness that the working the Spirit produces in me). Instead, God came to me directly and I had the immediate experience of God working on me to change my views and my life. I have no more reason to question this than I have to question that the light shines when I see it; the experience itself is self-validating in an uncontestable way. As Richard Sibbes makes the point in a way that became fodder for more radical Puritans:

> How do you know the word to be the word? It carrieth proof and evidence in itself. It is an evidence that the fire is hot to him that feeleth it, and that the sun shineth to him that looks on it; how much more doth the word ... I am sure I felt it, it warmed my heart, and converted me. There is no other principle to prove the word, but experience from the working of it.[13]

So the more radical Congregationalist Walter Cradock can exclaim:

> For as in natural things, you know, that by the same light whereby I see the Sun, by the same light I know that I see him: So there is in the very manifestation of God to the soule, it carries a witnesse in it self, it is so cleare, that when I have it, though I never had it before, and I cannot demonstratively speak a word what it is, yet I know as it is Gods sight, so I know as I see him.[14]

The Presbyterian and eventual non-conformist John Owen makes a similar affirmation:

---

[13] Sibbes, *Works*, vol. IV, pp. 334–5, 363; vol. II, p. 495, cited by Nuttall, *Holy Spirit*, p. 39.
[14] Walter Cradock, *Gospel-Holinesse* (1651), "To the Reader," and p. 32, cited by Nuttall, *Holy Spirit*, p. 40.

Let the Sun arise in the firmament, and there is no need of Witnesses to prove and confirme unto a seeing man that it is day ... Let the least child bring a candle into a roome that before was darke, and it would be madnesse to go about to prove with substantiall Witnesses, men of Gravity and Authority, that Light is brought in. Doth it not evince its selfe, with an Assurance above all that can be obteined by any Testimony whatever?[15]

If you were not there to experience these things – and by definition you were not since these were experiences that singled me out personally, experiences shielded from public view in the depths of my interior life – you have no grounds to challenge them – no more than a blind man has the right to question what a sighted person sees. As Peter Sterry in the more radical Puritan party affirms, "I can no more convey a sense of this difference (between Reason and Spirit) into any soule, that hath not seen these two Lights shining in it self: than I can convey the difference between Salt and Sugar; to him who hath never tasted sweet or sharp. These things are discerned only by the exercise of senses."[16]

Upholders of the second view of the Spirit – even when they share this same empiricist bent – typically attack the self-evidence of the Spirit's influence on individual persons and reinstate fallible human judgments, often from public evidence, into every claim to divine sanction. Even in the case of a private revelation of the Spirit to me personally, beyond anything found in scripture or church teachings and therefore beyond the range of those usual public tests, I am drawing the conclusion that the Spirit is at work on me from the evidence of my own private experience – for example, from the overwhelming way I become convinced of something, out of the blue, on the occasion of reading a Bible verse, in the prayerful search

[15] John Owen, *Of the Divine Originall, Authority, Self-evidencing Light, and Power of the Scriptures* (1659), pp. 72–3, cited by Nuttall, *Holy Spirit*, p. 41.
[16] Peter Sterry, *The Spirits Conviction of Sinne* (1645), p. 24, cited by Nuttall, *Holy Spirit*, p. 139.

for divine direction, subsequently confirmed for me by my ability
to lead a markedly different way of life. The inferential process of
human judgment here properly admits of question – perhaps even
more than in other forms of religious authorization since I am
thrown on my own resources in forming these judgements without
the help and correction of others in making them. As Jeremy Taylor
maintains, "it is true, reason is fallible; or ... subject to abuse and
deception ... but if reason ... be fallible, so are the pretences of
revelation subject to abuse; and what are we now the nearer?"[17] My
vanity, my pride – even my simple credulity – might easily be at
work here leading me astray, making me think I have been touched
by the Spirit when I have not. Although "revelations and inspirations
seem to fall upon us from heaven," John Donne suggests, "they did
ascend from the earth, from our selves, from our own melancholy,
and pride, or too much homeliness and familiarity in our accesses
and conversation with God, or a facility in believing, or in often
dreaming the same thing."[18] Appeals to the direct working of the
Spirit on individual persons are therefore no better able to avoid
critical questioning than claims to divine sanction based on scripture
or church teaching. As John Locke says,

> he, therefore, that will not give himself up to all the extravagance of
> delusion and error must bring this guide of his *light within* to the
> trial. God when he makes the prophet does not unmake the man. He
> leaves all his faculties in the natural state, to enable him to judge of
> his inspirations, whether they be of *divine* original or no.[19]

The second account of the Spirit's working simply accepts (with
critics of the faith) the unavoidable fallibility of religious ways of

---

[17] Jeremy Taylor, *Works*, ed. R. Heber (1828), vol. XI, p. 462, cited by McAdoo, *Spirit of Anglicanism*, pp. 64–5.

[18] John Donne, *Fifty Sermons* (London, 1649), p. 201, cited by Steffan, "Social Argument," p. 47.

[19] John Locke, *An Essay Concerning Human Understanding* (1689), ed. Alexander Campbell, 2 vols. (New York: Dover, 1959), vol. II, Book 4, chapter 19, section 14, p. 438.

authorizing human claims; but understands this (against both the critics and those appealing to an unmediated personal working of the Spirit on them) to be part and parcel of the very old view of what appeals to the Spirit bring with them: the need for a complex process of testing and discernment in community. Again, Locke makes the point:

> If this internal light ... be conformable to the principles of reason, or to the word of God ... we may safely receive it for true ... If it receive no testimony nor evidence from either of these rules, we cannot take it for revelation ... till we have some other mark that it is revelation, besides our believing that it is so. Thus we see the holy men of old, who had revelations from God, had something else besides that internal light of assurance in their own minds to testify to them that it was from God. They were not left to their own persuasions alone ... but had outward signs to convince them of the Author of those revelations. And when they were to convince others, they had a power given them to justify the truth of their commission.[20]

But the story told so far is inadequate – even at the level of gross generality at which it remains. Appeals to the Spirit in modern times, as in earlier ones, are generally not for the purpose of supplementing and shoring up contested forms of religious authority, but ways of furthering that attack. The direct inspiration of the Spirit becomes an alternative source of religious authority with which to contest the usual ones – appeals to the authority of scripture, church teaching, and the God-given light of reason as that might find expression in the long-standing opinion of educated clerical elites. Perhaps most moderately expressed in the words of the early Puritan Richard Sibbes:

> There is a great difference between us and our adversaries ... They say we must believe ... because of the church. I say no. The church, we believe, hath a kind of working here, but that is in the last place.

---

[20] Locke, *Essay*, Book 4, chapter 19, section 15, p. 439.

For God himself in his word, is chief. The inward arguments from the word itself, and from the Spirit are the next. The church is the remotest witness, the remotest help of all.[21]

Or more radically by John Owen: "There is no need of Tradition … no need of the Authority of any Churches … A Church may beare up the light, it is not the light. It beares witnesse to it, but kindles not one divine beame to further its discovery."[22] And more radically still by Peter Sterry:

> The Papists … perswade us to receive the testimony, not of the Spirit but of the Church, for a Touchstone of Truth … Thus the Church's authority, not the Demonstration of the Holy Ghost, shall be the light of Faith to Truth … But wee need no visible Judge on earth, to determine our consciences; what is Scripture; what is the essence of Scripture. We have an invisible Judge and Witnesse in our own breasts.[23]

Appeals to the direct personal inspiration of the Spirit are not as much answering challenges posed to the usual sources of religious authority (as I have been suggesting so far) as putting themselves in league with such challenges. They are generally part of a minority Christian attack on established religious views and practices that use scripture or tradition as a defense against criticism. Appeals to the direct working of the Spirit are proffered as a means of prophetic dissent against otherwise entrenched scripture-based religious views or traditional church teachings. They also work as a defense against the persecution of dissenting religious opinion when such persecution is authorized and fomented by the idea that the majority view has the divine sanction of either scripture or church teaching behind it.

This remains, nonetheless, a distinctively modern dynamic. It does not easily fit, in the first place, with the analysis of

---

[21] Sibbes, *Works*, vol. III, p. 374, cited by Nuttall, *Holy Spirit*, pp. 43.

[22] Owen, *Divine Originall*, p. 44, p. 76, cited by Nuttall, *Holy Spirit*, pp. 43–4.

[23] Sterry, *Spirits Conviction*, p. 28, cited by Nuttall, *Holy Spirit*, p. 44.

charismatic-versus-institutional authority so often employed, usefully I believe, in discussions of earlier periods in the church. In the early church, the authority of those holding institutional office might be contested by individuals claiming special gifts from the Spirit of wisdom or moral and religious virtuosity.[24] But these are qualities that, for all their personal character, are publicly evident and communally recognized. Their acquisition, moreover, is generally recognized to require slow and patient processes of training – for example, ascetic disciplines. Nothing rides, in short, on their interiority or lack of mediation by ordinary human processes.

What the insistence on interiority or lack of mediation does is make the attack on other forms of religious authority much more thoroughgoing – more extensive and fundamental – than anything previously seen. The attack on public mediations of the Spirit is no longer equivalent to a simple attack on institutional authority in virtue of office or role in the church. Nor does it only bring with it the ability to bypass ordinary sacramental forms and stale interpretations of scripture when communicating with the Spirit, in the attempt to uncover more profound truths about God and more rigorous requirements for human life. It is also an attack on the authority of all communally and socially validated forms of intellectual, religious, and moral achievement that take their rise from long, slow processes of training or learning. It is in short a way of issuing a religious challenge to all the usual sources of religious authority on the part of persons without any obvious, communally recognized gifts of the Spirit – those without education and socially recognized graces of a religious or moral sort. Appealing to the direct influence of the Spirit upon them, people need not wait for gifts of the Spirit to be developed and recognized through the usual channels that church authorities control. And the hidden interiority of the Spirit's working effectively deflects attention from the

---

[24] For these conflicts between different sources of authority in the early church, see, for example, Rowan Williams, *Arius* (Grand Rapids, Michigan: Eerdmans, 2002).

publicly recognized character or reputation of such persons; it is a working that makes up for their lack of authority according to commonly accepted standards on all other social, educational, moral, and religious fronts.

The range of persons who are able to claim religious authority is not only expanded here beyond what was hitherto possible – beyond, for example, the extremes represented in the early church by those claiming an authority of spiritual virtuosity and wisdom apart from established institutional position, on the one hand, and those claiming the authority of office, however weak their preaching, theological teaching, or moral virtue, on the other. This expansion of who can claim authority presupposes a more thoroughgoing attack on the usual sources of religious authority themselves across the board. Appeals to the Spirit are not a way of taking sides in a controversy between one commonly accepted way of justifying religious authority and another commonly accepted one, in which the primary question is how to rank them in relation to one another. Instead, an appeal to the direct working of the Spirit amounts to a fundamental questioning of all of them.

The extensiveness of this attack on the usual sources of religious authority – whether person specific or institutional – has everything to do with the fundamental level at which sources of religious authority were challenged in modern times.[25] A general skepticism about the usual sources of religious authorization was fomented from within the Christian fold by Reformation controversies that pitted scripture (and private conscience in the reading of it) against established church traditions in ways that apparently precluded argumentative settlement. The controversies took place here at too fundamental a level to be effectively resolved. The most basic or bedrock criteria of religious truth, merely presumed hitherto, became subject to questioning by one's co-religionists in ways that

---

[25] See Richard Popkin, *The History of Scepticism from Erasmus to Spinoza* (Berkeley, California: University of California Press, 1979).

only encouraged a skeptical regress of mutual recrimination. How does one know church teaching is reliable? Church teaching purports to conform to scripture but perhaps it does so only according to a corrupt tradition of interpretation that makes a habit out of misreading it. The clear teaching of scripture might trump church traditions but what, besides the normative principles for reading it supplied by the church, is to prevent wildly disparate and arbitrary interpretations of scripture according to the unconstrained opinions of individual fancy? Without argumentative avenues of resolution, these intractable disputes over religious authority break out into a century of violence – religious persecution of dissenting views and religious warfare – that only further discredits and undermines all the usual sources of religious authorization. Unchecked religious fervor or zeal for competing religious viewpoints that divine sanction prevents any of the warring parties from questioning promotes the use of force on all sides and becomes, thereby, a simple recipe for ongoing bloodshed.

Appeals to the immediate working of the Spirit, occurring as they so often do (for example, in the English Civil War) among unlettered and socially disreputable lay religious dissenters, might be understood, in keeping with these worries about the violence-prone character of the usual sources of divine sanction, to be an attempt to break open the ossified rigidity of religious claims made on the usual grounds.[26] New voices need to be included; religious views, held onto ever so tightly by way of appeals to an unbending scriptural witness or unwavering church tradition, need to be open for the unpredictable revisions of a Spirit on the move again in the present day, in expected persons and places. The stultifying fixity of a written word or unquestionable teaching office would in this way be contested so as to invalidate the use of force against dissenting religious minorities.

[26] See, for example, Michael Walzer, *The Revolution of the Saints* (Cambridge, Massachusetts: Harvard University Press, 1965); and Christopher Hill, *The World Turned Upside Down* (London: Penguin, 1975).

Understanding the appeal to an immediate working of the Spirit in individual lives in this way – as a counter to authoritarian justifications of religious persecution – one could conclude that the second view of the Spirit is merely designed to blunt, even crush, its prophetic spirit. The second view of how the Spirit works is not directed with the same force as the first against the usual sources of religious authority; it seems to dull the very attack on those sources that the first appeal to the Spirit makes possible, by now extending the workings of Spirit to the usual sources themselves. The Spirit is not simply at work directly in individual persons to say a new thing, but at work in the institutional forms of the established churches, in the reason of an educated clergy entitled by their training to draw conclusions about how scripture is to be read, in all sorts of patient processes that require skills formed over time by some people more than others, in fundamentally unequal fashion.

No doubt the second understanding of the way the Spirit works can have a conservative effect.[27] It can be used to restrict the working of the Spirit to the regular, predictable channels of church tradition and church life – for example, to sacraments routinely administered by an ordained clergy. Anything out of the ordinary – anything novel or "singular," in the language of the day – becomes in this way suspect, simply because it fails to conform to the common and the run-of-the-mill. The unusual is taken for a sign, not of the Spirit, but of the demonic. Advocates of the first view of the Spirit would then be holding out for a free Spirit against its domesticated captivity in rigidly controlled institutional forms. What they properly object to, in the way the second account of the Spirit reconciles the Spirit with institutional forms, is this:

> the infinitely abounding spirit of God, which blows when and where it listeth, and ministers in Christians according to the gift, and pro-phesies according to the will of the Almighty God … is subject to the Laws and ordinances of men … to outward ceremonies, as

[27] For examples, see Steffan, "Social Argument," pp. 53–60.

Ordination, etc. God must not speak till man give him leave; not teach nor Preach, but whom man allows, and approves, and ordains.[28]

This second account of the working of the Spirit can also, however, be an effort to do better what the first view is trying to do: attack dogmatism and fanaticism in claims for divine sanction. The conservative potential of the second understanding of the Spirit is often altered, indeed, in the confrontation with so-called enthusiasm, so as to incorporate its concerns and give them their due. Rather than attack the usual sources with unmitigated ferocity from the outside (as the account of the immediate working of the Spirit encourages), the appeal to the Spirit on the second view would loosen up the usual sources of religious authority by increasing their flexibility, tolerance for diversity of opinion, and openness to change. By talking about the Spirit at work in them, one would be trying to increase the complexity of the usual sources to bring about their greater inclusiveness and internal diversity. More open-ended processes of religious formation would ensue, with stability no longer secured, in a top-down fashion, through enforced redundancy and mechanical repetition of a neat linear sort – that is, by simply insisting others believe what one tells them to believe.

So as to reconcile it with the anti-authoritarianism of the first, the second way of appealing to the Spirit opens up the usual sources of religious authority to criticism on grounds that, while requiring practice, are commonly exercised in some form or other by everyone. For example, consenting to the teachings of established church authorities is a particular case of putting one's trust in what other people say. Rather than rejecting that sort of authority altogether and relying on your own personal experience – what the Spirit has witnessed to you personally – one can subject those authorities to critical standards for trust employed in everyday life. That is just what it would mean to follow the directives of the Spirit in this case. One would ask oneself: "Are they in a better

---

[28] John Saltmarsh, *Sparkles of Glory* (1647), p. v., cited by Nuttall, *Holy Spirit*, p. 84.

position than you to know? Do they have reason to lie to you? Are their faculties impaired or their views compromised by moral corruption and narrow self-interest?" Or when considering the extent to which the Bible is an authoritative report about Jesus' life, one could employ the common standards for witnesses in ordinary trials: "In the testimony of others, is to be considered: 1. The number. 2. The integrity. 3. The skill of the witnesses. 4. The design of the author, where it is a testimony out of a book cited. 5. The consistency of the parts, and circumstances of the relation. 6. Contrary testimonies."[29]

The Spirit at work everywhere – in the teachings of the church, in one's personal religious experience, and in the complex processes of bringing them together for purposes of mutual adjudication – would in this way only open up the life of the church to greater flexibility and greater appreciation for the surprise of the new. Taking the other route – reserving appeal to the Spirit, as the first view does, to cases where the Spirit comes directly to individual persons – tends, to the contrary as we have seen, only to solidify the association of the highest forms of religious authority with simple self-evidence of an uncontestable sort. The Spirit trumps all those other purported authorities because I cannot doubt it; my experience of the Spirit speaks for itself in an indubitable fashion. Far from countering fanatical zeal, and a dogmatism of religious viewpoint that excludes all possibility of criticism from the outside, appeal to the direct working of the Spirit in one's personal experience would in this way simply reinstate fanaticism and dogmatism on new grounds. Uncritical fervor for what the Spirit has revealed to you personally would enter the fray, along with all the other competing claimants to similarly absolute forms of divine sanction, bringing with it its very own justification for violence. Enthusiasm would only aid and abet that "zeal for opinions that hath fill'd our hemisphear with smoke and darkness" – a reference to religious

[29] Locke, *Essay*, Book 4, chapter 15, section 4, p. 366.

warfare in England and elsewhere in the sixteenth and seventeenth centuries.[30]

Chastened by this criticism of its own violent and dogmatic potential, insistence on the immediate working of the Spirit in the interior of individual lives can itself easily be modified to stress the need for external tests and complex public forms of accountability. Both sides in the modern controversy over how the Spirit works would in this way be transformed in a kind of dialectic of mutual learning through opposition to one another.[31] External critique becomes the impetus for reform among advocates of the immediate working of the Spirit. Scripture, a public test of quite long standing, is certainly held up:

> The breath of the Spirit in us is suitable to the Spirit's breathing in the Scriptures; the same Spirit doth not breathe contrary notions. But there be, you will say, strong Illusions. True. Bring them therefore to some rules of discerning. Bring all your joy, and peace, and confidence to the word. They go together. As a pair of indentures, one answers another.[32]

Rational investigation provides another public test:

> If we give to reason, memory, study, books, methods, forms, etc, but their proper place in subordination to Christ and to his Spirit, they are so far from being quenchers of the Spirit, that they are necessary in their places, and such means as we must use, if ever we will expect the Spirit's help ... He that hath both the Spirit of sanctification, and acquired gifts of knowledge together, is the complete Christian, and likely to know much more, than he that hath either of these alone.[33]

[30] Joseph Glanville, *The Vanity of Dogmatizing* (1661) (New York, 1931), p. 209, cited by Steffan, "Social Argument," p. 41.
[31] See Heyd, "Reaction to Enthusiasm," pp. 262, 273, 276, 280; and James R. Jacob and Margaret C. Jacob, "The Anglican Origins of Modern Science: The Metaphysical Foundations of the Whig Constitution," *Isis* 71/257 (1980), pp. 254, 255, 258, 267.
[32] Sibbes, *Works*, vol. v, pp. 427, 441, cited by Nuttall, *Holy Spirit*, p. 43.
[33] Baxter, *Works*, vol. v, p. 567 and vol. xx, p. 179, cited by Nuttall, *Holy Spirit*, p. 84.

The working of the Spirit can remain here in its immediacy and interiority quite distinct from the public tests that check for the authenticity of appeals to it. At the very least the Spirit in its immediate working within the depths of one's own heart still tends to be privileged as a source of insight over the working of the Spirit through public media: for example, personal experience of the Spirit must underpin any public media that are reliable sources. In this respect the two views of the Spirit continue to be opposed. They fundamentally identify the working of the Spirit by different markers: the Spirit is still referenced more narrowly on the first view, in terms, for example, of direct personal experience however broadly extended or construed, and in an all-encompassing way in the second, so as to be inclusive of the internal and the external, the direct and the indirect, the personal and the institutional, the routinized and the spontaneous, and so on. But the more that the first view of the Spirit converges with the second in recognizing the fallibility of immediate experiential appeals to the Spirit, and therefore the need for public testing, the more it becomes for practical purposes indistinguishable from the second in all but emphasis.

How might the second, very broad view of the Spirit's working bridge old and new – a modern scientific outlook and a classical Christological one? The first view of the immediate working of the Spirit is clearly influenced, as I mentioned earlier in passing, by the empirical philosophies and scientific methods of the early modern period. This is an "experimental" approach in its reliance on personal experience and its suspicion of traditional and textual authorities. But with the end of the English Civil War and the restoration of the establishment church along with much of the old structures of national governance, scientific opinion in Britain, as represented by the Royal Society, clearly aligned itself against "enthusiasm."[34] In contrast to all immediate insight, "scientific progress would come

---

[34] This is the major thesis of Jacob and Jacob, "Anglican Origins." See also Heyd, "Reaction to Enthusiasm," pp. 272–3, 277.

through painstaking inquiry, the collection of evidence, and the testing of hypotheses. Knowledge then was not ... the result of ... God's direct revelation to the saints. God instead revealed Himself indirectly, [by means that] required close study in order to bear fruit."[35] "Patient, industrious scrutiny" was necessary to uncover the working of God in the order of nature; there would be no "easy shortcuts" to either religious or scientific truth, as enthusiasts hoped, via direct revelation.[36] In place of private truth, science offered publicly reproducible experiment, and conclusions that might be corroborated by any trustworthy witness.[37]

Truth mediated in complex fashion, through indirect revelation in the workings of the world, conforms, then, with both the second understanding of the Spirit and methods of inquiry in modern science. Such resonance between science and the second view of the Spirit is only heightened by the sort of conclusions about the world drawn by present-day science. This is a world of "intrinsic unpredictability," whose characteristically "open grain" nevertheless has the "self-organizing power to generate spontaneously large-scale patterns of remarkably ordered behavior," in and through contingent happenstance.[38] This is a world in which the Spirit might work "modestly," in continuous fashion throughout the totality of natural processes.[39] Contrary to the often socially and politically conservative character of the Royal Society after the 1650s, this is also a world open, as the second view of the Spirit insists, to an unpredictable future, beyond any ultimate human

[35] Jacob and Jacob, "Anglican Origins," p. 256.
[36] Ibid.; Heyd, "Reaction to Enthusiasm," p. 277. Robert Boyle is a fine example of this opinion. See J. R. Jacob, *Robert Boyle and the English Revolution* (New York: Burt Franklin, 1977), pp. 98–112.
[37] For the class connotations of trustworthiness in reporting, see Steven Shapin, *A Social History of Truth: Civility and Science in Seventeenth-Century England* (University of Chicago Press, 1994).
[38] John Polkinghorne, "The Hidden Spirit and the Cosmos," in Michael Welker (ed.), *The Work of the Spirit* (Grand Rapids, Michigan: Eerdmans, 2006), pp. 173, 176, 178, 180.
[39] This is a central claim of Polkinghorne, "Hidden Spirit."

control and beyond any self-serving human interest in fixed orders or rigid institutional mechanisms for enforcing the status quo.[40]

But if the second view of how the Spirit works is appropriately modern in its respect for the methods and conclusions of contemporary science, it is also the recovery of a quite classical account of the way God works in the world. This is a view of the Spirit stripped, as we have seen, of a modern either-or between the workings of God and creatures, an either-or that would turn what God does for the world into a merely miraculous exception to the general rule. As such it has everything to do with the understanding of incarnation in evidence throughout this book. The Spirit works in much the way God works in Christ. Christ becomes the key to it.

Just as in the second account of the working of the Spirit, in Christ God does not evacuate the human or push it aside. Rather than forming competing powers like water and fire that extinguish or evaporate one another, humanity and divinity are present together in Christ. This lack of competitiveness from God's side, indeed, is the very prerequisite of incarnation: if the divine is to be one with the human in Christ, the presence of divinity cannot entail the removal of the human. The same lack of competitiveness from our side, moreover, is the prerequisite of the incarnation's point: if we are to be fulfilled by God's intimate relationship with us in Christ, the human cannot require independence from God to be itself.[41]

Divinity and humanity in Christ are, indeed, fully themselves in being together. Even if in Christ divinity seems to retreat beneath the appearance of human frailty and failure on the cross, one must nevertheless assume its full presence in power to rework the human, to heal and elevate the human beyond itself. "The wonders evident in his actions we regard as sufficient proof of the presence of the Godhead, and in the deeds recorded we mark all those attributes by

---

[40] Jacob and Jacob, "Anglican Origins," especially pp. 253, 265–7.
[41] See Kathryn Tanner, *Jesus, Humanity and the Trinity* (Minneapolis, Minnesota: Fortress Press, 2001), chapter 1.

which the divine nature is characterized"[42] And humanity is only more fully itself in being thoroughly reworked by divine power. Refashioned by divine power, humans are more fully human in knowing the truth and choosing the good as they were meant to. Humans, as Thomas Torrance affirms, "are completed beyond themselves in God, so that instead of thinking that human minds and wills are crowded out by the presence of God [in Christ] ... we must think of them as reaching completeness in him and thus being established as human minds and wills. Properly speaking, therefore, in the Incarnation the presence of the complete God does not mean the absence of man, or the presence only of incomplete man, but rather the presence of man in his completeness as man in God ... Because the presence of God is creative, instead of excluding or overwhelming what is human, it posits it, upholds, and renews it"[43] Elevated beyond the human through participation in divinity, the human nevertheless remains itself. When we enjoy eternal life, for example, we do so as the human beings we still are. We participate in powers that are not our own by nature; we enjoy what remains beyond our ken as mere human beings. That is just to say we are not ourselves turned into God in the process.

God works in Christ as the Spirit works in us: in and through the human. Christ works the salvation that only God can bring, but in a thoroughly human way – through his speech, spit, touch, his blood poured out. The divine and human operate in Christ at the very same time in the very same acts. A man dies and in that dying the divine acts to save – in virtue, indeed, of its very togetherness with a human life so sacrificed. In much the same way, the Spirit directs our lives as we attempt to direct our own, in and through our efforts, together with us.

---

[42] Gregory of Nyssa, "An Address on Religious Instruction," trans. Cyril C. Richardson, in Edward Hardy (ed.), *Christology of the Later Fathers* (Philadelphia: Westminster, 1954), section 12, p. 289.

[43] Thomas F. Torrance, *Theology in Reconciliation* (London: Geoffrey Chapman, 1975), p. 155.

One should not expect the Spirit to bypass the problematic features of our lives in working to guide us, anymore than Christ does in working to save us. Christ saves, not by a divine life exempt from the mess, conflict, and loss of human life, but by one given over without reserve to those very features of it; he takes them, utterly and completely, to himself for his own. Christ's immersion in them poses no dangers to his ability to save; in the same way the messiness and conflict of our lives in community pose no ultimate impediment to the Spirit's working an unheard of good for us in and through them. Indeed, immersion in them forms a very step in the process by which good comes. In Christ, divinity conquers death by dying as a man, overcomes temptation by being humanly tempted, surpasses failure by suffering it. Life in all its agony and ignominy – the history of human life running down to its death in conflict with others – is all assumed by the divine Word in Christ in order, thereby, to be healed.

If anything it is not the human quality of Christ's life that is evacuated but its divinity, submerged as that is beneath a human life only gradually transformed by intimacy with it. The hiddenness of the Spirit in and under the human is therefore no exception. Divinity in Christ remains in all its power unabated as the source of human transformation, but that divine power is certainly not evident from the first. In keeping with the historical extension of human life and the resistant forces of sin within it, divine power only gradually makes its presence felt in reworked features of human life itself – and only very clearly in the end, the flesh resurrected, reconciled with its enemies, healed. The human is already elevated in union with Christ above itself to enjoy the very life of God, but this will be fully manifest in us only at a time of some unknown future reckoning. Sin will ultimately be extinguished in our lives; sin is indeed the water here and God the fire. But this will happen only ultimately in some disturbed, unpredictably non-linear process, comparable to the conquering of the effects of sin on Jesus' own life – what looks like final defeat, simple loss under sin's crushing weight, is not. The Spirit, we might hope, works through sinful historical processes in much the same way, prompting us neither to despair of our failings, nor forcing us to flee the very humanity of our condition. Rather than try to short-circuit the messy course of human history in a rush for certainty, or narrowly channel history's pluriform course with a demand for control, we can therefore continue in such human processes, however painful and otherwise disheartening they may be, with patience and without anxiety, in the confidence that, even in our ignorance of it, God's Spirit is making its way in and through them.

The Spirit's working in us is invisible in much the way divinity in Christ is invisible. The divine in Christ comes with no fanfare, no evident power and glory; what one sees is an obviously human life and really not much more than that. The divinity of Christ appears after the fact, as a kind of inference from this particular human life's effects: "believe me from the works I do," to paraphrase John 14:11. Athanasius makes the point: "Just as, though invisible, he is known through the works of creation; so having become man, and being in the body unseen, it may be known from his works that he who can do these is not man, but the power and Word of God."[44] The Word is "visible now because of his being one with the man who is visible … not in his invisible Godhead but in the operation of the Godhead through the human body and whole man, which he has renewed by its appropriation to himself."[45] Sunk as human life has been in sin and death, this renewal of human life is so unexpected that it can have only God for its source. We believe it therefore, even

[44] Athanasius, "On the Incarnation of the Word," trans. Archibald Robertson, in Philip Schaff and Henry Wace (eds.), Nicene and Post-Nicene Fathers, vol. IV, Second Series (Grand Rapids, Michigan: Eerdmans, 1957), section 18, p. 46; see also section 14, p. 44; section 16, p. 45; section 32, p. 53; section 21, p. 59; and section 54, p. 65.

[45] Athanasius, "Four Discourses against the Arians," trans. John Henry Newman and Archibald Robertson, in Philip Schaff and Henry Wace (eds.), Nicene and Post-Nicene Fathers, vol. IV, Second Series (Grand Rapids, Michigan: Eerdmans, 1957), Discourse 4, section 36, p. 447.

if we see no obviously divine hand at work. In virtue of what we know of Christ, we can be similarly confident of the Spirit's invisible efficacy for the good in our own inadequate efforts; we will know it for a fact, however, only after the unheard of and unexpected good happens by way of the Spirit's power.

The divinity of Christ is invisible, too, in that it has no specific location in Jesus' life. It is instead effective everywhere. In just this way the Spirit works, we have said, in and through the whole of the human and not simply in hidden revelations to the human heart.

The divinity of Christ cannot be specifically located, for example, in supernatural powers of an exceptional sort that stand out from among his more ordinary ones. Instead, he heals with the spit he commonly swallows and by way of the hem of the cloak he drags through dusty streets. While Christ enjoys divine powers in addition to his ordinary human capacities, those divine powers do not appear as some supernatural addition to his ordinary ones, their presence felt in exceptional events outside or apart from his ordinary human dealings with others. Divine powers instead appear in and through the regular human happenings of his life. In the incarnation of the Word in Christ, we consequently see "the endless pressure of God through the events, the things and the people and the situations, of his world."[46] In much the same way, we have suggested,

> the Spirit ... is not an addition to this concatenation of events and clashing wills ... set above the confused and changing world of concrete ... events and situations. The basic Christian material permits of no flight from history, but it draws us back again and again to the singularity, the particularity, the temporality, in a word, the genuine historicity which is its dominant characteristic.[47]

In the same way that the Spirit does not come on the scene when human processes vacate it but appears in and through them, the

---

[46] Ronald Gregor Smith, *The New Man: Christianity and Man's Coming of Age* (London: SCM, 1956), p. 110.

[47] *Ibid.*, p. 32.

divinity of Christ does not start where his humanity ends, but shines through its entirety. That divinity is evident, for example, in the whole of his flesh resurrected – as the eternal life of his full, finished humanity, complete with all its wounds. It appears, not alongside it, but in and through this human life's very own special character – the distinctive form or organization *of* the whole. Divinity is indeed what gives this human life the only human character it has, the character that makes it what it is. Because Christ is the Son of God, trinitarian life constitutes, as we have said, the very shape of his human life. Similarly, in and through our humanity as that participates in Christ's own, our whole lives are to gain a new character in the Spirit. From the depths of sin and death, out of the very occurrence of conflict, suffering, and loss in our lives together, which all but renders the Spirit invisible, will have to come what one would never expect and could never predict: a new human manner of existence; human lives re-formed, reworked as a whole by the Spirit into a life-giving, Spirit-filled form.

Index